THE

Illustrated Field Guide to

VINTAGE TRAILERS

Bob Thompson & Carl Jameson

First Edition

23 22 21 20 19 5 4 3

Published by

Gibbs Smith
P.O. Box 667
Layton, Utah 84041

1.800.835.4993 orders

www.gibbs-smith.com

Designed by Bob Thompson

Printed and bound in China

Gibbs Smith books are printed on either recycled, 100% post-consumer waste, FSC-certified papers or on paper produced from sustainable PE-FC-certified forest/controlled wood source. Learn more at www.pefc.org.

Library of Congress Control Number: 2018951251

ISBN: 978-1-4236-4888-8

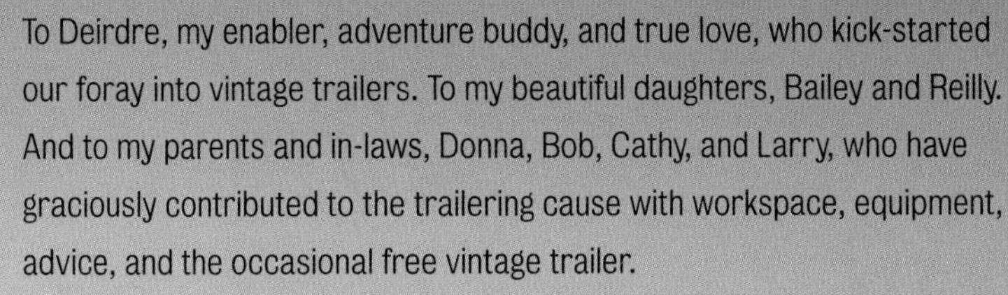

To Deirdre, my enabler, adventure buddy, and true love, who kick-started our foray into vintage trailers. To my beautiful daughters, Bailey and Reilly. And to my parents and in-laws, Donna, Bob, Cathy, and Larry, who have graciously contributed to the trailering cause with workspace, equipment, advice, and the occasional free vintage trailer.

—Bob Thompson

To Sharon, who chose to travel with me on a lifelong journey of discovery. And to my mom, Audrey, and stepdad, Chuck, who courageously took a blended family of seven trailer camping all those summers ago. I learned a lot on that trip, mostly that I liked to play outside. And that my affection can be bought with a Suzuki 125 dirt bike.

—Carl Jameson

OPEN

CONTENTS

Color plate sections begin on pages 108, 208, and 288.

INDEX *of* MANUFACTURERS

ON THE ROAD *to the* FIELD GUIDE

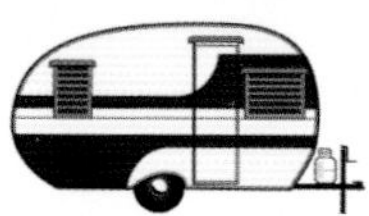

What do a creative director and video producer know about vintage travel trailers? Apparently not much. When we teamed up to restore a dilapidated trailer we had no idea what a DIY education it would become. We discovered that finding any information about vintage trailers is an archaeological dig back to midcentury art, science, and technology.

In the beginning we believed that owning a trailer would be akin to camping in a vintage trailer advertisement: a warm summer spent camping by the lake, canoeing, swimming, and fishing—along with a cool, refreshing brew. A return to a simpler time. A simpler time, indeed!—if simpler means no directions, plans, or map. What were we thinking?

We were thrilled when, on our first trip to look at a trailer, the seller told us to head to the red barn out back. We slid open the barn doors to reveal what we thought was a "barn find," one of those hidden gems that has been undisturbed for decades. Upon inspection we could tell the trailer was no barn find. Ugh! The smell of mildew and cats permeated the interior. The dinette cushions and couch were chewed down to the metal springs. The rotten walls, cabinets, and floors fell apart in our hands. But the pictures we took of the trailer in its rustic setting did make it look pretty enticing. After conferring at a local watering hole we bought it for full price . . . and it didn't even have a title.

Vintage trailer wisdom: never, ever, ever buy a trailer without a clear title. In order to get a new title we needed to identify the trailer for the Department of Motor Vehicles and confirm the trailer's ownership. The bill of sale, written in purple crayon because we couldn't find a pen, said it was a 1958 Cardinal.

We headed to the local DMV with our bill of sale, pictures, and a shaky knowledge

We s-l-o-w-l-y drove our trailer home, for fear it might fly apart at any moment, and stopped often. Here's the trailer posing for its first photo op at Multnomah Falls.

of our trailer's lineage. The DMV clerk was adamant about needing the trailer's vehicle identification number before we could get a new title. She said that the VIN could be found on the trailer's tongue and to only return once we had it. When we walked out of the DMV we heard laughter.

Long story short, we found the VIN and then after three more trips to the DMV, several registered letters, and a death certificate we got our new title.

In our excitement we had purposely glossed over the fact that we had purchased a trailer that needed to be completely rebuilt and neither of us had a place to work on it. So now we scrambled to find a space somewhere, anywhere, in town. We ended up renting a work bay down by the slough. The other bays were rented by auto body shops, scrap metal recyclers, and undisclosed business endeavors. It was hangover quiet in the morning when we got to work, but by noon the sound of grinders, cutting torches, and heavy metal blared from all sides.

So we took the trailer apart from the inside out, confident that by making detailed drawings and taking thousands of pictures we could resurrect it. This was easy, we told ourselves and each other at every opportunity. In fact, our trailer would be better than original when we were done. No problem. Soon we had taken the trailer down to the frame and its parts were scattered around the work bay.

Over the next several months we rebuilt our trailer. It took time and perseverance. We calculated that if you thought you needed to go to Home Depot once, you really needed to go three times, not including the returns. We decided to keep the trailer in the style of the original, but to update its look and its systems. We added a battery, DC power, a water pump, a radio, and walnut wood inlays.

Along the way we took time out to celebrate with friends. We couldn't wait to finish the trailer to have a Spam and eggs breakfast, so we did it sans roof. Note that trailers become much cozier when you add a roof. We even took time to christen it the Canned Ham Project.

The trailer, taken down to its frame, barely had its walls up when we hosted breakfast in it. Carl grilled egg and Spam ala Monty Python.

Left to right: Elle Poindexter (8½ months pregnant with Paloma), Kyle LeMire, Bob, and Deirdre Thompson.

The mostly finished trailer on its maiden voyage to the Oregon coast.

We're still adding the final touches. When we exchanged its dull painted skin with shiny new aluminum, the graphics and logo disappeared. Bob re-created and replaced the original logos on the trailer's front and back. What was once a generic canned ham became instantly identifiable as a Cardinal. Before that it was mistaken for a number of other trailers.

The finished interior has warm, fishing cabin-like touches.

As we rebuilt the canned ham we got hooked on vintage trailers. We read, searched, and joined vintage trailer groups to learn more about our trailer—and to plan our next purchase. We faced the conundrum of vintage trailer enthusiasts everywhere: we had a lot of questions and not a lot of answers. The little information we did find was scattered throughout books, the Internet, and old magazines.

What we needed was a field guide. Since we had learned a ton while rebuilding our trailer we thought,"Why not do it ourselves? How many years of research, rallies, road trips, and writing could that take?" The answer to the latter question is about five years. Now you know why we created *The Illustrated Field Guide to Vintage Trailers* for beginners, the experienced, and all of the curious travelers out on the road (and us).

IDENTIFICATION *in the* FIELD

When you look at a vintage trailer what do you see?

The look of a decades-old trailer, stored in less-than-ideal conditions, can make it difficult to identify. A vintage trailer's paint can be worn, its logo nearly invisible, and if it's a common type, easy to confuse with similar models of the era.

But even without those markers you can identify a trailer's brand, model, and year. Start by looking at the whole trailer, then narrow your focus to details like windows and running lights. Take photos for future reference as you research your find.

Vintage trailers can be spotted most anywhere you travel. These trailers were found in a grassy lot, a driveway, a field, near a highway, and even on a disused ferry in Washington State's Puget Sound.

Shape

The shape of a trailer is your biggest clue to its origin. Take a good look at it, then with the field guide in hand, compare it to the Vintage Trailer Body Styles and Body Style Examples on pages 22–25.

Length

The length of a trailer is closely related to the trailer's use. Some manufacturers specialized in building shorter vacation trailers, while others made longer travel or park models.

Skin Material

What is the trailer made of? Wood? Aluminum? Fiberglass? The skin, depending on its material, type, and use, will give you information about the manufacturer and the trailer's age.

Graphics

Vintage trailer brands often used identifiable bold designs on their complete line of trailers. If a graphic can still be seen, search through the field guide to see if there's a match to your model.

Badges and Logos

Badges can provide some or all the information about your trailer. They can be found near the entry door or frame. Logos are often affixed outside in the front and back and/or routed in cabinetry.

Wheel Wells, Tires, and Hubcaps

Look at the cut of the wheel well. Its shape was generally consistent within a line. Some manufacturers had their own branded hubcaps, but most original hubcaps have likely been lost or changed out.

Windows

Windows are a major aspect in a vintage trailer's appeal. Check out the iconic wraparound window of a Holiday House or the jalousie windows on many trailers from the late 1950s and '60s.

Doors, Handles, and Knobs

The door and its handle can reveal a trailer brand and period by its form, location, and hinge side. Wooden screen doors were standard until aluminum ones were introduced in 1960.

Taillights and Running Lights

The design of taillights and running lights are more than decoration; they date the period of a trailer. In addition, some manufacturers created their own lights or used common ones in a distinct pattern.

Interior

Peek through the windows or get inside a vintage trailer. Check out the color scheme, wall material, cabinets, and fixtures. Look for manuals in drawers or specification sheets glued inside cabinets.

Uncovering the Vehicle Identification Number

The story of the vehicle identification number begins in 1954. A VIN is a coded series of letters and numbers that has two parts. The first part contains manufacturer and specific vehicle information. The second part of the code is the vehicle's serial number.

A trailer built before 1954 does not have a VIN; it has a serial number. The serial number gave the trailer a unique number, but didn't contain any useful identification information.

Between 1954 and 1981, VINs were used on all types of vehicles, but the coded information contained in them was up to the manufacturer. They might or might not have put their name in the code, along with trailer length, year, and model information.

In 1981 the sequence and information encoded in a VIN was standardized. Any information you can decode from a VIN created before 1981 is an educated guess, unless you have specific manufacturer code keys. Depending on where you live, you may need to register your trailer with the DMV. If so, you'll need to make sure that the VIN on the title and the VIN on the trailer match.

A VIN can often be found on the trailer's passenger side tongue, but every trailer is different. The front entrance, inside cabinets, above the front or rear windows, the trunk, the tongue, and the frame are other possible spots.

Above: Stripping multiple layers of paint in search of a VIN stamped into the trailer's tongue. **Below:** The VIN on a 1963 Fireball presented itself more readily.

How to Measure a Vintage Trailer

When you measure your vintage trailer you may notice that its length is different than what brochures or model numbers might have led you to believe. The way mid-twentieth-century trailer makers measured their trailers varied between manufacturers. Some would measure only the body, while others would include the tongue in their specifications.

Why they did this may be more about marketing than anything else. If a manufacturer measured only the body of a trailer, then it would seem shorter, lighter, and easier to tow. If they included the tongue in their measurements, then a buyer might think a trailer had more living space.

Whatever their reason for measuring trailers the way they did, the way to measure a trailer today is simple: measure it from the front of the tongue to the rear bumper. If the trailer doesn't have a rear bumper, measure it to the most extended part of its rear end.

That's the measurement the DMV and your insurance company will want to know. And more importantly, it's the number you'll want to know when you choose a campsite. If you know your trailer's length it will save you the trouble of backing it into a too-short or too-long site. Better yet, you'll be able to find just the right-size pull through.

VINTAGE TRAILER BODY STYLES

Over the decades there have been hundreds of trailer manufacturers and thousands of individual models. However, the majority of vintage trailers fall into a few basic categories. While the aircraft style popularized by Airstream has been enduring since the 1930s, most others tend to reflect the style of the decades from which they came.

Unique

Some notable trailers defy categorization, as their creators pushed boundaries of design and construction techniques of the era.

Fiberglass Egg

These lightweight molded trailers are named for their rounded and typically white fiberglass bodies.

Aircraft-style trailers were born out of the 1930s and '40s aviation industry and were built and styled using aircraft construction techniques.

As the name implies, bread loafs are long, flat-sided trailers rounded off at the top like a loaf of bread.

The smallest of all trailers, teardrops provide the bare essentials of sleeping quarters and a rear galley.

With flat aluminum sides and a round profile, their striking resemblance to a can of ham make these trailers aptly named.

The 1960s and '70s saw many manufacturers opting for a squared-off body style for ease of construction.

Body Style Examples

This graphic shows examples of vintage trailers organized by body style. The trailers in each category have similar shapes, but there is variation depending on the manufacturer, model, and year.

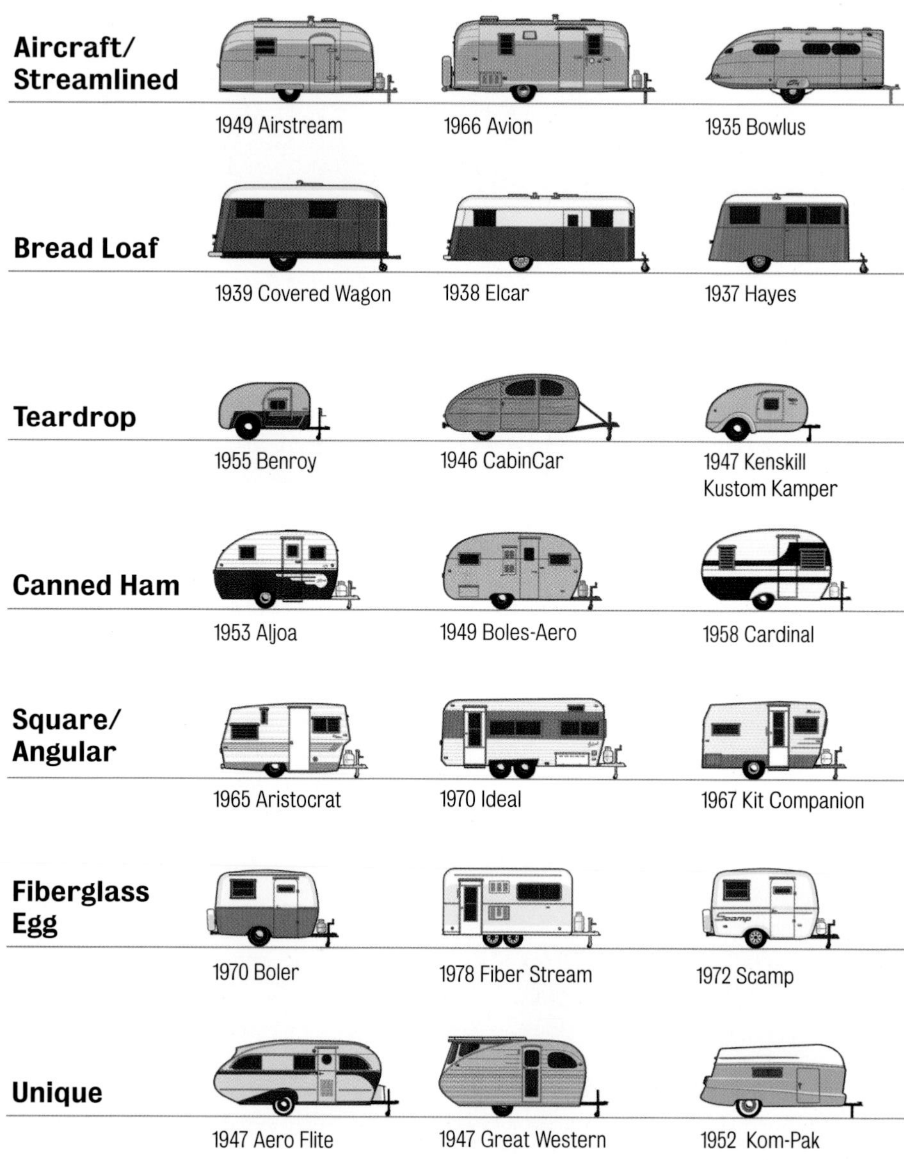

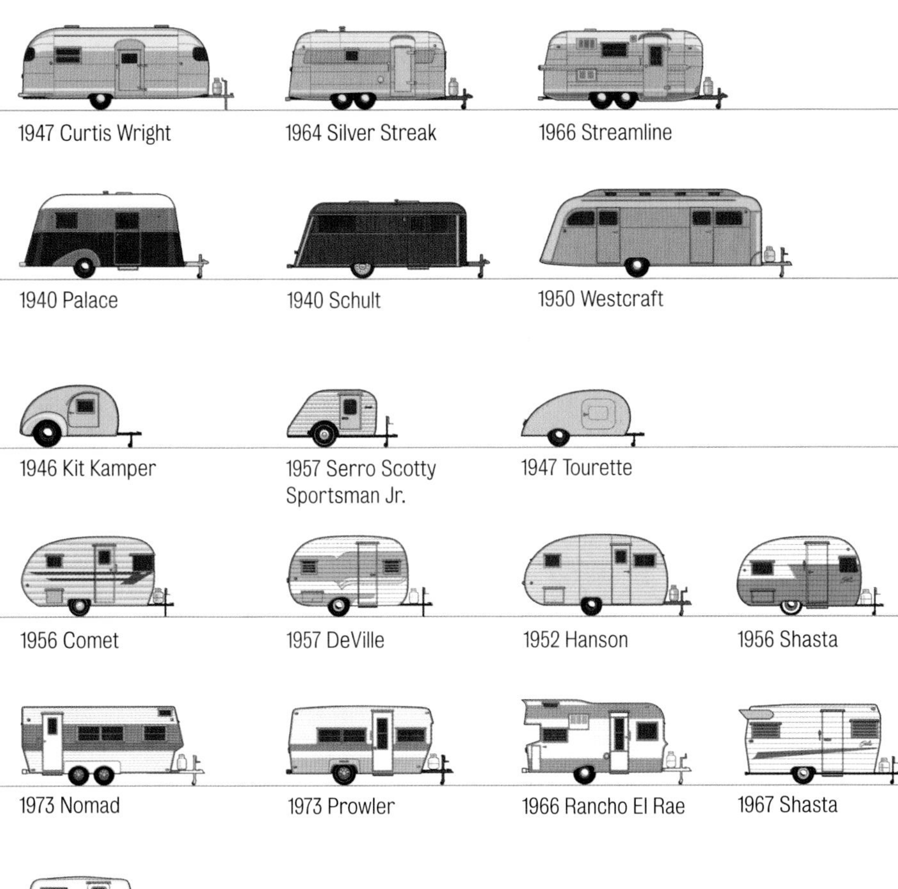

1947 Curtis Wright

1964 Silver Streak

1966 Streamline

1940 Palace

1940 Schult

1950 Westcraft

1946 Kit Kamper

1957 Serro Scotty Sportsman Jr.

1947 Tourette

1956 Comet

1957 DeVille

1952 Hanson

1956 Shasta

1973 Nomad

1973 Prowler

1966 Rancho El Rae

1967 Shasta

1975 Trillium

1961 Holiday House Geographic

1936 Masterbilt

1958 PleasureCraft

1961 Trailorboat

HOW *to* USE THIS GUIDE

If you've ever used a field guide for bird identification, you know the basics of how to use *The Illustrated Field Guide to Vintage Trailers.* The field guide is organized for quick reading and as a starting point for further research. It includes valuable information with titles like Identification in the Field, Uncovering the Vehicle Identification Number, and How To Measure a Vintage Trailer.

The identification section of the field guide starts with Vintage Trailer Body Styles, followed by trailer manufacturers that include full entries like the sample on the facing page. The full entries are alphabetized together in the front of a letter's section. Smaller manufacturers, unique, and rare trailers are in alphabetical order after the full entries.

It may be easier to look a manufacturer up in the index or you may find yourself looking at the hundreds of eye-catching photographs of trailers in the field guide. They range from barn finds to "best in show" models. The pictures show a cross-section of brands, trailers, and a variety pack of models. Those with sharp eyes will spot ones that have no written entry.

There's a glossary that defines terms trailerites need to know when sitting around a glamper's campfire, followed by an update on Trailers in the Field, a Where the Trailers Were Made map, and a Vintage Trailer Check List to fill out when you identify a trailer in the field.

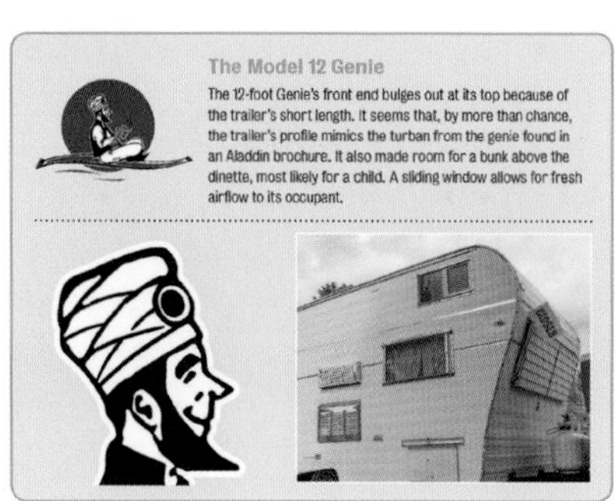
The Model 12 Genie

The 12-foot Genie's front end bulges out at its top because of the trailer's short length. It seems that, by more than chance, the trailer's profile mimics the turban from the genie found in an Aladdin brochure. It also made room for a bunk above the dinette, most likely for a child. A sliding window allows for fresh airflow to its occupant.

Googie Style

The bright logo and geometric ornamentation of the Holiday House are excellent examples of the modern futurist style known as Googie—atomic and space age design infused with a heady mix of prosperity and optimism.

Throughout the field guide are spotting notes that highlight trailer models of specific interest, as well as significant features, events, and trivia.

Style and Identifying Features

Body style silhouette(s) of the brand helps to quickly categorize a manufacturer's line. Photographs focus on the unique features that aid in identifying a trailer brand or model in the field.

Logo

Oversized, in sharp detail, and redrawn based on original materials, a brand's logo appears at the top of the entry.

Company Name and Years

The original or most recognized company name is listed. The dates of the company or a trailer brand's life help narrow the age of a vintage trailer.

Key Models

Trailers are illustrated in fine detail, making it easy to distinguish specific models and become familiar with manufacturer brand attributes.

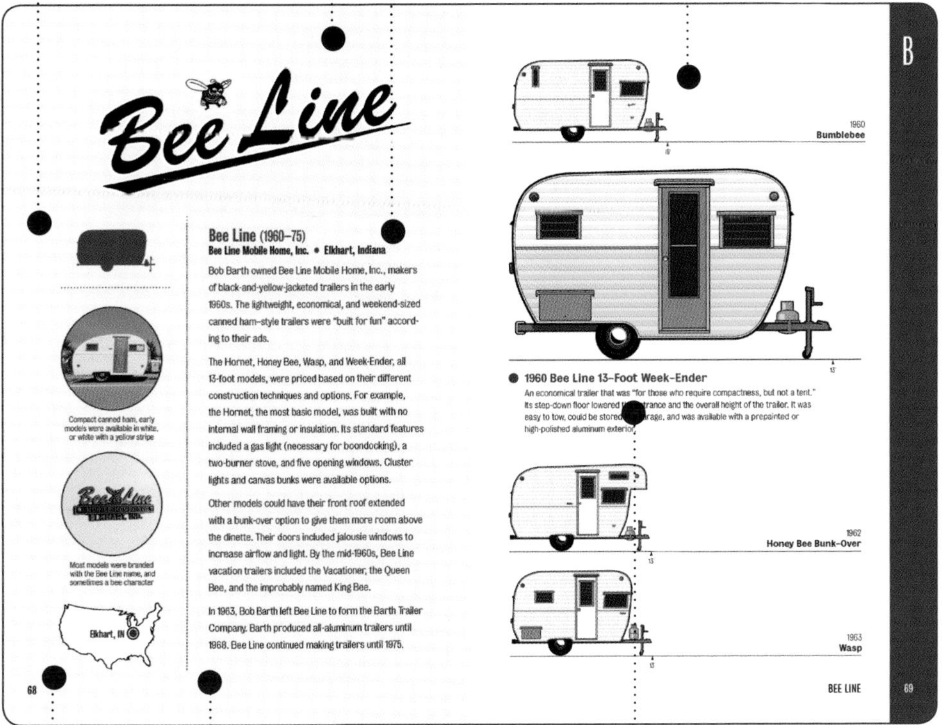

Bee Line

Bee Line (1960–75)

Bee Line Mobile Home, Inc. • Elkhart, Indiana

Bob Barth owned Bee Line Mobile Home, Inc., makers of black-and-yellow-jacketed trailers in the early 1960s. The lightweight, economical, and weekend-sized canned ham–style trailers were "built for fun" according to their ads.

The Hornet, Honey Bee, Wasp, and Week-Ender, all 13-foot models, were priced based on their different construction techniques and options. For example, the Hornet, the most basic model, was built with no internal wall framing or insulation. Its standard features included a gas light (necessary for boondocking), a two-burner stove, and five opening windows. Cluster lights and canvas bunks were available options.

Other models could have their front roof extended with a bunk-over option to give them more room above the dinette. Their doors included jalousie windows to increase airflow and light. By the mid-1960s, Bee Line vacation trailers included the Vacationer, the Queen Bee, and the improbably named King Bee.

In 1963, Bob Barth left Bee Line to form the Barth Trailer Company. Barth produced all-aluminum trailers until 1968. Bee Line continued making trailers until 1975.

Compact canned ham, early models were available in white, or white with a yellow stripe

Most models were branded with the Bee Line name, and sometimes a bee character

Elkhart, IN

68

B

1960 **Bumblebee**

1960 Bee Line 13-Foot Week-Ender

An economical trailer that was "for those who require compactness, but not a tent." Its step-down floor lowered [illegible]trance and the overall height of the trailer. It was easy to tow, could be stored [illegible]rage, and was available with a prepainted or high-polished aluminum exterior.

1962 **Honey Bee Bunk-Over**

1963 **Wasp**

BEE LINE 69

Historical Brief

An outline of the manufacturer's origins, technical and model highlights, and up-to-date information.

Models of Interest

Enlarged illustrations are used to call out key models that exemplify a brand or style, or are of interest for their design, function, innovation, or historical significance.

Manufacturing Origin

The city or cities of manufacture are pinpointed on a simple US map. This is useful for seeing regional trends and major centers of trailer manufacturing activity.

WHAT TRAILERS ARE INCLUDED *in the* FIELD GUIDE?

Hundreds of companies made trailers from the 1930s through the 1970s. Many were started in warehouses, barns, or even single-car garages. Some of the companies grew into bigger regional and national companies whose brands are still around today, others stayed small and made trailers for decades, and others faded away in years or even months. Every one has a great story.

We set out to tell them all in *The Illustrated Field Guide to Vintage Trailers*, but soon discovered that goal was wildly unrealistic. Information about many trailers, even from the largest makers, is often spotty and unreliable. So we cut down our encyclopedic ambition to field guide size. It took many conversations, the use of our limited math skills, and several rounds of adult beverages for us to come up with the following questions as the basis for inclusion in this guide.

We're sure you can imagine sitting across the table from us as we drew up our list of questions and wrote down our thoughts behind each one. They're all pretty common sense. The list ultimately provided the direction we needed to discover the best candidates for the guide. We found answers at trailer rallies, on the Internet and by using original sources in the RV/MH Hall of Fame library.

1. Was the trailer built between 1930 and 1980?

We consider the golden age of vintage travel trailering to be between the end of World War II in 1945 and the 1973–74 oil embargo that slowed the industry to a trickle.

2. Was it a travel trailer?

We didn't include park models or mobile homes. Some larger models might be included as part of a manufacturer's line or if they are of historical significance.

3. Is the travel trailer large enough to stand up inside?

This leaves out most teardrops, except those that might be part of a manufacturer's larger line of trailers. We left out truck-bed campers too.

4. Is the trailer still seen on the road and at rallies?

If a trailer brand has been seen on the road or at rallies it was included in the field guide. Some manufacturers have full histories, some are mentioned in short entries, and the hardest to research are represented in photographs only.

5. Was the trailer mentioned in industry publications?

We researched the many publications available at the RV/MH Hall of Fame library. If enough information could be found about a trailer in industry magazines, marketing materials, and advertisements, it's in the field guide.

6. Is there currently a group or organization devoted to the trailer?

We searched the Internet for trailer groups and organizations. We added them to a weighted spreadsheet to help us determine what brands to include in the field guide.

7. Is the trailer unique or unusual in its design or engineering?

Any trailer that we feel represents a step forward in design or engineering, or is one of a kind in a technical sense, is included in the field guide.

8. Is the trailer historically significant or otherwise collectible?

A trailer could be historically significant or collectible for any number of reasons, such as who built it or who might have owned it.

We're not perfect!

If you find a mistake or omission in *The Illustrated Field Guide to Vintage Trailers,* send us an e-mail at **oops@vintagetrailerfieldguide.com** with any photographs and supporting documents. We'll make changes to the next edition of the field guide and announce the correction on our website and social media pages. Make sure to send us your name so we can give you credit for your contribution.

MANUFACTURERS A *to* Z

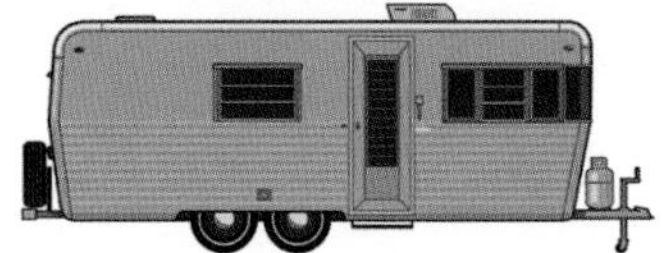

A

Art moderne design with a sleek, sporty profile

A tail wing window juts from the rear of the trailer

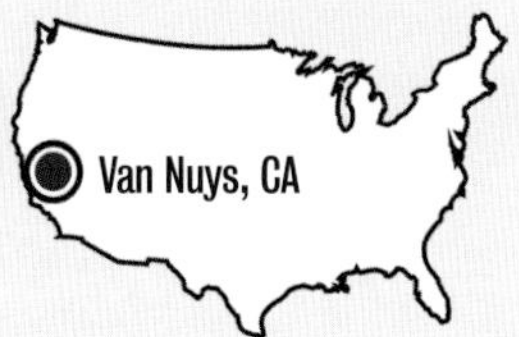

Aero Flite (1945–49)

Aero Lines • Van Nuys, California

Metropolitan Airport in Van Nuys, California, was a defense manufacturing center during World War II and home to Aero Services, an aircraft repair center that retooled after the war and added a travel trailer division, Aero Lines.

Legend has it that the final scenes in the film *Casablanca,* when Humphrey Bogart says goodbye to Ingrid Bergman, were shot at the airport. So it must have seemed natural that the Beverly Hills Hotel provided the backdrop for Aero Flite's public debut on December 8, 1945.

Aero Flite trailers were patented by Frederick C. Hoffman, an aircraft designer who brought his expertise in aircraft construction and applied it to all-aluminum trailers. His background is evident in their rigid aircraft-style structure, the red wing graphic that wraps the wheel hub, and the art moderne louvers on the front. The louvers are part of a filtered air flow system worthy of high-altitude flight.

Aero Lines built an estimated 110 to 120 trailers between 1946 and early 1949; as many as 25 of those trailers are known to have survived until today. Those still on the road are highly coveted restoration projects.

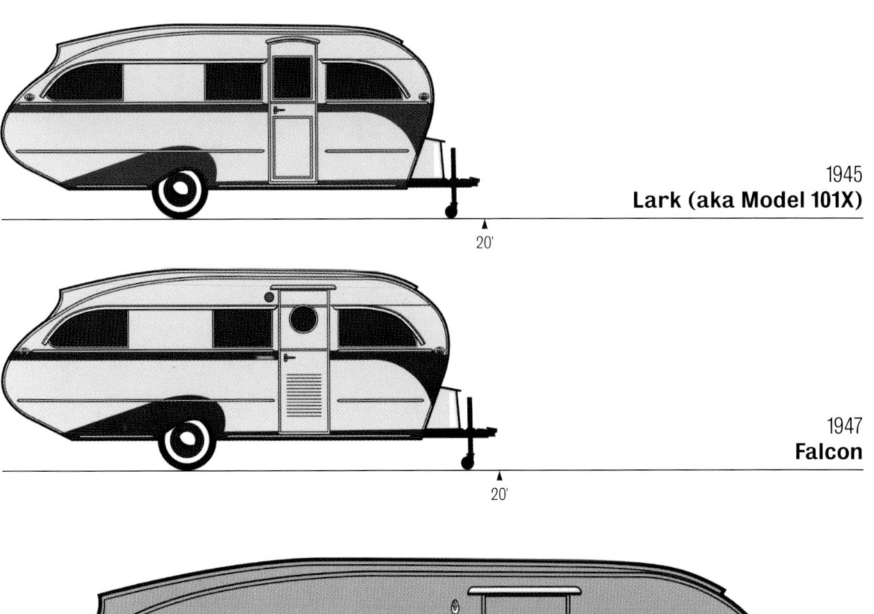

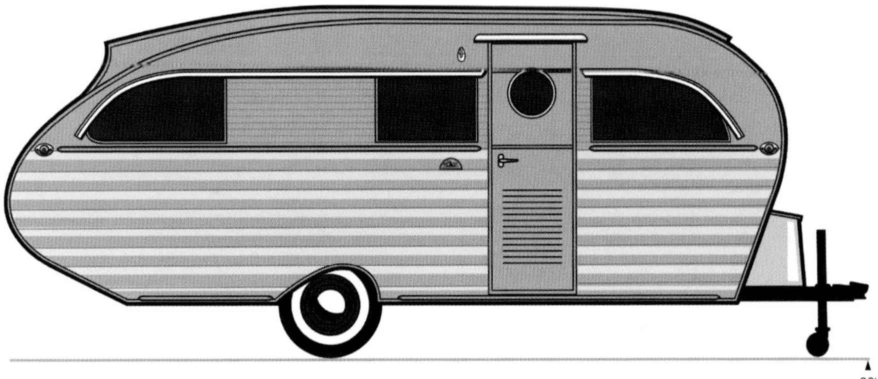

1948 Aero Flite Falcon

Late model Aero Flites are distinguished by a few subtle design changes, including ribbed side panels and an absence of painted stripes.

Extended Rear Window

The raised roof and extended rear window on Aero Flite trailers add interior height, roominess, and improved airflow. This feature can also be found on the very rare Great Western, one of Frederick C. Hoffman's other notable trailer designs.

Airfloat

Elongated canned ham body shape with porthole windows

Thin corrugated siding with a smooth band behind windows

Airfloat (1930–57)

Airfloat Coach Manufacturing Co. • Los Angeles, California

Omar Suttles launched Airfloat Coach Manufacturing in 1930. The former automotive engineer and inventor soon landed on Airfloat's canned ham–shaped body covered in Masonite and porthole window design. By the end of the decade models had titles like Master, Commander, and President. Airfloat stopped production on that line from 1943 through 1945 to build bread loaf–style trailers during World War II.

In 1947, Airfloat debuted the Landyacht, with all-aluminum skin, a one-piece roof, corrugated panels, and "the most advanced air conditioning system of its kind." It used a "thermo-air passage" in the trailer's 3-inch hollow walls and roof. The roof vent adjusted how much fresh air flowed through the hollows, and in doing so regulated the temperature.

Airfloat invited customers to visit their factory, where they could choose to buy an existing trailer or to commission one with personalized interior colors and features. The company closed in 1957. Omar Suttles was inducted into the RV/MH Hall of Fame in 1974. He was one of the founders of the Trailer Coach Association, a predecessor to the Recreational Vehicle Industry Association.

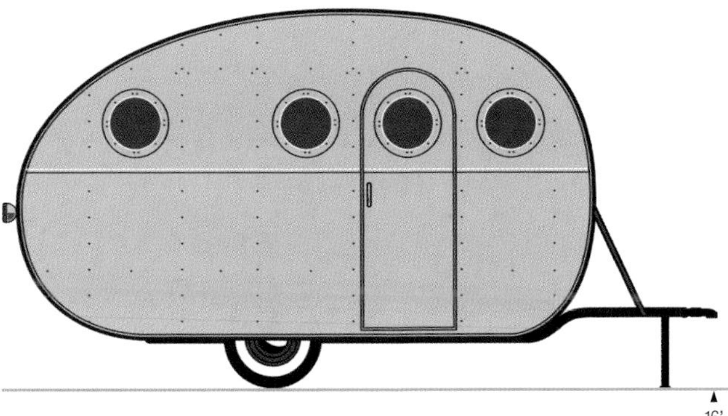

1935 Airfloat Coach

The nautically inspired Airfloat Coach was unveiled at the 1935 Outing Show in Los Angeles. It had porthole windows, a rounded body, and a Masonite skin. Airfloats wouldn't gain their unique corrugated aluminum look until after World War II.

1938
Skipper

The 3rd Wheel

The 1942 Commodore 3rd Wheel launched with a dolly wheel anchored beneath the trailer's tongue and coupler. It decreased the weight bearing down on the hitch and increased a tow vehicle's ability to pull longer and heavier loads. In a few years it became standard on most Airfloat models.

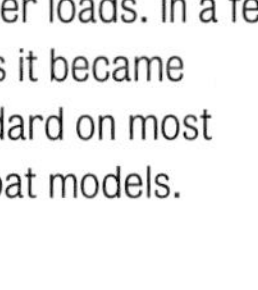

1949 Landyacht

Clinton and Merle Twiss commissioned a 28-foot Landyacht to be built for their road trip across the lower 48 states. Their misadventures inspired the book *The Long, Long, Trailer* by Clinton Twiss. A longer 1953 Redman New Moon 36-foot trailer starred in the Lucille Ball and Desi Arnaz 1954 film based on the book.

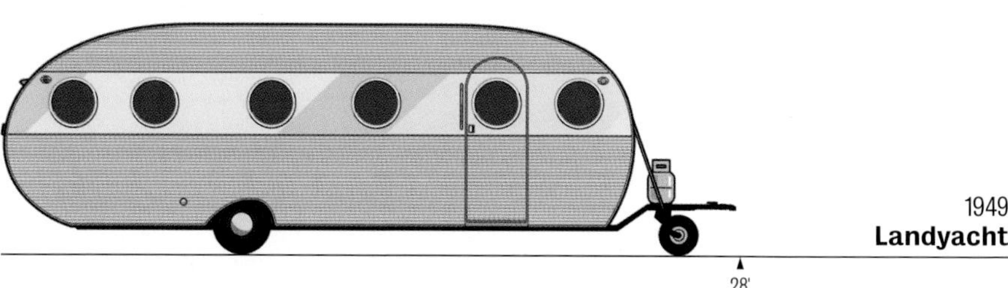

1949
Landyacht

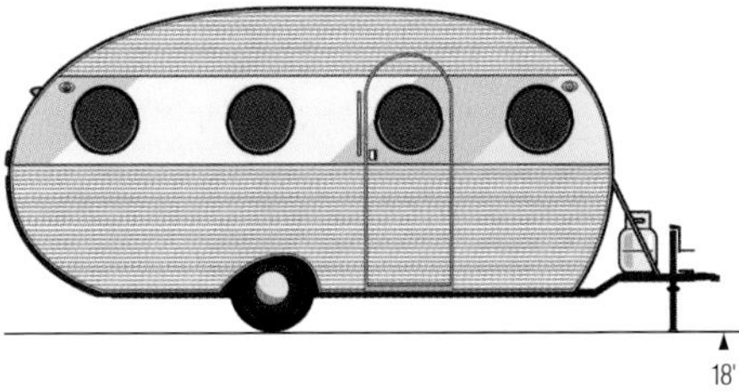

18'

1951
Skipper

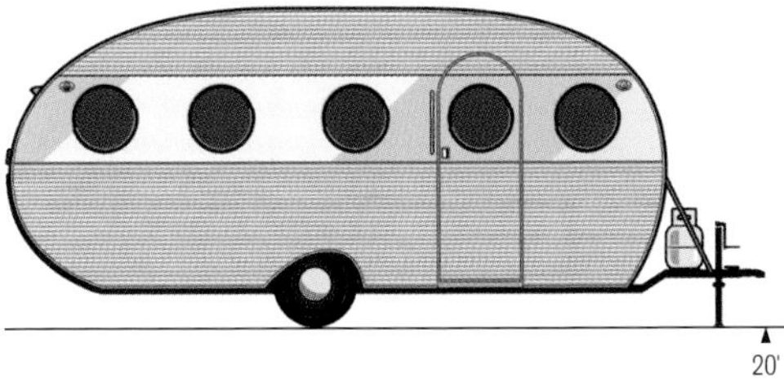

20'

1955
Navigator

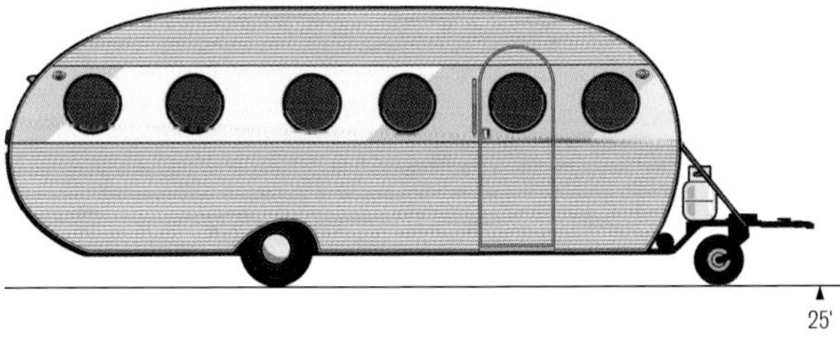

25'

1955
Cruiser

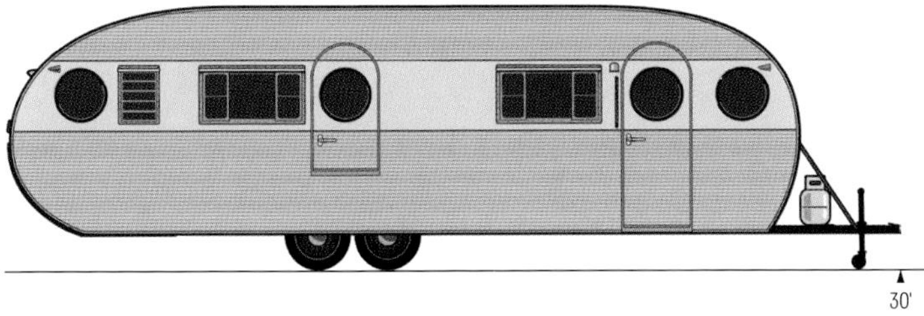

30'

1957
Landyacht

45'

1957 Airfloat Presidential Yacht

In 1957, Airfloat introduced anodized gold siding to their model line, touting it as nonfading and element proof. At 45 feet long, the patriotic-themed Presidential Yacht Golden Eagle was a powerful symbol of Airfloat's top-of-the-line status.

AIRSTREAM

Rounded aluminum aircraft-style construction

Badges that identify the brand, model, and/or interior package

Airstream (1936–present)

Airstream, Inc. • Los Angeles, California / Jackson Center, Ohio

You wouldn't guess in 1929 that the first incarnation of the Airstream trailer, a tent mounted on a Model-T chassis, would eventually define the best in modern American engineering. It's canvas flaps, through many iterations, grew into a smooth aluminum shell by the mid-1930s.

Airstream's founder, Wally Byam, designed them to be light enough to be towed by a car, while providing first-class accommodations anywhere in the world. With built-to-last riveted aluminum construction and names like Clipper, Whirlwind, and Flying Cloud, there's no doubt that early Airstream trailers were marketed as a way to fly down the road in style.

Its classic fuselage shape has only been modified a few times in its nearly 90-years-young existence. Many vintage Airstreams are still on the road with original, restored, or completely redone interiors. So many, in fact, that to join the Vintage Airstream Club owners have to have a trailer that's at least 25 years old.

Vintage Airstreams can often be seen put to use as working trailers. They've been turned into food carts, mobile offices, and one-of-a-kind backyard rentals.

1936 Silver Cloud

Bearing little resemblance to the famed aluminum models, the earliest Airstreams were offered either as plans for do-it-yourselfers or preassembled. Silver Clouds were constructed of wood and Masonite and sold by Airstream dealers as finished units.

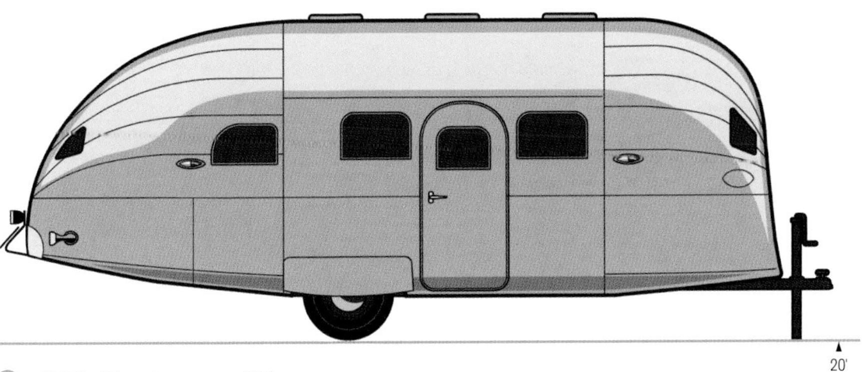

1936 Airstream Clipper

Airstream founder Wally Byam had been selling plans, kits, and assembled Masonite trailers when the struggling Bowlus Company went out of business. Byam redesigned the riveted aluminum Bowlus Road Chief and renamed it the Clipper, establishing the template for all Airstreams to come.

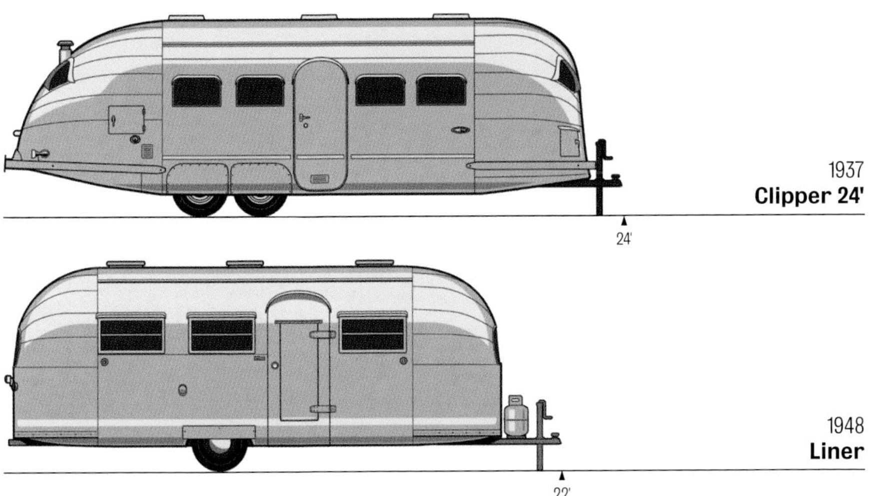

1937
Clipper 24'

1948
Liner

1948
Weewind
16'

1948
Whirlwind
28'

1951
Cruisette
15'

California

Ohio

California vs. Ohio

In the 1950s, Airstream made the same trailer models in California and Ohio, but the model names and some style elements varied between the two. The shapes of the wheel wells are distinct: California wheel wells are teardrop shaped, while the Ohio models have square or peaked ones. Another difference was the nine-panel "whale tail" end cap found only on the back of California models of the mid-1950s. Ohio models of the same era had 13 panels that converged around the rear window. The number of panels decreased over time, to only seven by 1957–58.

Wally Byam Caravan Club International

The red numbers on Airstream trailers are issued by the Caravan Club. The club formed in 1955 to encourage people to get out and use their travel trailers, to see and enjoy the world around them, and to test Airstream trailers' quality. New members can reactivate a former member's number that remains on their now vintage trailer. Wally's membership number was 1. It is not up for reactivation.

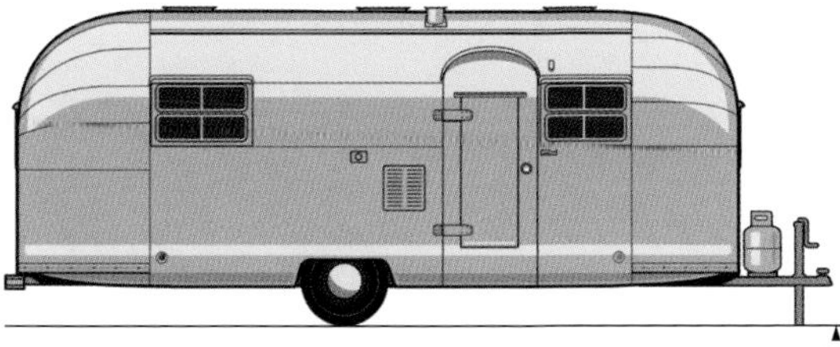

20'

1952
Flying Cloud

16'

1956
Bubble

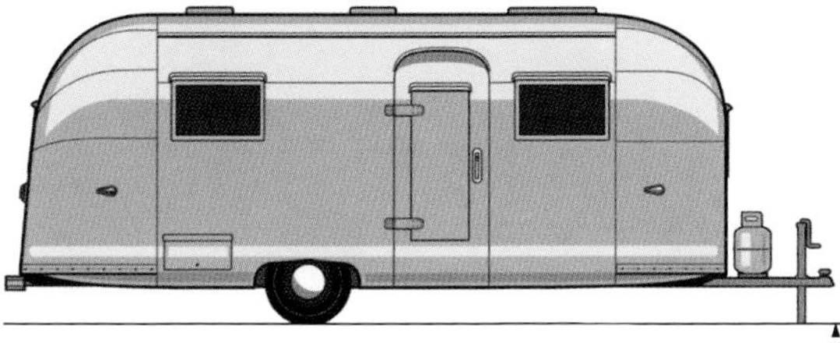

22'

1959
Safari

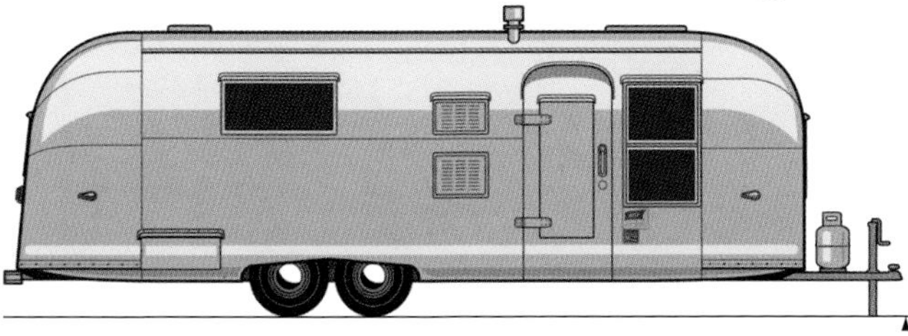

26'

1959
Overlander

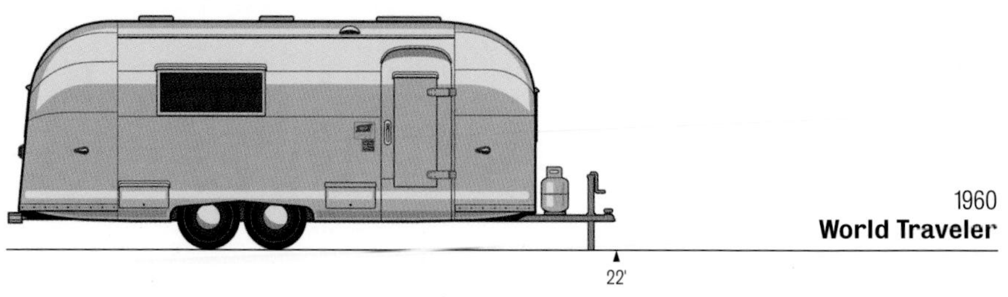

1961 Airstream Bambi

The compact, self-contained, and affordable Bambi was one of the most popular of all Airstreams. It continues to be popular and highly sought after by enthusiasts today, which unfortunately means "affordable" is no longer a word one would use to describe a Bambi.

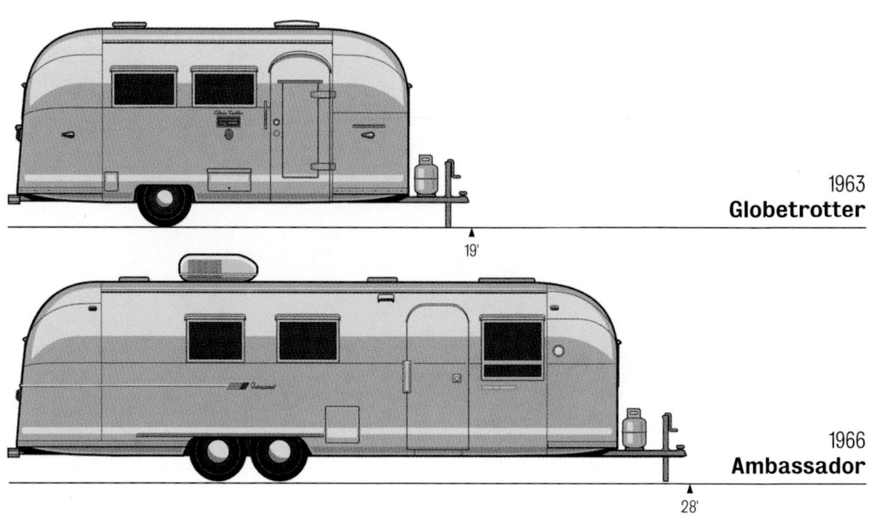

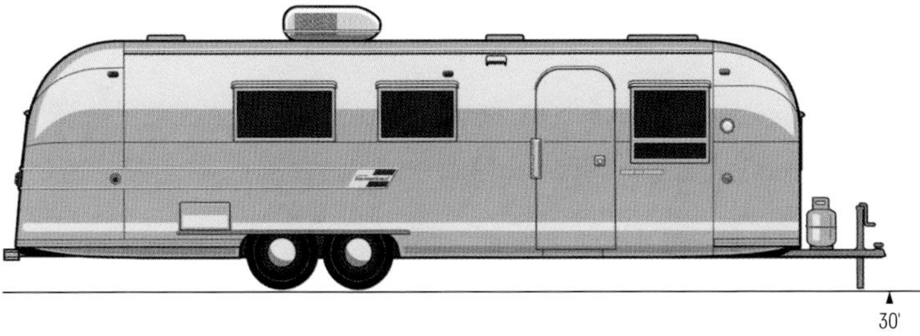

30'

1968
Sovereign of the Road

18'

1969
Caravel

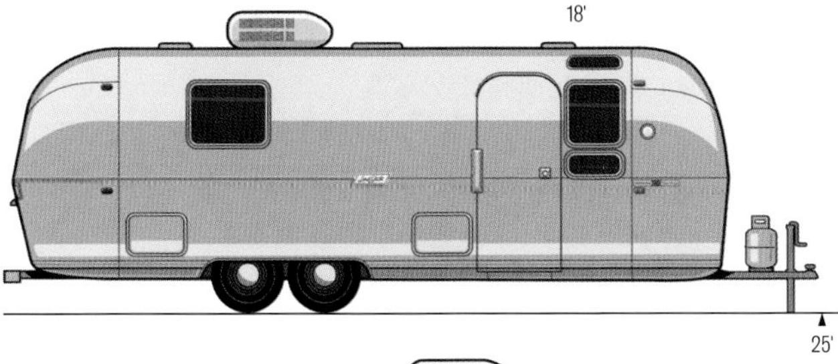

25'

1971
Tradewind

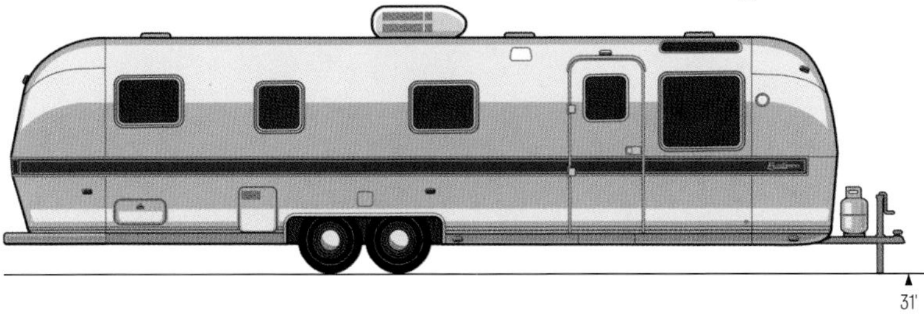

31'

1979
Excella 500

Evolution of the Airstream Body Style

Considering how many decades these aircraft-inspired trailers have been in production, their appearance has changed very little since the first Clipper rolled off the line in 1936. Over the years, the aluminum fuselage body has undergone subtle refinements in curvature and the number of aluminum panels, giving a characteristic look to each model era.

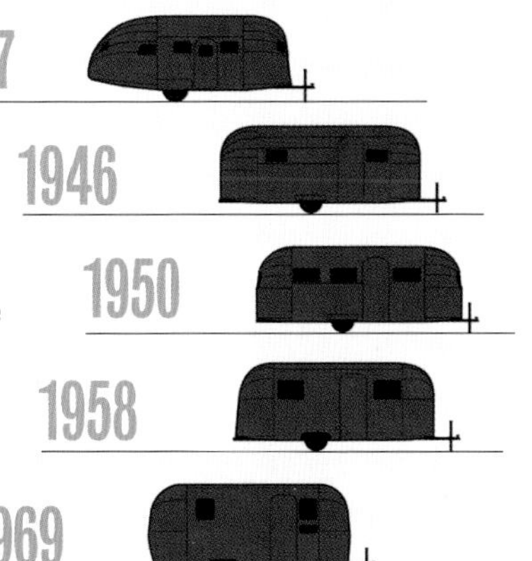

Many models from 1963–67 feature an exaggerated crown

Wheel wells angle down toward the rear of the trailer

Aladdin (1963–early 1970s)

Aladdin Trailer Company • Hillsboro, Oregon

The Aladdin Trailer Company was short lived. Their trailers first hit the road in 1963, the same year that Allan Sherman was topping the charts with the song "Hello Muddah, Hello Fadduh"—a classic letter home from Camp Granada.

Aladdin made vacation trailers meant for family weekend outings, but their slogan and model names promised great adventure. They were advertised as a "Magic Carpet to Vacationland" and had names inspired by the Arabic folk tales in *One Thousand and One Nights*: Genie, Hideaway, Magic Lamp, Magic Carpet, Sultan's Castle, Allah's Choice, and Arabian Night.

Spotting an Aladdin trailer is easy, even if its nameplate has faded, as many of the 1963–67 models feature an exaggerated crown made to accommodate a top bunk above the dinette.

The original owners sold the company in 1969—the year thousands of the nation's mud-covered youth camped out at Woodstock. The new owners made them until the early 1970s. The Aladdins still on the road today are treasured family members at rallies and events across the western United States.

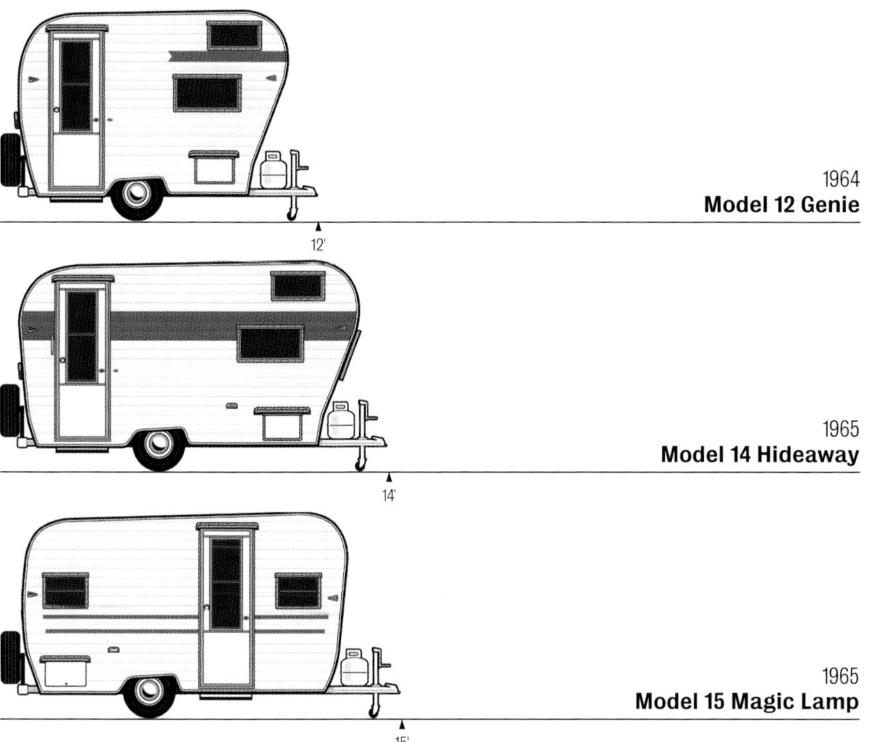

The Model 12 Genie

The 12-foot Genie's front end bulges out at its top because of the trailer's short length. It seems that, by more than chance, the trailer's profile mimics the turban from the genie found in an Aladdin brochure. It also made room for a bunk above the dinette, most likely for a child. A sliding window allows for fresh airflow to its occupant.

1965
Model 19-5 Arabian Night

1966
Model 15 Magic Carpet

1967 Aladdin Sultan's Castle

While not the largest in the Aladdin line, the Sultan's Castle was made for boondocking vacations. It had twin propane tanks, gas stoves, and fridges, gas and electric (AC/DC) lights, and a marine toilet. There is ample storage space and room for six people to sleep when the dinette and daveno areas are converted to beds.

1968
Hideaway

Aladdin's Magic Lamp

The Aladdin magic lamp logo, simplified and routed into a few lines, adds flair to kitchen cabinets in most models and is a unique mark for identification.

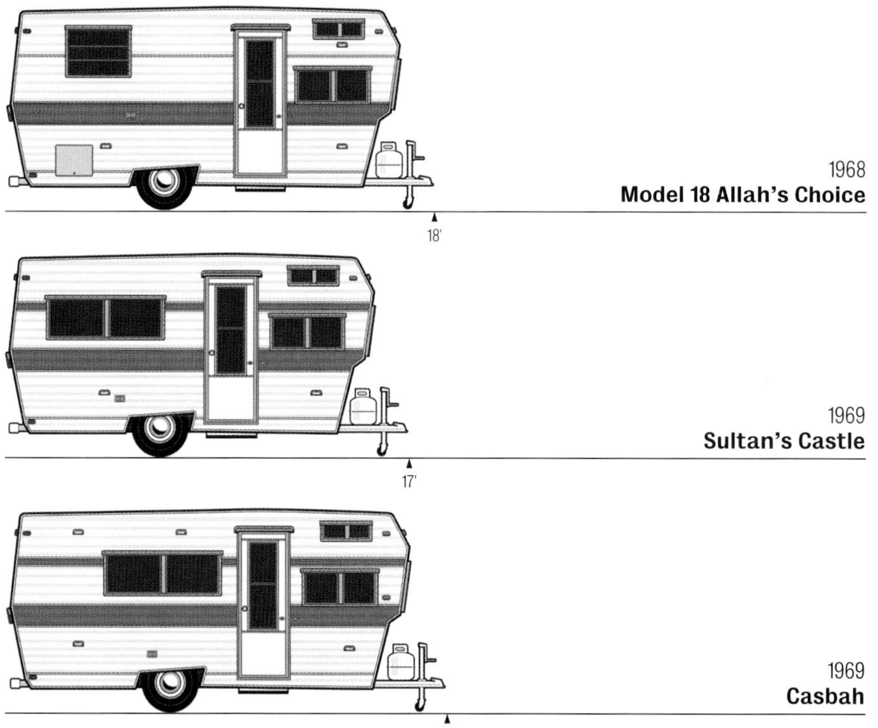

1968
Model 18 Allah's Choice

1969
Sultan's Castle

1969
Casbah

Aljoa / Aljo

Early Aljoas have flat-sided bare aluminum canned ham bodies

Mid-1950s to 1960s models are painted and feature either the Aljoa or Aljo logo in a winged medallion on their flanks

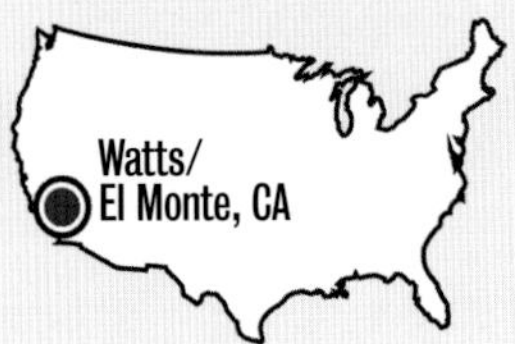

Aljoa (1945–56) / Aljo (1956–78)

Modernistic Industries • Watts / El Monte, California

Modernistic Industries founder C. T. McCreary built the first Aljoa trailers in a small shop in Watts, California, from 1945 to 1949. The company then moved to the center of trailer manufacturing at the time: El Monte, California. In 1949, Al Rose, the self-titled "Trailer King," bought out the entire run of Aljoa's 14-foot canned hams.

When aluminum manufacturer Alcoa discovered advertisements touting "All Aluminum Aljoa Trailers," it sued for trademark infringement. A name change soon followed.

Aljo trailers migrated across the United States, eventually growing into the second-largest trailer brand in the nation by 1957. The Forest City, Iowa, branch of Modernistic Industries molted into Winnebago Industries.

By the late fifties, Aljo offered several floor plans and interiors: the Mikado, an Oriental modern style; the Betsy Ross, a provincial style; and the Florentine, a midcentury contemporary blend of pink and black. The Aljo brand was sold to Skyline Industries in 1978. C. T. McCreary was inducted into RV/MH Hall of Fame in 2004. The Aljo nameplate went extinct in 2016.

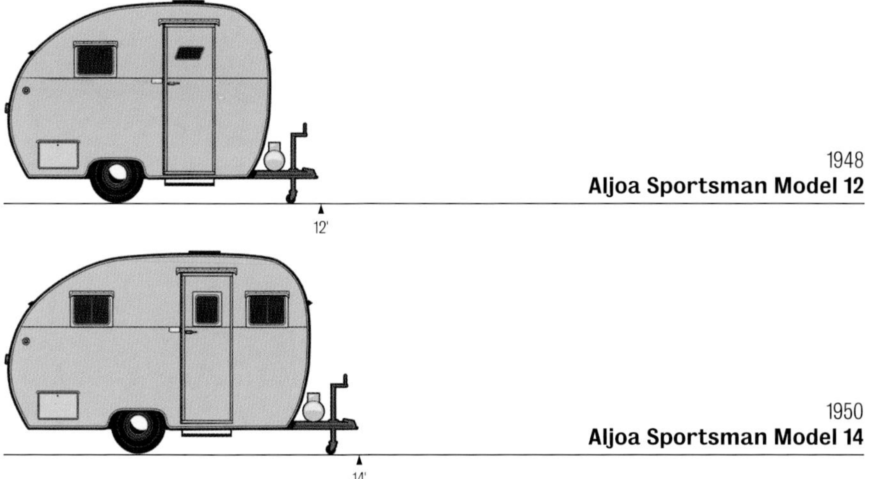

1948
Aljoa Sportsman Model 12

1950
Aljoa Sportsman Model 14

1953 Aljoa Sportsman Model 16

The canned ham shape and bold comet-inspired medallion of the 1950s-era models make them the most recognizable and sought after by Aljoa/Aljo enthusiasts.

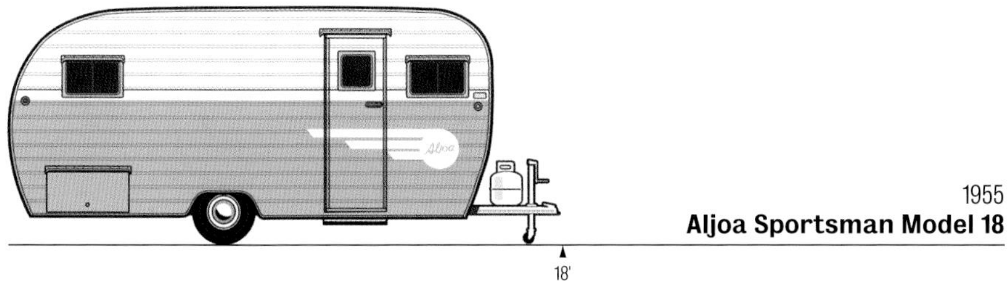

1955
Aljoa Sportsman Model 18

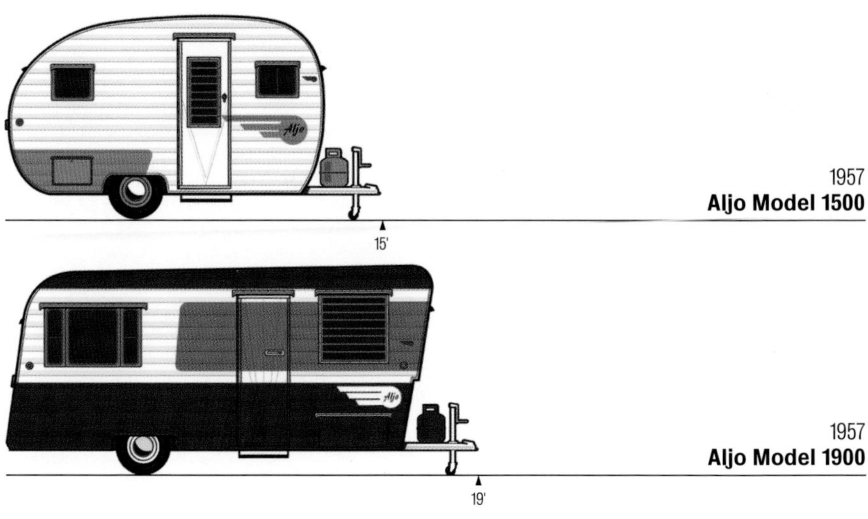

1957
Aljo Model 1500

1957
Aljo Model 1900

The Change from Aljoa to Aljo

Though rumors abound concerning the origin of the Aljoa name, it's a known fact that aluminum manufacturing giant Alcoa sued for trademark infringement in the mid-1950s. In response, the second "a" was dropped and the trailer company became Aljo. Models from 1956 onward bear this name.

1959
Aljo Model 1800

The 1958 Aljos

This print ad from the January 1958 edition of *Trail-R-News* is an interesting study in the evolution of body styles. As the 1950s came to a close, the classic canned ham trailer was still represented in the Aljo line with the Model 1500, while the rest of the line became increasingly square—a style that would become typical of most trailers into the '60s and '70s.

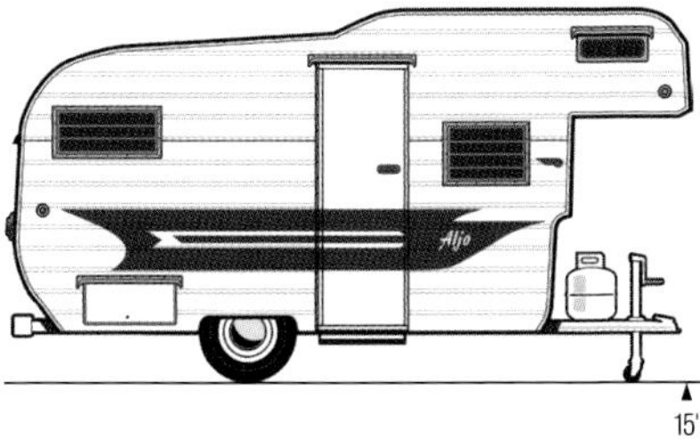

15'

1961
Aljo Model 1500x

17'

1964
Aljo Model 1700

15'

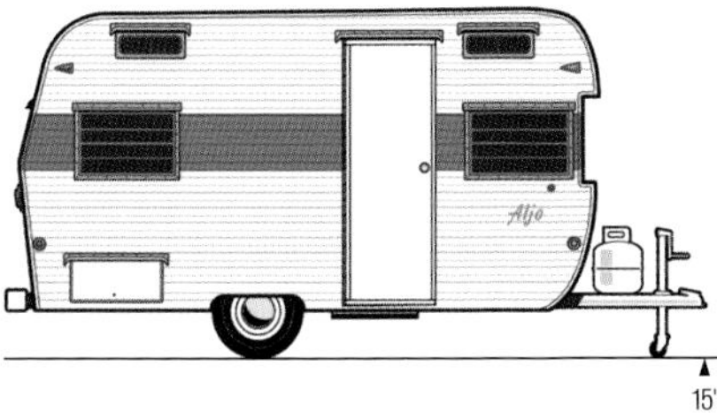

1968
Aljo Model 15

Compact bare aluminum canned ham body (mid-1950s)

Squarish canned ham body, often with quilted diamond stripe or arrowhead painted graphic (early 1960s)

Aloha (1954–mid-1970s)

Aloha Trailer Company • Aloha / Beaverton, Oregon

The Aloha Trailer Company was founded in Aloha, Oregon, in 1954. The locals there pronounce it Ah-lo-WA rather than Ah-lo-HA, but that didn't stop the company from exploiting the mispronunciation into a regional brand.

Tiki pop culture was flourishing on the United States mainland when Glen Gordon and a business partner bought the company on July 6, 1959—weeks before Hawaii became the 50th state on August 21, 1959. Polynesian-themed restaurants, bars, and bowling alleys were filled with bamboo, rum cocktails, and palm trees.

Mixing tiki culture and "get away from it all" trailer culture proved a winning combination for Aloha in the northwestern United States and Canada. At the height of its production in the 1960s, Aloha built 17 to 19 trailers a day, had several hundred employees, owned their buildings, and added a night shift.

The company also made truck campers and custom motor homes. The Aloha brand even made it onto house barges. Gordon sold the company in 1969.

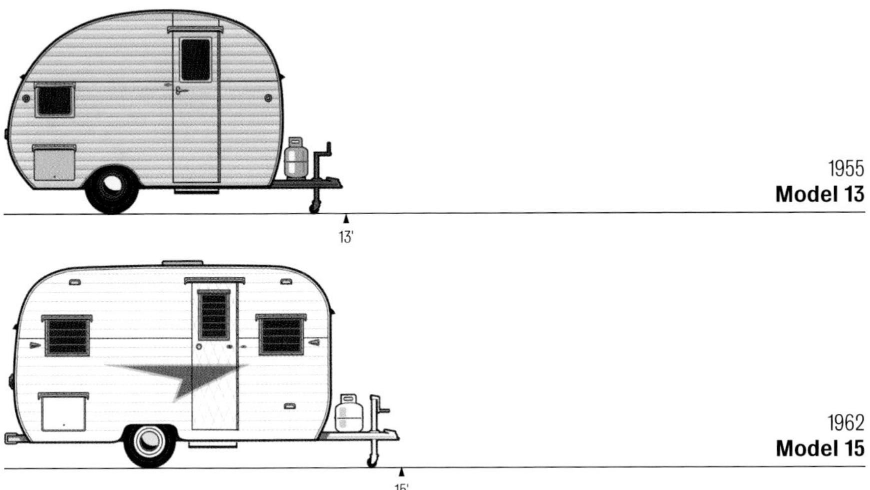

NORTHCRAFT VINTAGE TRAILER RESTORATION

1962 World's Fair Model

Made to help alleviate housing shortages during the Seattle World's Fair, this updated version of the Space Age–themed trailer has rounded front windows, a whale tail, and a cosmic paint scheme.

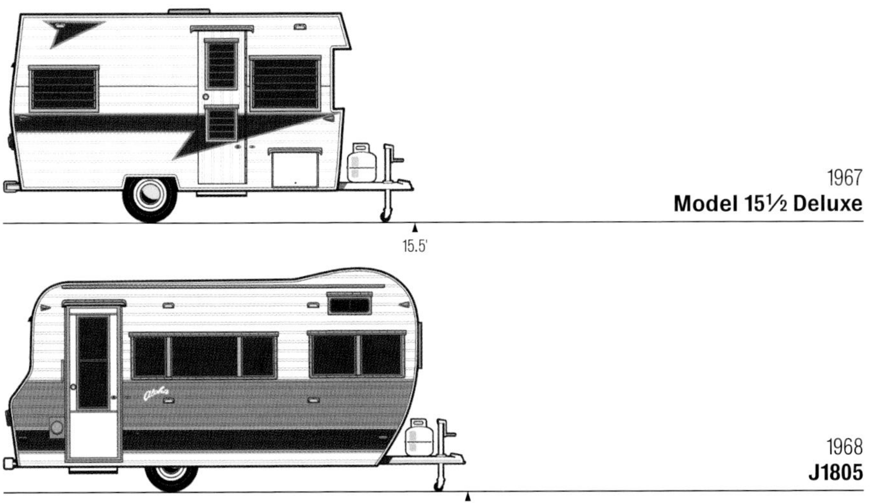

Aristocrat trailers

An angular body style distinguishes most of the models in the Aristocrat lineup

Model names and the Aristocrat logo are often attached emblems displayed on the front, back, and sides of the trailer

Aristocrat (1956–73)

I. B. Perch Co. • Morgan Hill, California / Boise Cascade • Weiser, Idaho

In 1956, *The Wizard of Oz* was first broadcast nationwide on CBS television stations, Elvis Presley swiveled his hips for the first time on the *The Ed Sullivan Show,* and the first Aristocrat trailers manufactured by the I. B. Perch Co. rolled off the line.

Irving Perch, the founder of the company, moved operations to Morgan Hill, California, in 1957. The Lo-Liner, a luxury trailer that could fit into a garage, propelled sales, and by the '60s, I. B. Perch was the world's largest trailer manufacturer.

Aristocrat trailers were built using metal I beams, which along with corner cabinets, reinforced their structure. Most of the trailers in the line featured a toilet, convertible couch beds, and a lifetime guarantee. Note to vintage trailer enthusiasts: the lifetime guarantee only lasted for the life of the company, not the trailer itself.

Perch sold the company to Boise Cascade, which manufactured Aristocrats for the 1969 and 1970 model years. It was then sold to Bendix, which ceased trailer production in 1973. Irving Perch was inducted into the RV/MH Hall of Fame in 1997.

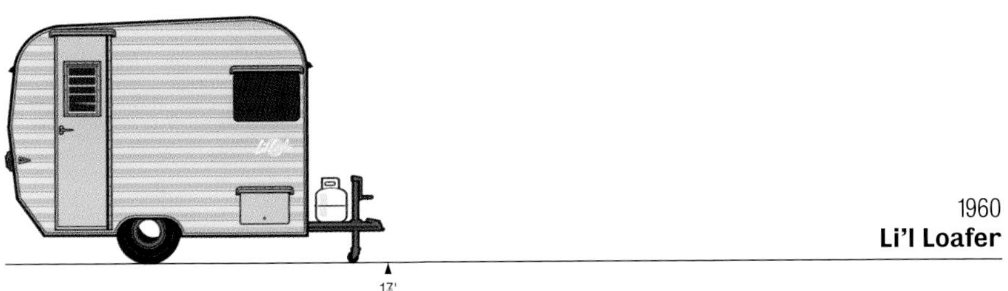

1960
Li'l Loafer

1962 Aristocrat Lo-Liner

Lo-Liner trailers could fit into a suburban garage by changing out its road tires with optional metal wheels that lowered its height. It was advertised for use as an extra bedroom, office, or children's playroom.

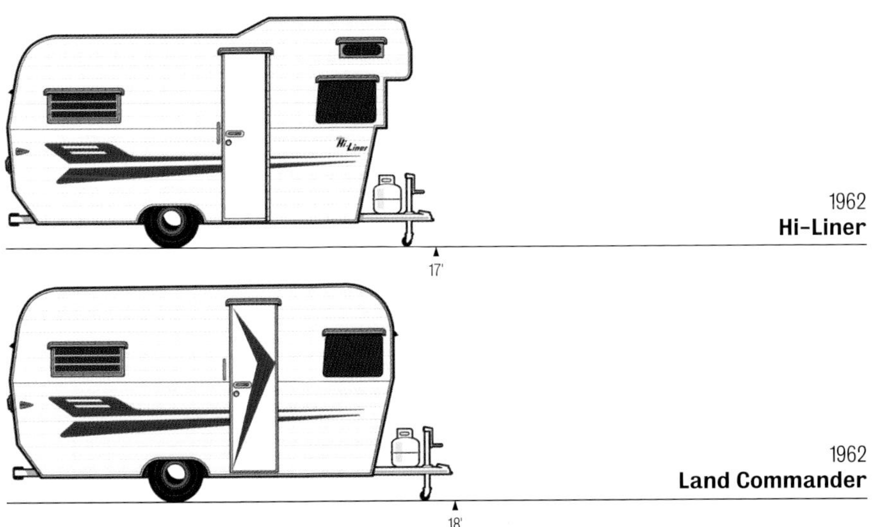

1962
Hi-Liner

1962
Land Commander

1963 Aristocrat Li'l Loafer

The diminutive Li'l Loafer was available in two versions. The standard version had a kitchen up front that included upper cabinets. The cabover version replaced the upper cabinets with a sliding bunk bed. Both were lightweight and maneuverable enough to be easily pulled by compact cars.

17'

1965
Mainliner

15'

1965
Lo-Liner

14'

1965
Travelier

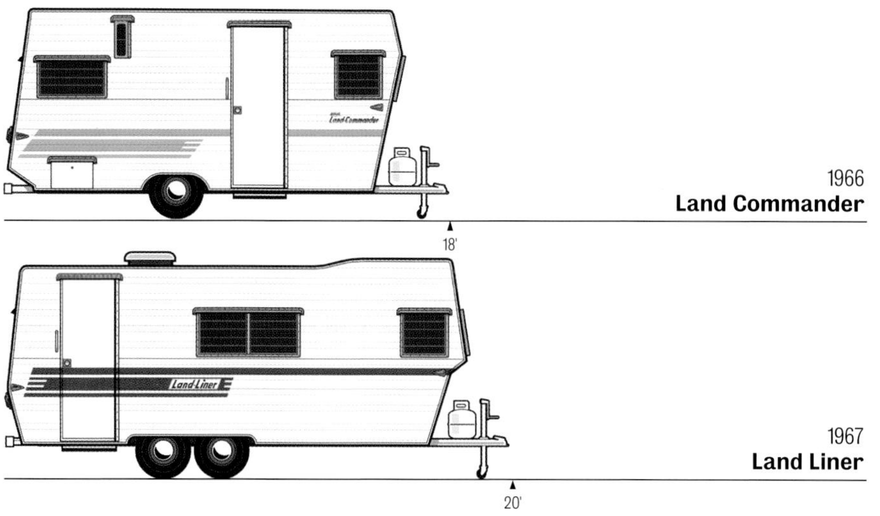

1966
Land Commander

18'

1967
Land Liner

20'

You're Following an Aristocrat

There's no better way to confirm you've spotted an Aristocrat trailer than by pulling up behind one and reading, "You're following an Aristocrat" embossed in black and white on a plastic sign riveted to Its tail end.

1972
Land Star

18'

AVION

An Airstream-like trailer distinguishable by ribbing on the curved panels, a square topped door, and Avion logo branding

Starting in 1968, models were fitted with tinted Astrovision windows inside black anodized aluminum frames

Avion (1955–2002)

Avion Coach Corporation • San Jacinto, California / Benton Harbor, Michigan

The Avion Coach Corporation, founded in 1955, purposely built aircraft-style aluminum trailers that mimicked Airstream trailers' appearance and design. According to a company brochure they decided to manufacture their luxurious coaches "on the premise that there were enough quality-minded people who would appreciate something infinitely superior to anything then available."

Airstream, Inc. filed a lawsuit before the first Avion trailer was off the line, but eventually lost its case in 1963 when it was determined that Airstream had no ownership of the design, shape, appearance, or construction of its trailers.

Avion went on to differentiate itself by changing the trailer shell to a satiny anodized aluminum. It took less maintenance and was meant to endure all types of weather and road conditions with less visible dinging and scratching. In 1967, the addition of tinted Astrovision windows cooled the outside appearance and controlled inside light. Other Avion firsts included Thermo-X polyurethane insulation and Smooth-Glide suspension.

Fleetwood bought the line in 1976. The aircraft-style trailers were replaced in 1991 with models built with more common materials and a more common shape. The brand was retired from service in 2002.

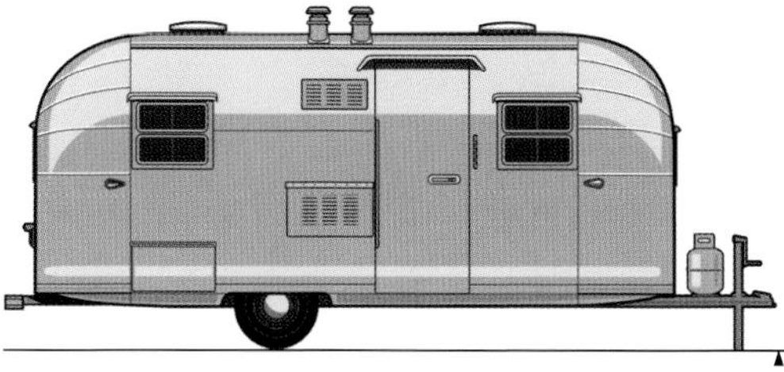

1957
Rambler

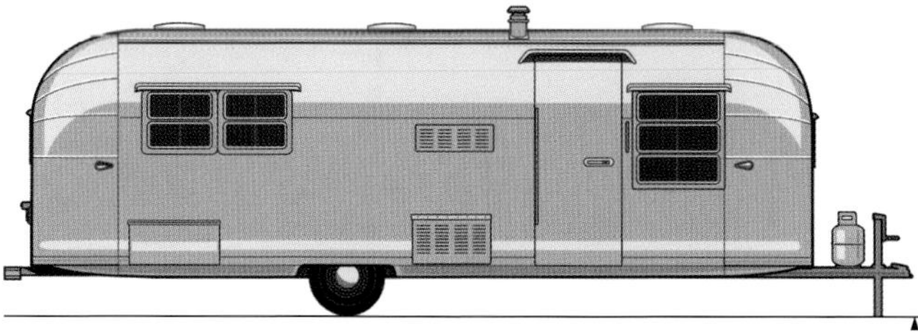

20'

1959
Regal

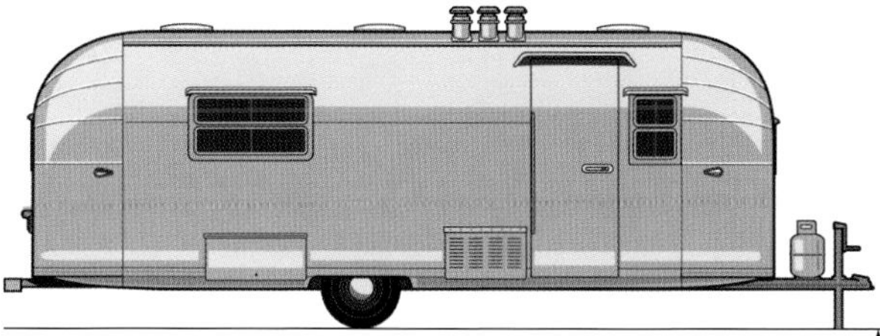

26'

1960
Holiday

24'

How to Tell an Avion from an Airstream

To the average person, vintage Avions and Airstreams are virtually identical other than their name badges. But there are a couple of details that help to differentiate them in the field: Avion models up to the early 1970s feature pronounced end-panel ribbing and a square-top door, compared to the smoother panel transitions and rounded door top found on Airstreams.

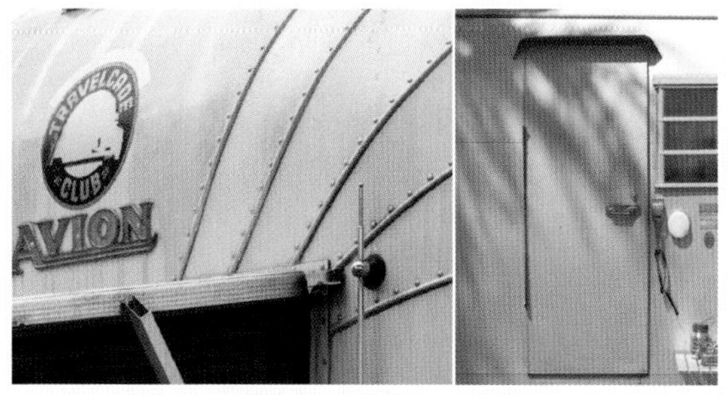

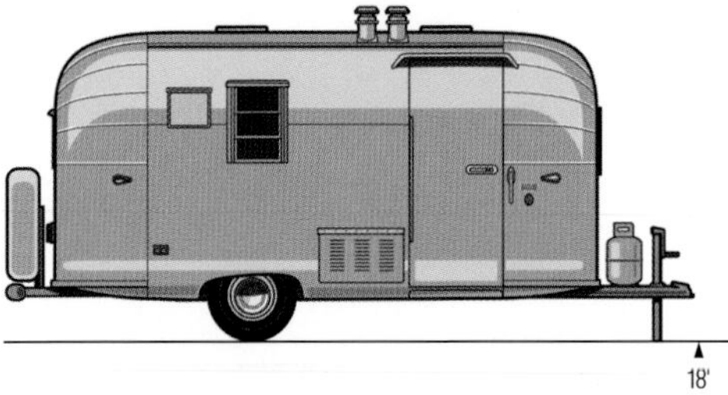

1963
Sportsman

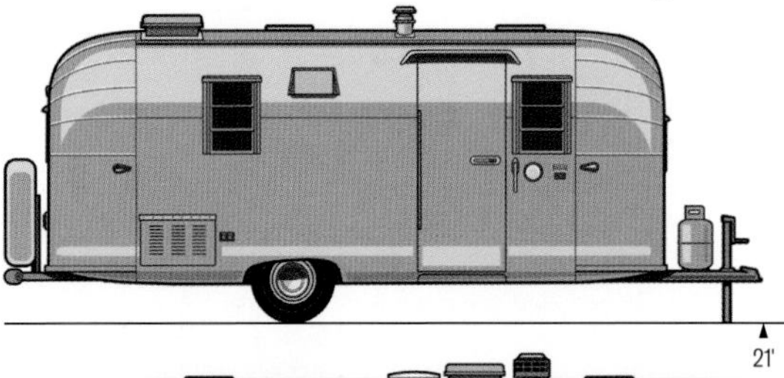

18'

1966
Tourist

21'

1968
Argonaut

25'

1968
Travelcader

28'

Smooth-Glide Suspension

Avion's marketing in the late 1960s and early '70s touted several "Great Ideas," including a unique suspension system, visible between the wheels on tandem models. The lifetime-warranted Smooth-Glide claimed zero maintenance, increased tire life, and an ultrasmooth ride.

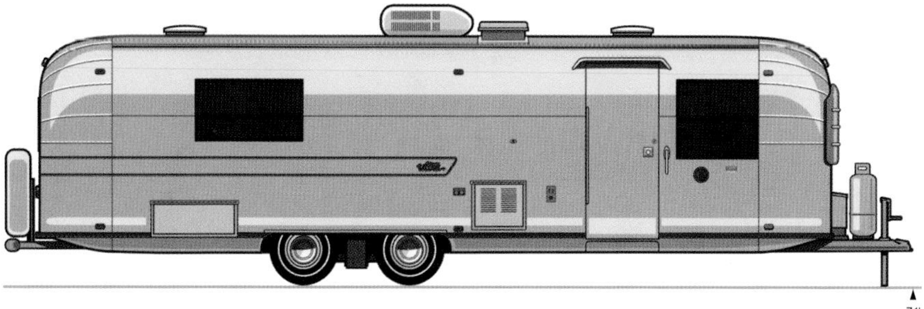

31'

1970 Avion Imperial Ultra

In 1970, Avion divided their lines into the Ultra, Classic, and Sports Special series. The Ultra series consisted of the Imperial, the Travelcader, and the Voyageur models. Their distinctive markings were red side trim, white sidewall tires, and a bay window.

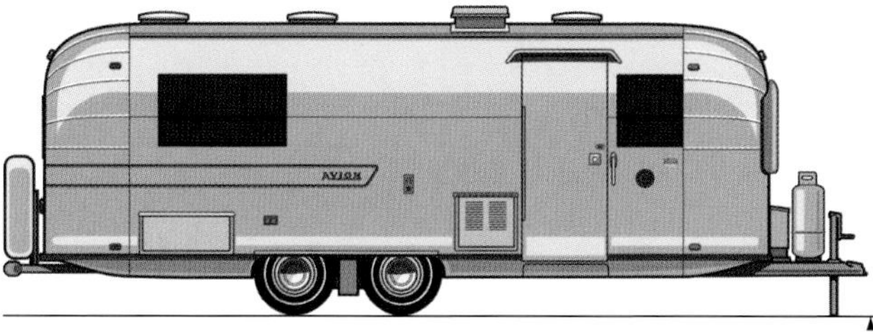

25'

1971
Voyageur

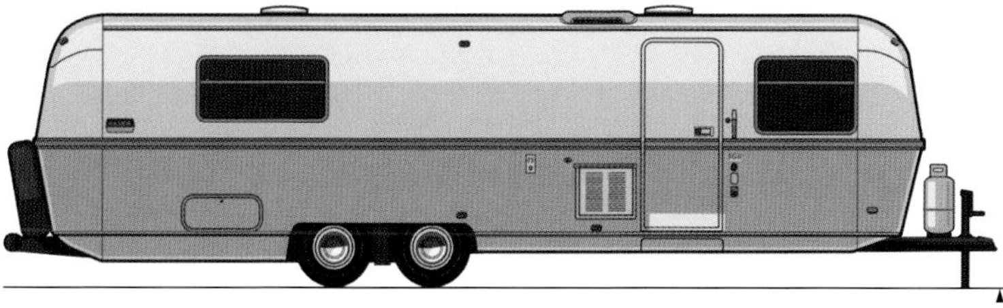

31'

1976
LaGrande

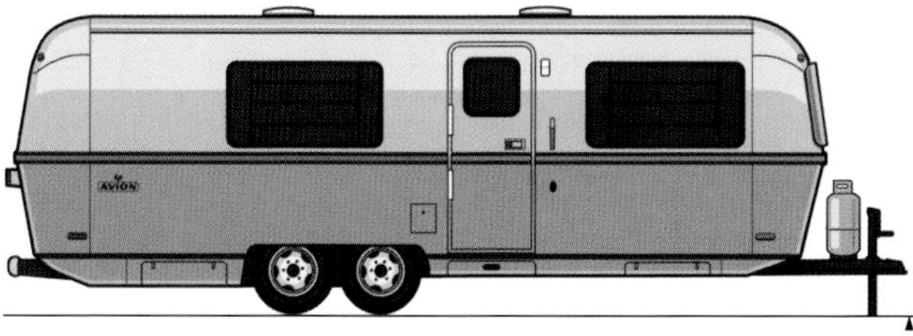

26'

1978
Model 26F

Ace (1960s–early 1970s)

Ace Traveler Corporation • Alfred, Maine

Ace had a full deck of travel trailers, including the 13-foot Heart, the 16-foot Diamond and self-contained Royal Diamond, and the 20-foot Royal Queen. They had a baked-on enamel aluminum skin outside. Inside, the walls and ceiling were covered with diamond-patterned aluminum, instead of the more typical choice of wood paneling that was common at the time.

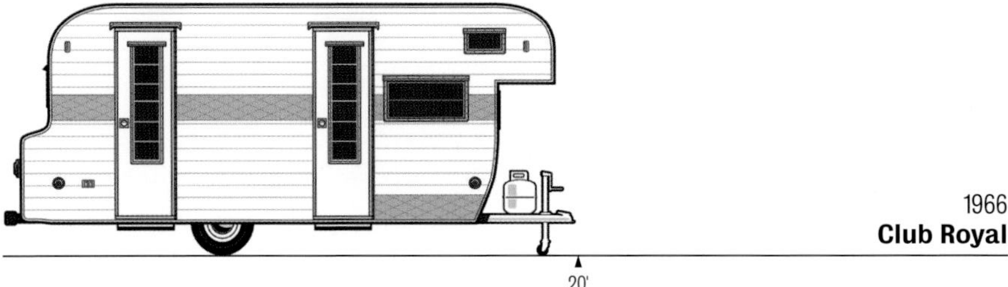

1966
Club Royal

Airlight (1954–55)

Airlight Trailer Company • Los Angeles, California

The lightweight all-aluminum aircraft-style trailers were offered in 15- and 24-foot lengths with two different floor plans. Although engineered and built by experienced teams, the Airlight brand was grounded after only one year on the market. The company went on to build more and larger models as the El Rey Trailer Company.

1955
Airlight 15' Rear Door

Alma Trailer Corporation (1934–57)

Alma Trailer Corporation • Alma, Michigan

Allen Hathaway, and William and Harold Redman founded the Alma Trailer Corporation in 1934. The Redmans left the company in 1937 to form the Redman Trailer Company. By 1944, Alma had the largest trailer plant in America. They manufactured Silver Moon trailers to house defense personnel during World War II. The company was bought by the Redman Trailer Company in 1957.

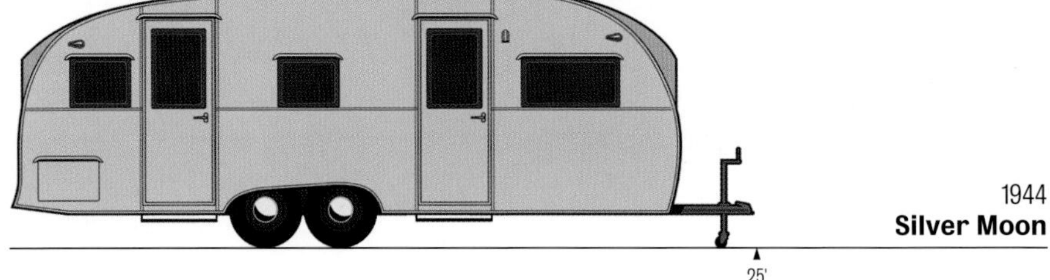

1944
Silver Moon

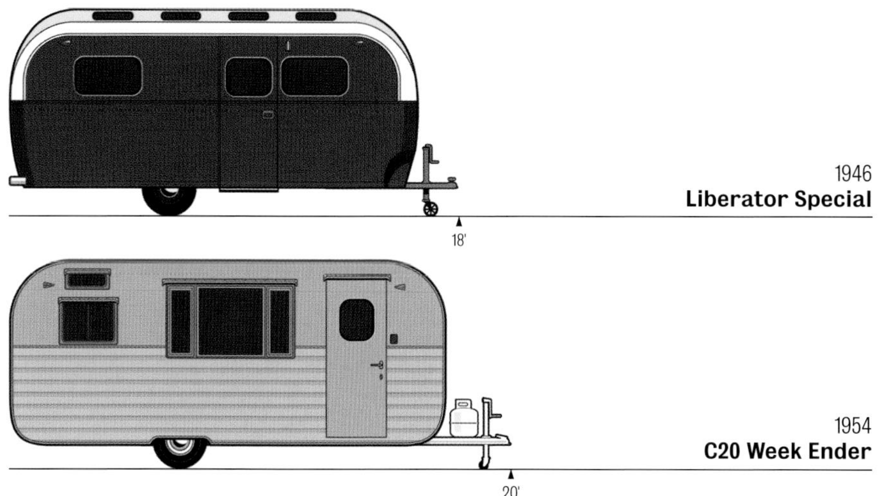

1946
Liberator Special

1954
C20 Week Ender

ALUMACOACH

Alumacoach (1969–72)

Alumacoach Industries, Ltd. • Richmond, British Columbia

The short-lived Alumacoach built two models of aircraft-style aluminum trailers: the 14-foot Mini-Cruiser and the 21-foot dual-axle Centennial Cruiser. Both trailers featured an oversized front window and sliding side windows. The 1971 Centennial Cruiser name celebrated British Columbia's 100th anniversary as a Canadian province.

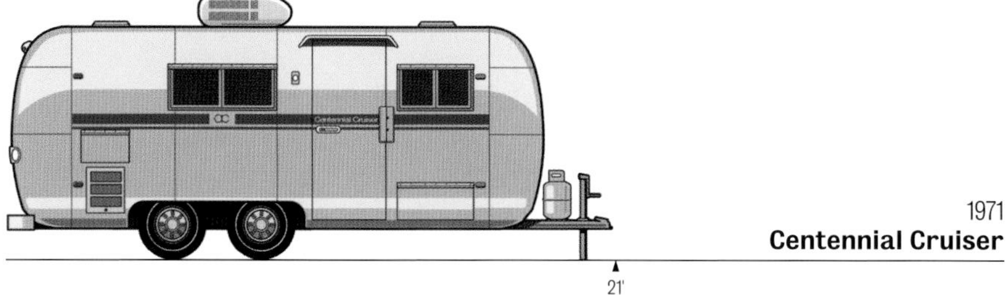

1971
Centennial Cruiser

Anderson (early 1940s–1957)

Anderson Coach Company • East Tawas, Michigan

Trailerites who lived in an Anderson park model felt right at home with its forced-air heating, fiberglass insulation, refrigerator with large freezer, and patented Expando snack bar. Anderson trailers used rigid stressing, a construction technique that made them both lightweight and strong. The Vent Wall—small windows near the ceiling—provided cross-ventilation in severe weather.

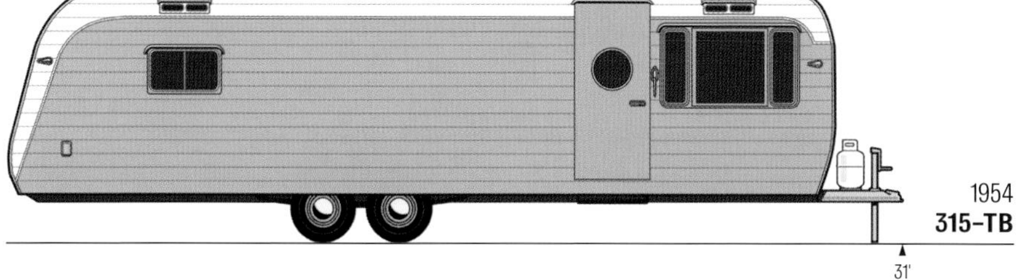

1954
315-TB

ARGOSY

Argosy (1972–79)

Argosy Manufacturing Co. • Versailles, Ohio

Argosy Manufacturing was a division of Airstream, and Airstream made both trailer brands. Moderately priced Argosy trailers, often called "Painted Airstreams," shared the shape and many features with their more expensive kin but had a painted fuselage and steel end caps. The Argosy Minuet line that launched in 1977 was narrower and had acrylic side windows.

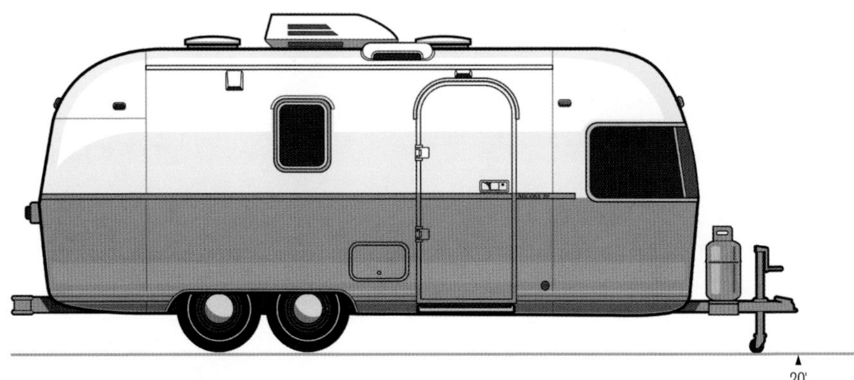

1972 Argosy 20

The shortest in the line, the Argosy 20 had a convertible front lounge that could sleep four comfortably. Two additional bunk beds were optional. Argosy furniture used "Perma-Tech" vinyl-covered hardwood with aluminum framing for its lasting beauty. All Argosy trailers came with a 12-month warranty that covered everything except for the tires and batteries.

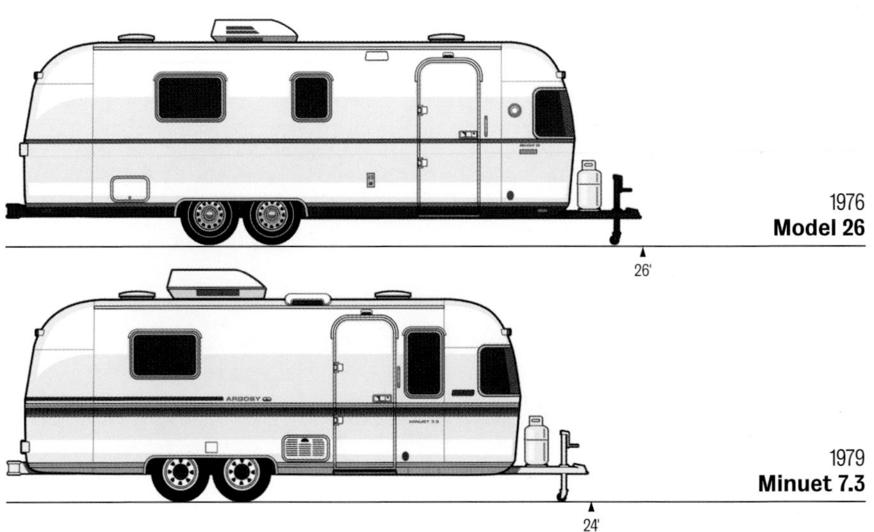

1976
Model 26

1979
Minuet 7.3

Arrow (1963–early 1970s)

Arrow Trailers, Inc. • Nappanee, Indiana

Only two canned ham–style models, the 13-foot Bow and the 15-foot Arrow, were built in Arrow's first year. They had a prefinished white aluminum exterior, jalousie windows, and mahogany interior. A small tribe of high-quality and low-priced models soon followed and continued the pointed theme: Little Chief, Dart, Lance, and Big Chief.

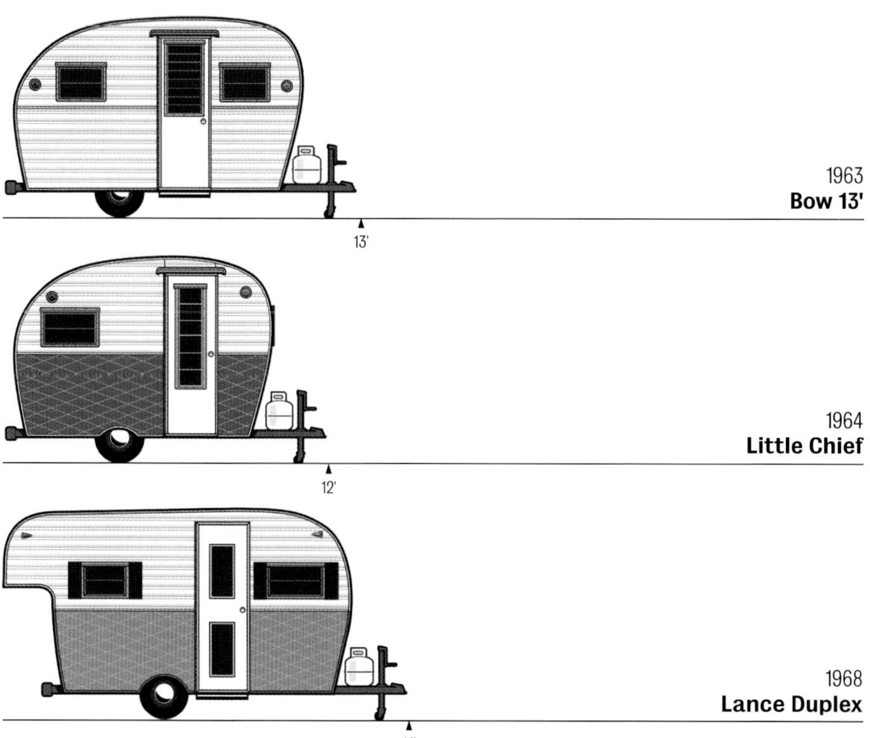

Arrowhead (1957–59)

Arrowhead Trailers • La Puente, California

Crown Sales, Inc. introduced a brother brand to Crown trailers in 1957, the Arrowhead. The company claimed to produce over 20 trailers a day in the most modern travel trailer factory in America. The bold arrow graphic that flies down the sides of the trailer came in a choice of seven colors. The 15- and 17-foot models could sleep five, while the 18-foot Queen of the Road slept four, but had a shower, toilet, and two doors.

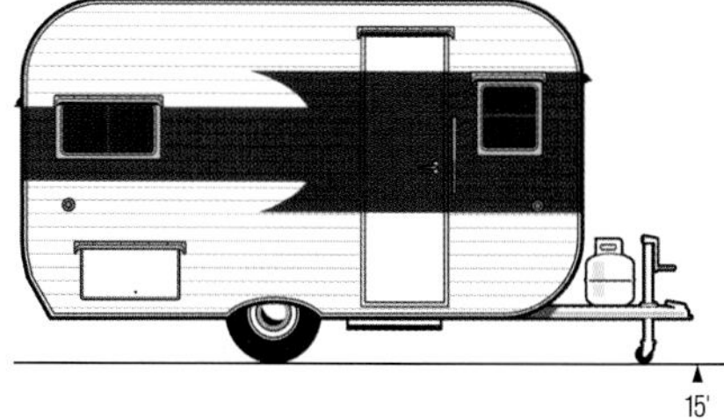

1958
Model 15'

15'

Avalair (1961–64)

Avalair Corporation • Baroda, Michigan

The first Avalair trailer was an aircraft-style model that boasted an outer shell made of Alcoa Acrylic aluminum. The advertised models included the 20-foot Venture, 22-foot Ranger, 25-foot Saber, 27-foot Wanderer, and 29-foot Voyager. The boxy aluminum Mark II, released in 1963, came in 17-foot and 19-foot models. They were self-contained, and had a large wardrobe and birch cabinets.

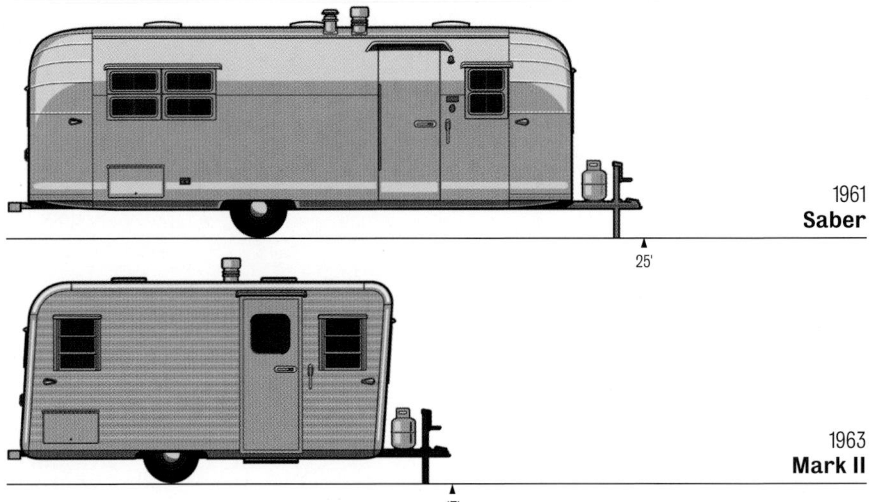

Avalon (1960–70)

Avalon Mobile Homes Corporation • Elkhart / Bristol, Indiana

Soon after the Avalon brand name first appeared on a canned ham–style trailer, it was emblazoned on a mobile office, a truck camper, and a motor home. The early Avalon vacation trailers had a tubular frame, an electrical system that used modern Romex wiring, and deluxe appliances. Later models added features like thermostatically controlled heat and grooved birch paneling.

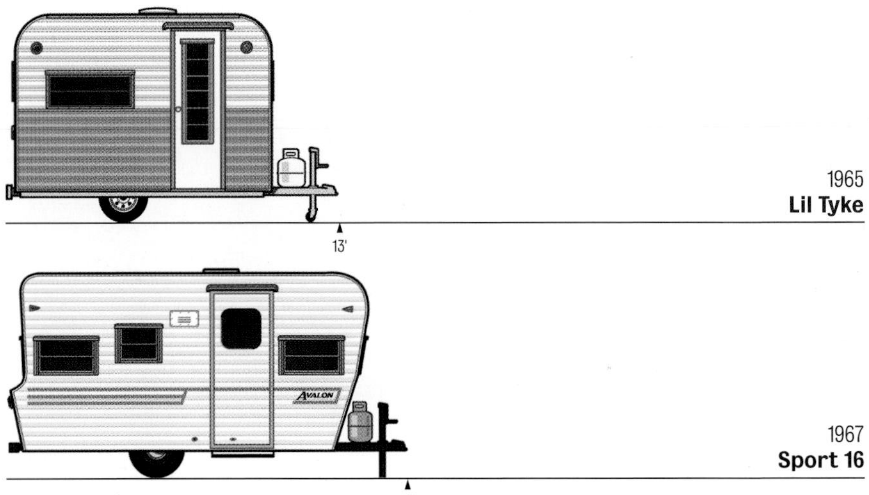

B

Bee Line

Compact canned ham, early models were available in white, or white with a yellow stripe

Most models were branded with the Bee Line name, and sometimes a bee character

Bee Line (1960–75)

Bee Line Mobile Home, Inc. • Elkhart, Indiana

Bob Barth owned Bee Line Mobile Home, Inc., makers of black-and-yellow-jacketed trailers in the early 1960s. The lightweight, economical, and weekend-sized canned ham–style trailers were "built for fun" according to their ads.

The Hornet, Honey Bee, Wasp, and Week-Ender, all 13-foot models, were priced based on their different construction techniques and options. For example, the Hornet, the most basic model, was built with no internal wall framing or insulation. Its standard features included a gas light (necessary for boondocking), a two-burner stove, and five opening windows. Cluster lights and canvas bunks were available options.

Other models could have their front roof extended with a bunk-over option to give them more room above the dinette. Their doors included jalousie windows to increase airflow and light. By the mid-1960s, Bee Line vacation trailers included the Vacationer, the Queen Bee, and the improbably named King Bee.

In 1963, Bob Barth left Bee Line to form the Barth Trailer Company. Barth produced all-aluminum trailers until 1968. Bee Line continued making trailers until 1975.

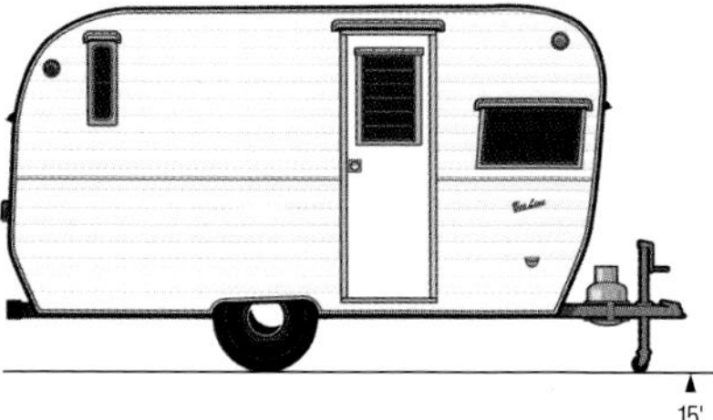

1960
Bumblebee

1960 Bee Line 13-Foot Week-Ender

An economical trailer that was "for those who require compactness, but not a tent." Its step-down floor lowered the entrance and the overall height of the trailer. It was easy to tow, could be stored in a garage, and was available with a prepainted or high-polished aluminum exterior.

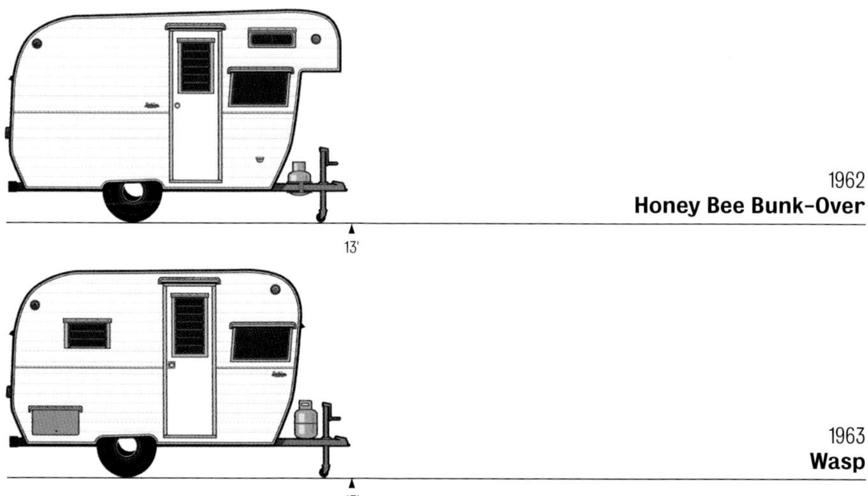

1962
Honey Bee Bunk-Over

1963
Wasp

1963
Hornet

13'

1963
Queen Bee

20'

1965
16' Self-Contained

16'

● 1965 Bee Line 18' SCRG

This self-contained model included a marine toilet with a holding tank. Bee Line, like many manufacturers, added a bunk-over option to give their standard models more sleeping space in the early 1960s. Bunk-overs jutted out over the front of the trailer but were built on the same frame length and had the same roof height as standard models.

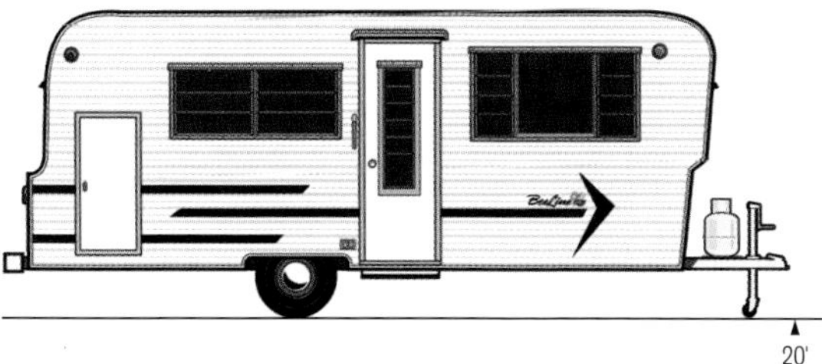

1967
Model 20

The Bees of Bee Line

Many trailer makers in the 1960s branded themselves by name, color palette, and cartoon characters. Bee Line's busy mascot began as a worker in 1960 and by 1965 had risen to queen bee. She crowned the line with a playful buzz through 1975.

1969
Model 16RB

1972
Model 220A-FTL

Canned ham shape with smooth riveted aluminum skin (1940s and '50s)

1960 models onward featured a gold anodized aluminum stripe on their sides

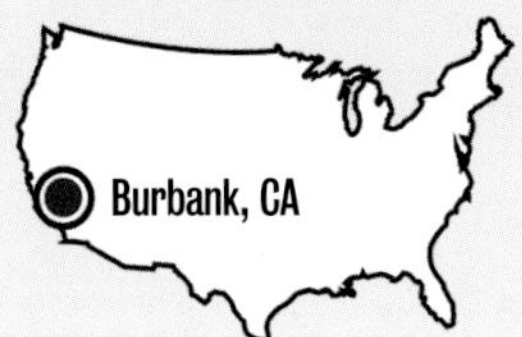

Boles-Aero (1947–80)

Boles Manufacturing Company / Boles-Aero Inc. • Burbank, California

The story of the Boles Manufacturing Company begins in a one-car garage in Burbank, California, circa 1946. This modest location is where Don Boles, using knowledge he'd gained in making aircraft for the Lockheed Aircraft Corporation, made his first all-aluminum trailers.

From the beginning, Boles made sure his trailers were built using the best materials and with outstanding craftsmanship. Boles-Aero trailers had aluminum frames and all-riveted construction, in common with other aeronautically named trailers, but not their fuselage-shaped bodies.

The first Boles-Aero trailers were simple 9-foot canned hams, but through the years they developed into 27- to 35-foot models called Nonpareil. Their boxiness made for more livable area and storage space. Constant improvement in their manufacture and in quality standards meant that later models offered forced-air heating, outside aluminum awnings, and "Scene-O-Ramic" wraparound front windows.

The last of the Boles-Aero trailers were the 1980 models. Although gone, they were not forgotten. Don Boles was inducted into the RV/MH Hall of Fame in 2005.

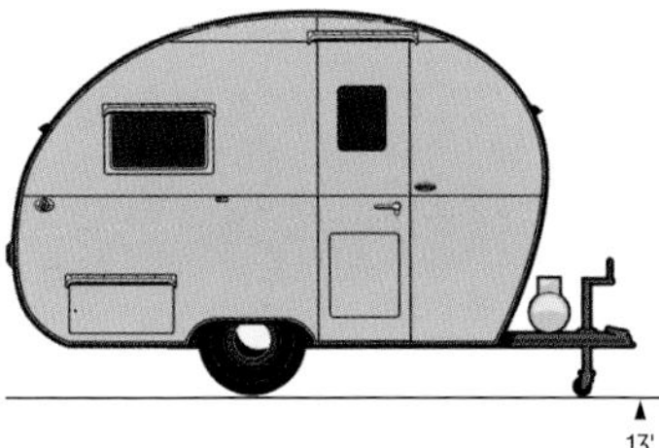

13'

1947
Model 13

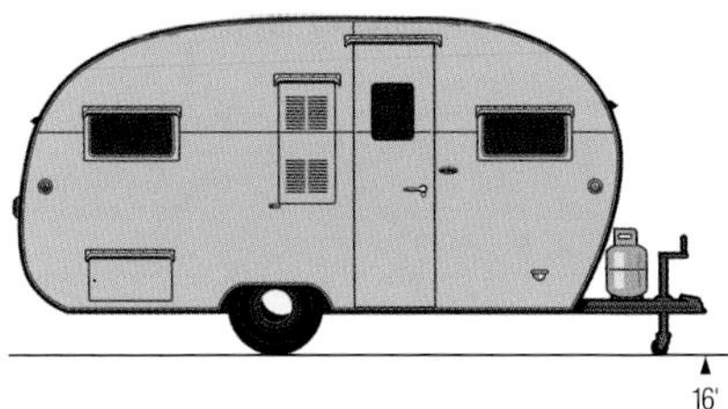

16'

1949
Model 16

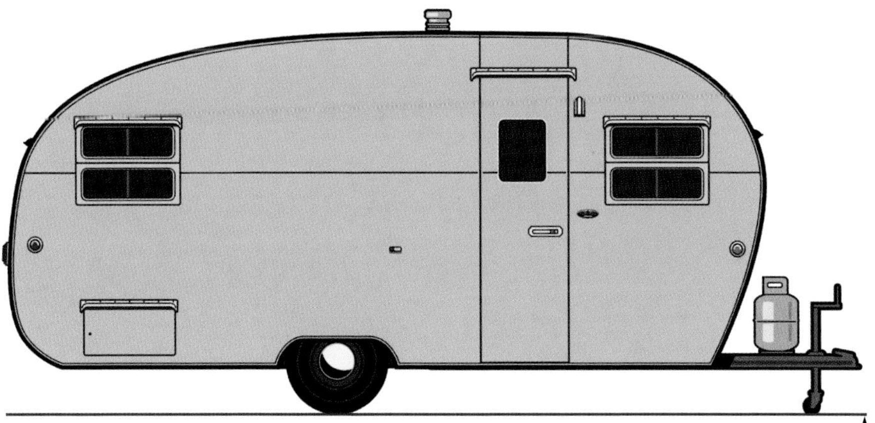

17'

1951 Boles-Aero Mira Mar

In 1951, Boles-Aeros were given Spanish names that mirrored the warmth and romance of Southern California and the Baja Peninsula. The Pacific Ocean would never seem far away in a Mira Mar, Montecito, Ensenada, Estrellita, La Paz, Monterey, or El Dorado. The naming convention faded away by the 1959 model year.

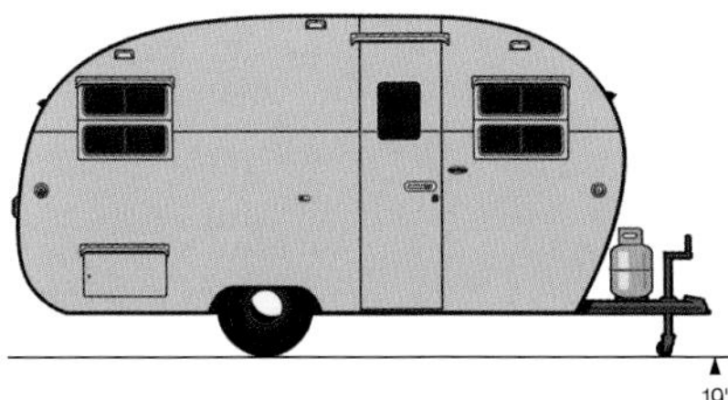

19'

1952
Monterey

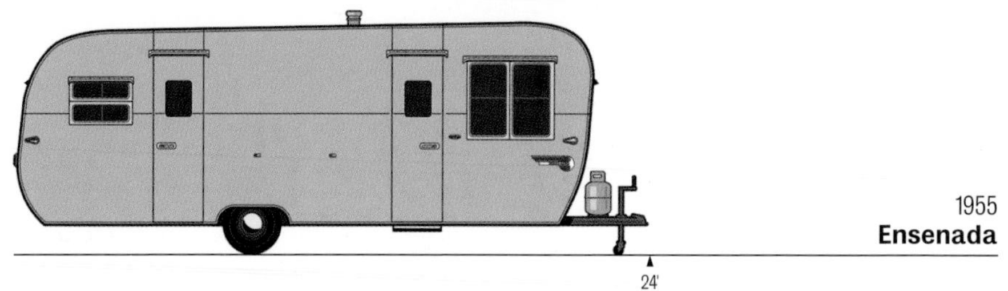

1955
Ensenada

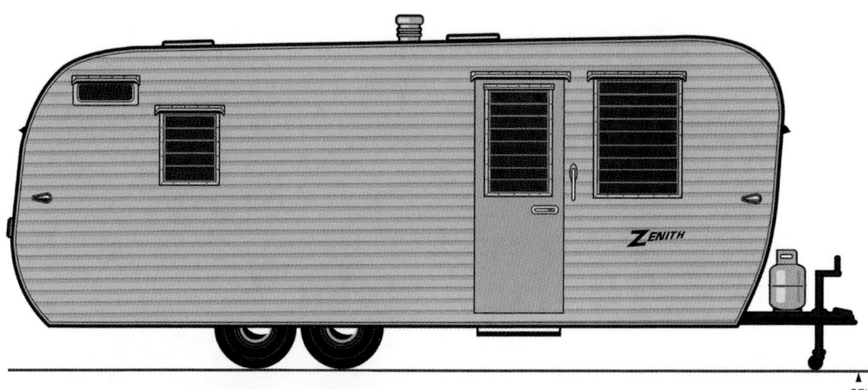

1956 Boles-Aero Zenith 23'

In 1956, Boles-Aero began advertising a "high in quality, low in price" line of trailers branded as Zenith. Similar in shape and style to their high-end counterparts, Zeniths ranged from 16 to 45 feet (see page 282).

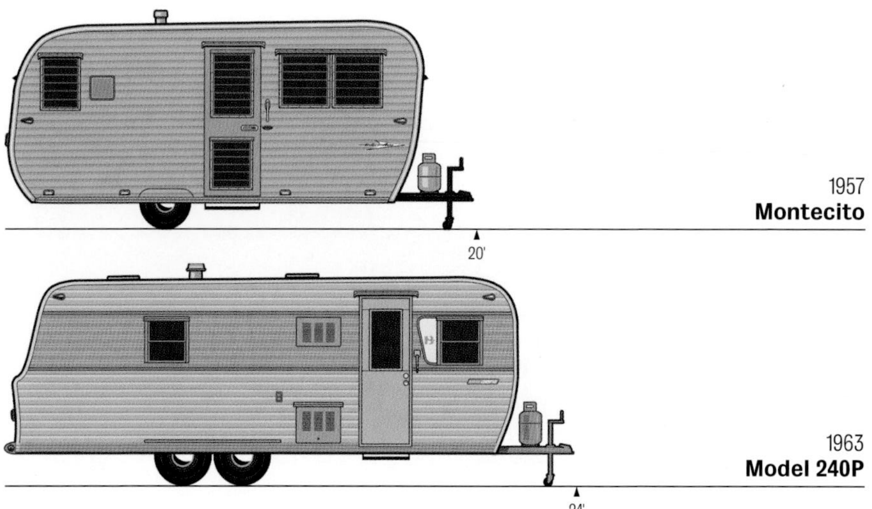

1957
Montecito

1963
Model 240P

1973
Nonpareil XL

27'

Boles-Aero Badges

The flying B Boles-Aero badges kept their wings for the company's life span. These few examples (there are more iterations) show the evolution of the logo and the brand.

The simple metal badge, like the trailers themselves, changed over time. It became a sophisticated golden bird as the trailer line became larger and more luxurious.

The original badge featured the wings of an eagle wrapping the B of Boles-Aero and seemingly lifting the badge up in flight. In later versions, the B flies toward the front of the trailer and to the horizon.

1977
Nonpareil XL

31'

BOWLUS "Road Chief"

Bowlus (1934–36)

Bowlus-Teller Manufacturing Company • San Fernando, California

The legendary aviation designer and builder Hawley Bowlus designed Bowlus-Teller trailers. Bowlus, who had experimented on gliders since 1910, was Superintendent of Construction at Ryan Airlines over Charles Lindbergh's *Spirit of St. Louis* aircraft in 1927.

Aerodynamic aircraft-style construction with unique front-of-trailer door placement

Bowlus-Teller Manufacturing was the first trailer company to use an aluminum and copper alloy with the trade name Duralumin. The aircraft-grade aluminum alloy provided a strong and lightweight skin for its trailers. Their flagship model, the Road Chief, took its rounded features and horizontal lines from art moderne and other transportation icons of the time: Zephyr Streamliners, Buck Rogers's spaceship, and the *Graf Zeppelin.*

Skirted fenders bearing the manufacturer and model names

The company struggled and soon fell into bankruptcy. Bowlus sold his designs for the Road Chief to Wally Byam, the founder of Airstream. Byam renamed it the Airstream Clipper and moved the front door to the side, making it more aerodynamic.

The Road Chief is the most elusive of vintage trailers. There is rumored to be only about 20 originals in existence of the 140 built between 1934 and 1936. Spotting an original on the highway is rare, but seeing a new one is a possibility. Bowlus Road Chief reintroduced the brand and makes a contemporary version of the trailer.

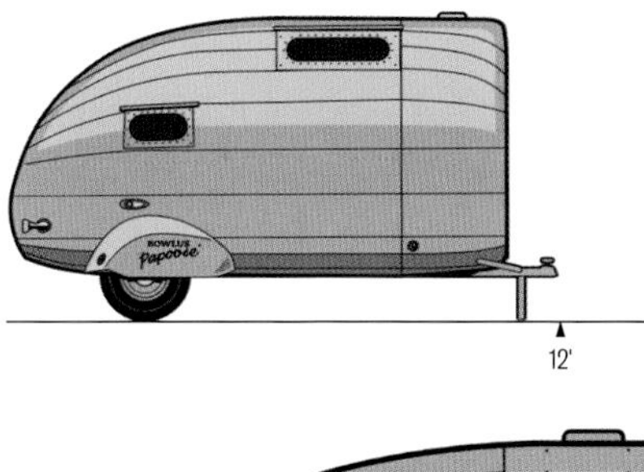

1934
Papoose

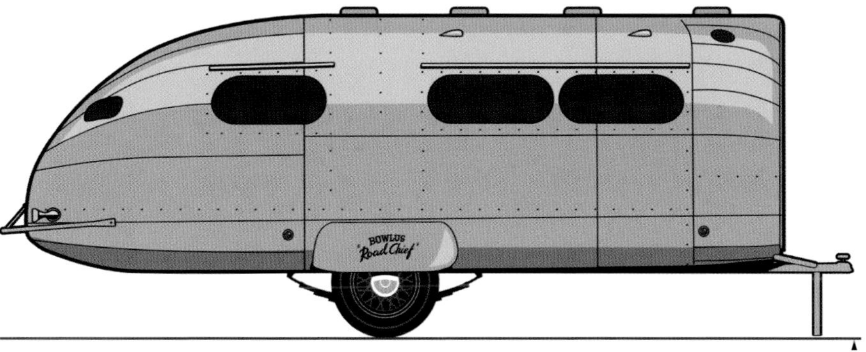

1935 Bowlus Road Chief

The Road Chief was a reflection of Hawley Bowlus's mastery of aircraft design and engineering. Beautifully crafted, its lightweight aluminum body was strong and aerodynamic. Though 19 feet bumper to hitch, it weighed only 1,100 pounds and could be easily towed by the average car of the era.

Along with the Road Chief line, the 1935 Bowlus-Teller catalog touted two other RV concepts: the 30-foot, V-8 powered Motor Chief and the 10-foot Trail-Ur-Boat, a versatile sportman's trailer constructed of two boats attached gunnel to gunnel.

Trail-Ur-Boat

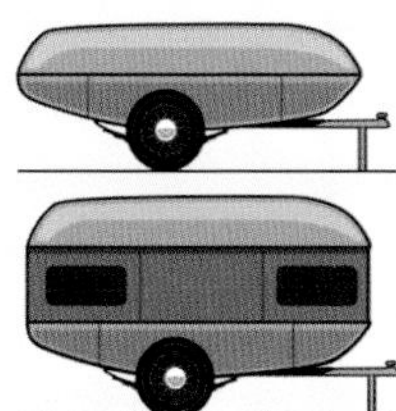

Motor Chief

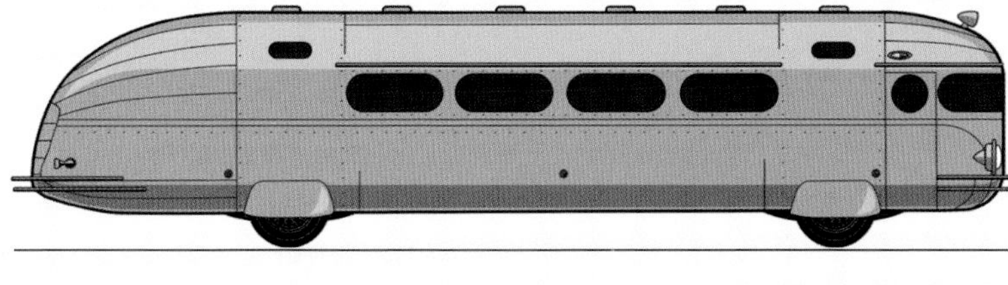

Banner (1963–80)

Banner Homes Corporation • Elkhart, Indiana

The "fit for a king" vacation trailers started small with the 13-foot Pennant series, then over the years crisscrossed the map with a complete range of price points, names, and lengths. Models that carried the Banner name included the Laredo, Madison, Waco, Buffalo, Houston, Tampa, Atlanta, Reno, and Sarasota. An optional rear bunk-over in 1960s models gave the line a unique jutting tail.

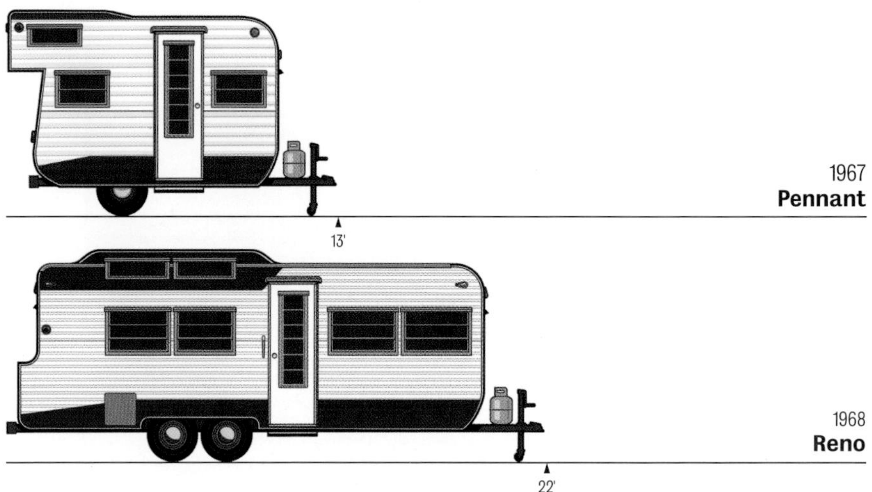

1967
Pennant

1968
Reno

Barth (1963–68)

Barth Corporation • Milford, Indiana

Bob Barth moved up the manufacturing ladder when he sold Bee Line Mobile Home, Inc., maker of modestly priced vacation trailers, to start the eponymous Barth Corporation. His new company built small quantities of high-quality all-aluminum bread loaf–style trailers. Prestige models were marketed to well-heeled customers as having first-class comfort, convenience, and price.

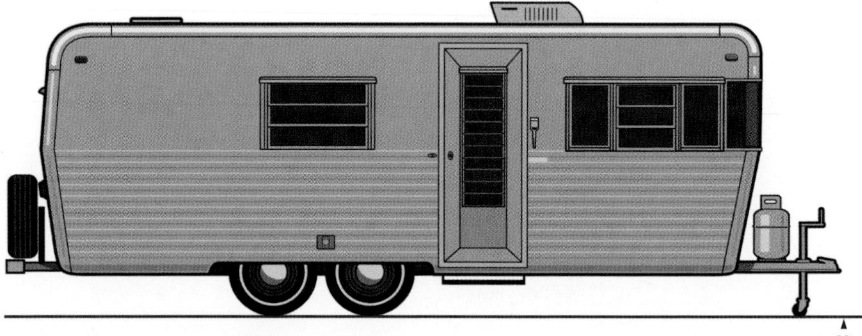

● 1966 Barth Air-Flo

The 1966 Barth line featured an Air-Flo design that incorporated an aluminum roof that wrapped over its smooth upper body. Barth trailers had a series of raised bands that ran down their lower sides, a uniquely beveled door, and a front end with indoor/outdoor Panavision windows.

Beemer (1953–mid-1960s)

Beemer & Grubb Enterprises • Mt. Morris, Michigan

A regional trailer manufacturer that kept a low profile during its lifetime. A 1953 advertisement from *Trailer Dealer* magazine offered a 19-foot, two-door trailer shell for $995 FOB factory for sportsmen and DIYers who wanted to outfit their own trailer. Beemer trailers generally fall in the canned ham family and have a straight-edged bottom that lacks wheel wells.

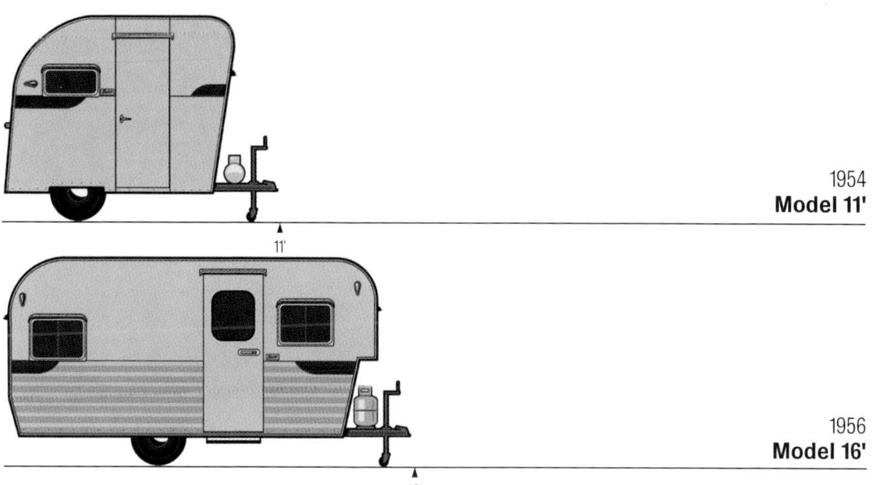

1954
Model 11'

1956
Model 16'

Bell (1961–77)

Bell Manufacturing Corporation • Kalispell, Montana

Bell "Distinctive Travel Homes" were well made, midpriced vacation trailers and truck campers that ranged across the highways of the 11 western states. The line, flat-roof, rounded-end variations of a canned ham–style trailer, offered models from 13 to 21 feet. Smaller models had a band of one or two coordinating colors on their sides, front, and tail.

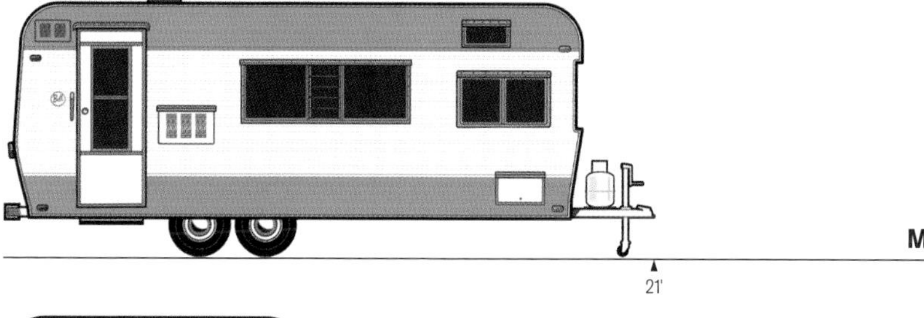

1969
Majestic

1973
Model 13'

Bellwood (1953–56)

Bellwood Trailer Coach • Phoenix, Arizona / Aloha, Oregon

The Bellwood canned ham is a twin with the 1956 Aloha Model 13. Both trailers were built in Aloha, Oregon, and are identical in shape and size. In the mid-1950s, the Bellwood Trailer Coach and Aloha Trailer Coach brand names appeared on similar badges. Coincidence? It's likely that the Aloha Trailer Company made both brands, but decided that the Aloha name was a better marketing opportunity during the tiki craze of the time.

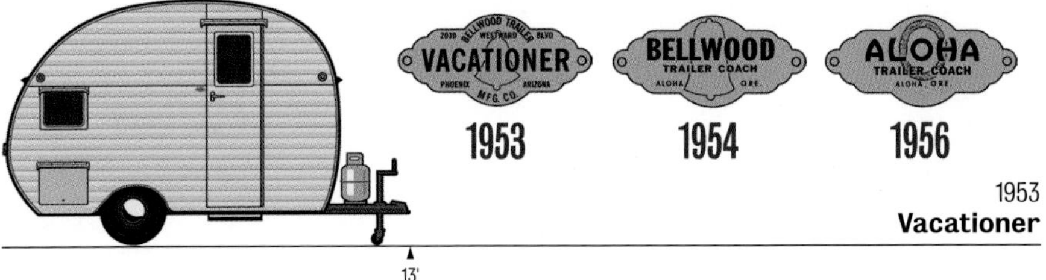

1953
Vacationer

Benroy (1953–55)

Benroy Trailer Products • Burbank, California

The 10-foot, 760-pound Benroy teardrop trailer was easy to tow and maneuver. Sportsmen of the 1950s found the small and basic camping unit to be a comfortable tent replacement. The inside was furnished with a three-quarter-size mattress, cabinets, and bookshelves. Its galley had a propane stove, running water, an ice box, and a drop-leaf table for stand-up meals.

10'

1954
DeLuxe

Blazon (1964–79)

Blazon Mobile Homes Corporation • Elkhart, Indiana

Blazon was one of the many RV manufacturers that hailed from Elkhart, Indiana, in the 1960s. Its brand was originally displayed only on vacation models, but as customers' tastes changed they built park models, fifth wheels, and motor homes. In 1971, Blazon added the economical Caper line for weekend camping and the expensive Elite line that stood out with its own coat of arms.

14'

1967
14' Front Kitchen

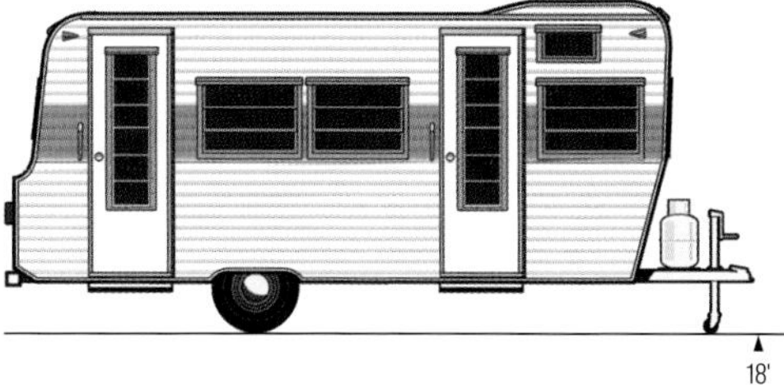

1968
Two-Door Rear Kitchen

boler

Boler (1968–88)

Boler Company • Winnipeg, Manitoba

A Boler fiberglass trailer could nest up to two adults and two children. The interior cupboards, closet, and bunks were made of fiberglass too. It was lightweight and easily pulled by a small car. The deceased Boler American, ECO, Love Bug, and Perris Pacer lines were made from imported Boler molds. Casita, Trillium, and Scamp trailers are the living descendants of the egg-shaped trailer.

● 1970 Boler 13'

A molded fiberglass shell provided the Boler a corrosion-free body with a durable finish. The color coordinated exterior needed minimal maintenance. Its basic amenities included a kitchen with a sink, a two-burner stove, and a small refrigerator. A dinette in the rear converted into a double bed, while a gaucho in the front converted into bunk beds.

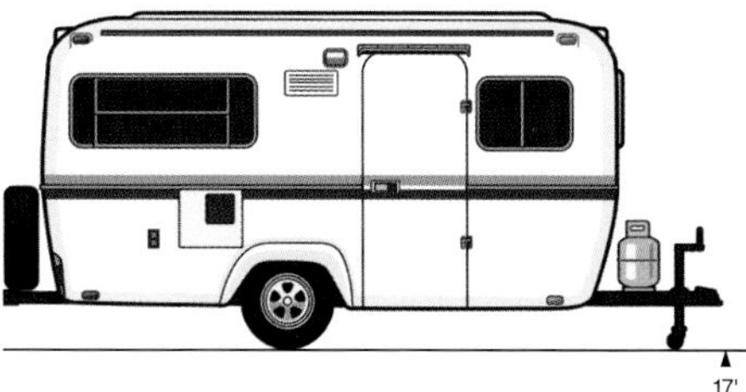

1978
Model 1700

Bonanza (1969–78)

Bonanza Trailers, Inc • Elkhart, Indiana / Coffeyville, Kansas

The Bonanza brand adorned several manufacturer's trailers during the mid-twentieth century, probably due to the popularity of the long-running western TV show of the same name. Bonanza models were herded into three series: the Pinto, the Standard, and the Deluxe. By the mid-1970s, fifth wheels and park models rounded out the stock and were sold as "a way of life."

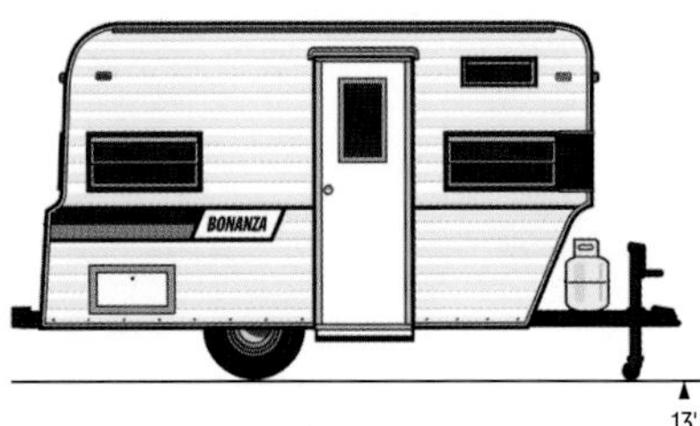

1973
Pinto

Broken Arrow (1960–73)

Broken Arrow Mobilhome Manufacturing, Inc • Broken Arrow, Oklahoma

The Broken Arrow Tepee and Wigwam were completely equipped and inexpensive canned ham–style trailers. Tepees generally came in 13-, 15-, or 16-foot lengths with a self-contained option. Wigwams were from 19 to 28 feet with optional tandem doors.

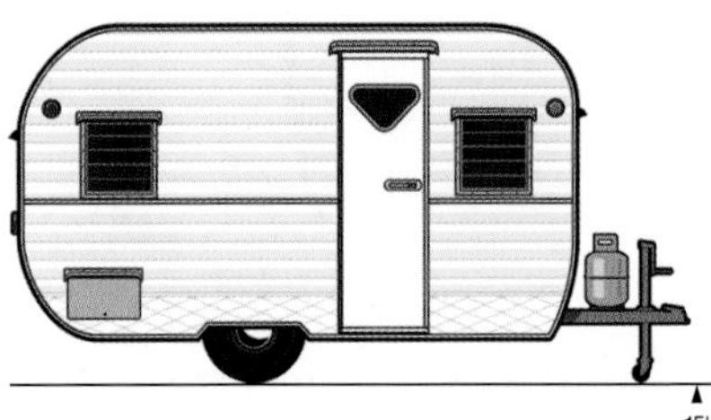

1960
Tepee

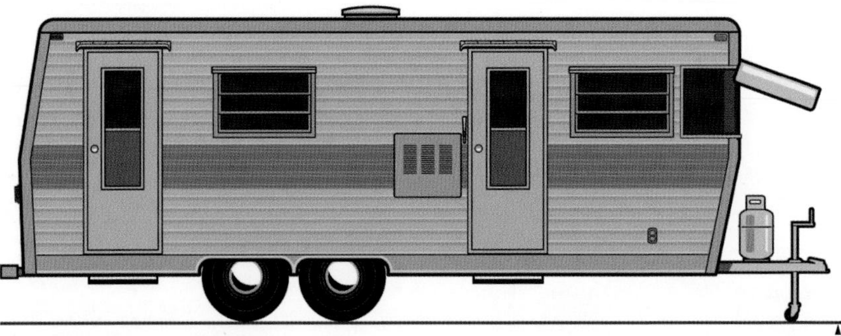

● 1972 Arrow-Flite

In the mid-1960s the all-aluminum Arrow-Flite line hit the market with its ultimate ruggedness, comfort, and beauty. Less standout was its name, which is easily confused with manufacturers like Aero Flite, Airfloat, and Airlight, and Shasta's Airflyte model.

C

Cardinal

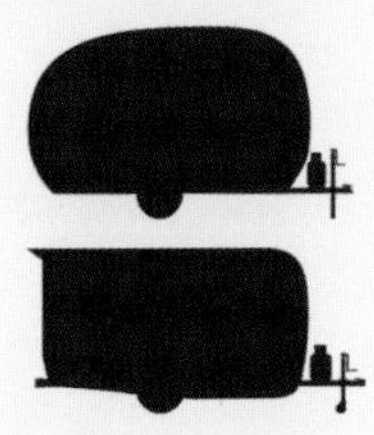

Canned ham body with various bold graphics (1952–64)

Boxy shape with wing-bar graphics and a cardinal crest projecting from the back roof (1965–78)

Cardinal (1954–78)

Adams Manufacturing Company • El Monte, California

The first Cardinals made by the Adams Manufacturing Company landed in the western United States in the early 1950s. The company name changed to Adams Trailer Manufacturing, Inc., then to Adams Vacation Trailer Manufacturing, Inc. as they became increasingly specialized.

The trailer's name honored the northern cardinal in its logo, color palette, and even the shape of later models. The male cardinal is bright red with a black face mask, while the female is tinged red on the tail, wings, and crest. Although the trailers were available in different colors, the line's dominant body color, like the bird, was red with black accents.

Cardinal vacation trailers were small, lightweight, and easy to tow. They displayed a sense of style by incorporating sporty lines and bold graphics. The early models' rounded canned ham shape never totally left Cardinals as they evolved by 1965 into a straight-tail version with a crest-like roofline.

The last model year that Cardinals were built by Adams was 1978. The Cardinal name is currently used by Forest River for luxury fifth wheels.

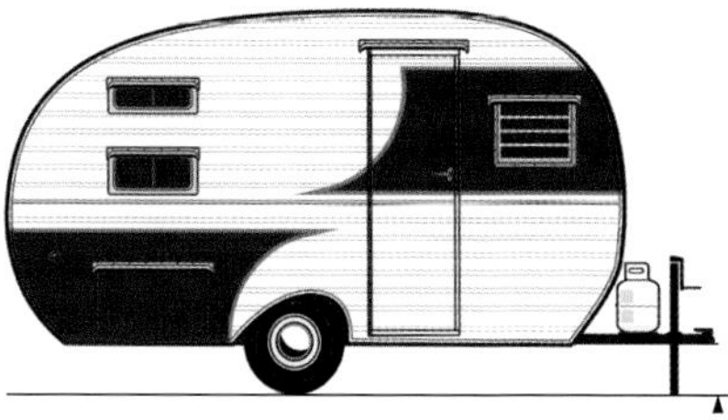

C

1956
Deluxe

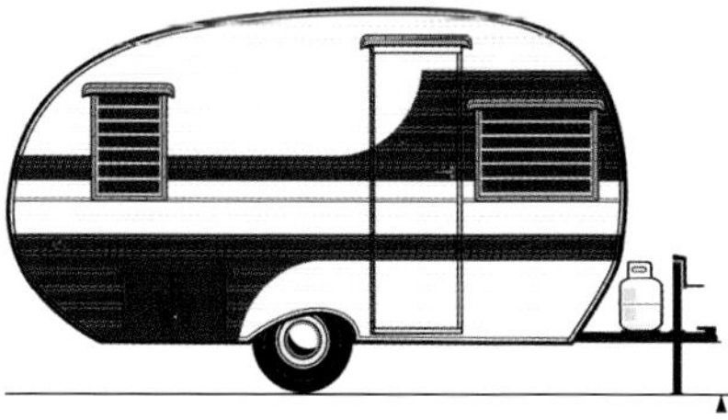

16'

1958
Model 16

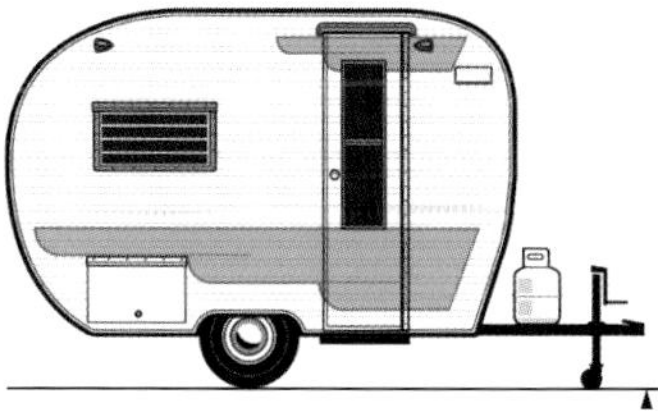

16'

1964
Model 13

13'

14'

1970 Cardinal Model 14 Love Bird

A lightweight and low-profile trailer, the 1970 Cardinal Model 14 was nicknamed the Love Bird because its compact size made it the perfect nesting site for two campers or a small family. While only 14 feet from tongue to tail, it managed to pack a dinette, two beds, a closet, and a full kitchen into its 11-foot cabin.

Bread loaf body style, with Masonite or leatherette siding and canvas top

Cast metal badge with artwork depicting a covered wagon can be found on many models

Covered Wagon (1932–68)

The Covered Wagon Company • Mount Clemens, Michigan

The Covered Wagon Company, founded in 1929 by Arthur G. Sherman, is credited with building the first travel trailer. Sherman patented his streamlined travel trailer in 1930, and by 1935 Covered Wagon was building them on the industry's first production line, based on Sherman's observations of the Ford Motor Company plant a few miles down the road.

The line produced between 35 and 40 of the Masonite-sided and canvas-topped trailers a day. Production and sales increased throughout the 1930s, eventually making Covered Wagon the country's largest travel trailer manufacturer.

Covered Wagon introduced Shermanite siding to their trailers in 1937. The zinc-coated steel and plywood covering weatherproofed the trailers' bodies. The company left the trailer business at the start of World War II to build truck parts and went out of business in 1946.

RV/MH Hall of Fame honoree Herbert Reeves Jr. acquired the rights to the Covered Wagon in 1958. The next-generation models were built until 1968. Arthur G. Sherman was inducted into the RV/MH Hall of Fame in 1974.

1933 Covered Wagon

After creating a patent model for the first "travel trailer" in 1930, Arthur Sherman made some revisions to his design and hand-built a few models in 1932. Assembly-line production of Covered Wagon trailers began in 1933.

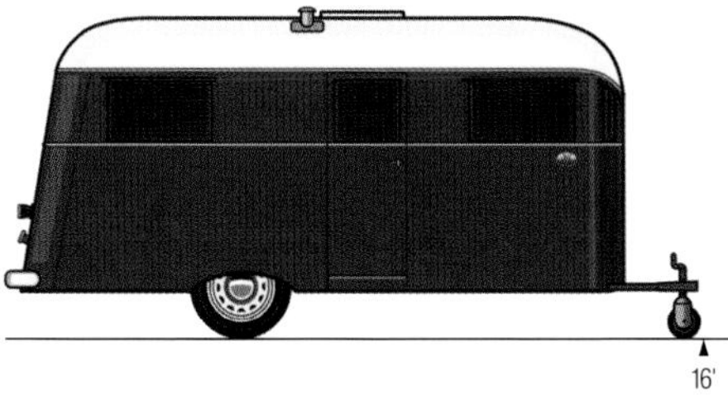

1936
Master

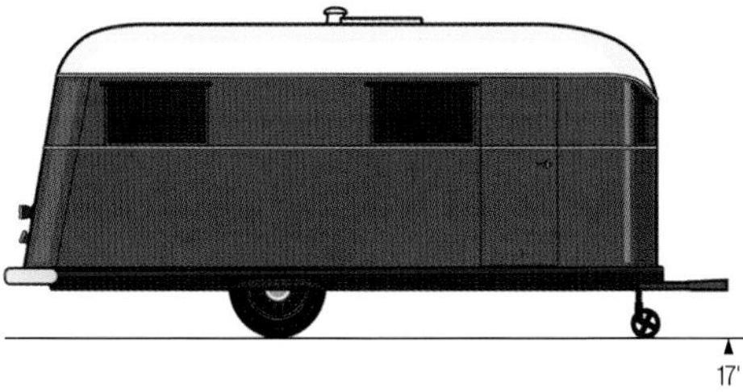

16'

1939
Road Master

17'

1959
International

18'

Curtis Wright

Two large eye-like windows stare out from the prow

Nameplate by door identifies manufacturer, model number, and serial number

Curtis Wright (1946–49)

Curtis Wright Industries • Los Angeles, California

Curtis Wright named his company after himself and, by coincidence, one of the best-known names in aviation, the Curtiss-Wright Corporation. There was no connection between the two. Although Wright did make some aircraft, his name has gone down in trailer history.

When the Curtis Wright Clipper landed in 1947 it seemed revolutionary. It was aerodynamic, all-aluminum, and looked capable of space flight. But it had pre-World War II progenitors: the Bowlus Road Chief and Wally Byam's Airstream Clipper.

Byam, working as a production supervisor, modified his trailer designs for Wright. The Clipper gained bigger plexiglass windows and a wider entry, but was much the same as its earlier incarnation. Their partnership lasted until early 1947. Byam went on to restart Airstream, Inc. The rest of the Curtis Wright trailers deepened the nautical theme with names like Flagship, Cutter, and Cruiser. Collectors today generally refer to them by the model number stamped into their badge.

Curtis Wright went out of business in 1949, but it was not the end of the line. The founders of the Silver Streak Trailer Company bought their assets at auction.

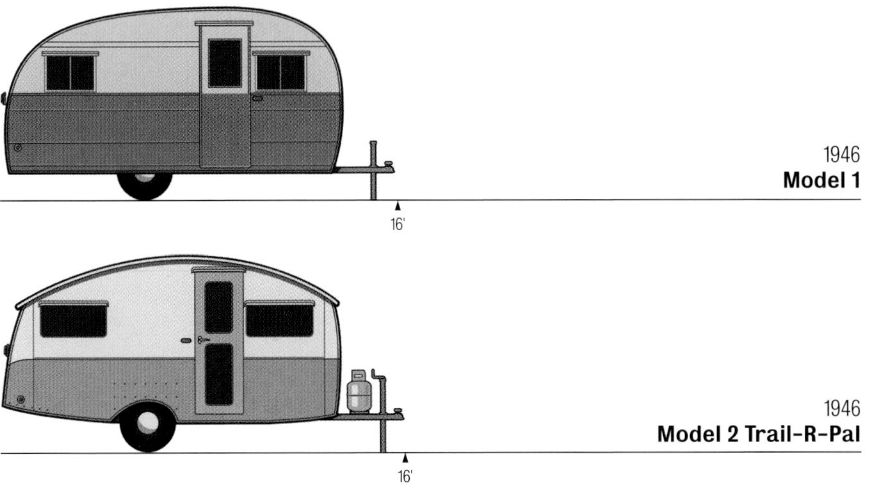

1946
Model 1

1946
Model 2 Trail-R-Pal

1947 Curtis Wright Model 5 Clipper

All Clippers built by Airstream, Curtis Wright, or Silver Streak were built according to Wally Byam's designs. Byam's pre-World War II Airstream Clipper was used as the basis for the Curtis Wright Model 5 and the subsequent Silver Streak Clipper.

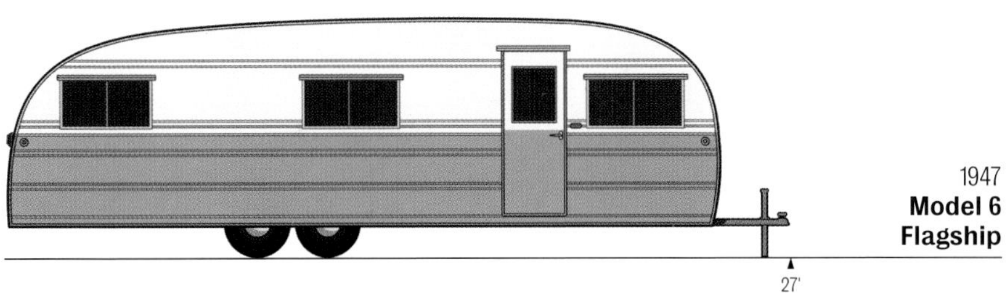

1947
Model 6 Flagship

CabinCar (1946–47)

Fleet Manufacturing, Inc. • Buffalo, New York / Fort Erie, Ontario

Fleet Manufacturing took their expertise in building small training airplanes during World War II and applied it to the CabinCar. Fleet, unlike most aircraft manufacturers that used leftover aluminum from the war to build their trailers, made the CabinCar out of Canadian plywood. It is estimated that less than 10 originals remain in existence. Luckily, the CabinCar's design has inspired many hobbyists to make replicas of it.

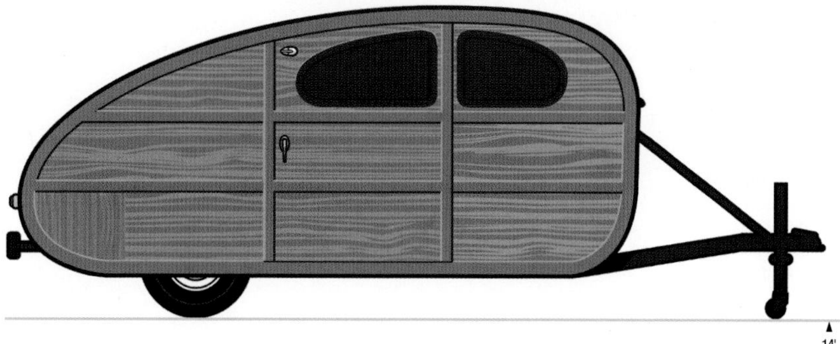

1946 CabinCar

CabinCar, a cross between a teardrop and a canned ham trailer, was no wider than a car, and because of its streamlined plywood construction weighed less than 900 pounds. It had a gracious wardrobe and storage space, a small cooking area, and a spacious double bed.

Cal-Craft (mid-1950s)

Cal-Craft Trailers, Inc. • El Monte, California

Cal-Craft, specialists in the mass production of vacation and travel trailers, was an offshoot of Ideal Industries. It made classic canned hams that were modestly priced, for their quality. Cal-Crafts had a one-piece aluminum roof, Pittsburgh seams, and deluxe birch cabinets. The 1954 15-foot model could sleep five and came with a stove, refrigerator, and water pump.

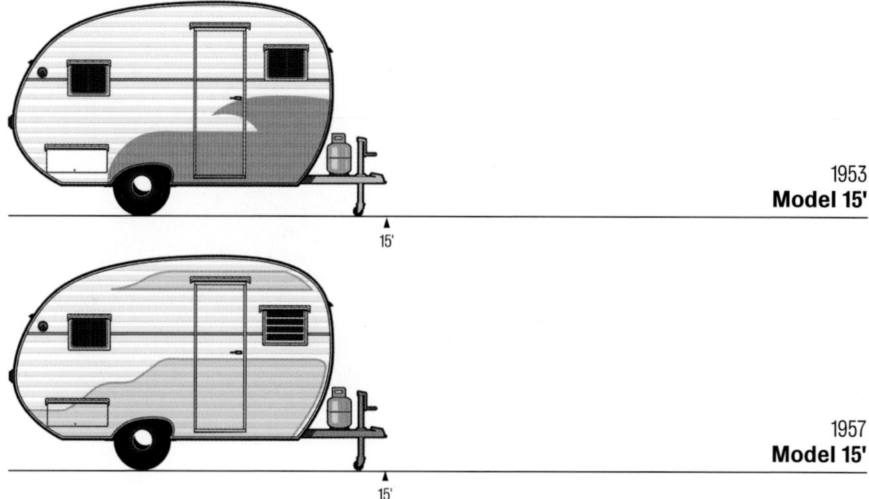

Caveman (1969–80)

Caveman Industries • Kalispell, Montana / Grants Pass, Oregon

The Neanderthal-branded manufacturer of RVs started building campers and Class C motor homes in 1969. By the 1972 model year it had added vacation trailers to its clan. The 1300, a compact model, could sleep up to four hunter-gatherers. It was 13 feet long, just under 7 feet wide, and weighed in at 1,490 pounds, making it the easiest-to-tow man cave of the era.

1973 Caveman 1300

The Caveman 1300 can be easily mistaken for the Bell 13' of the same year (see page 79). Both brands were owned by Di Giorgio Leisure Products of Kalispell, Montana.

Century (1950s–1978)

Federal Trailer Company • Detroit, Michigan

Custom-built Century travel trailers were not your typical canned ham. According to ads of the mid-1960s, "They had the look, sound, and feel of quality." A Century's body was made of 32-gauge anodized aluminum, had a fully enclosed underbelly, and sat on a five-inch box frame. Truck campers and fifth wheels joined the line in the late 1970s.

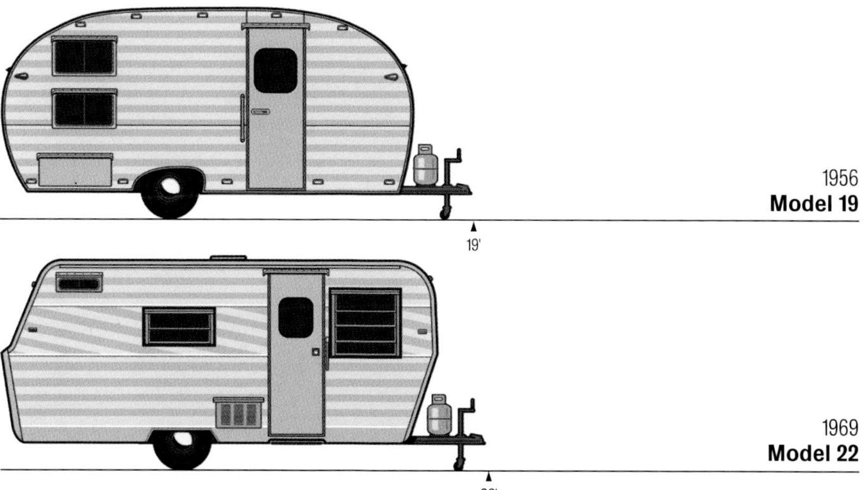

1956
Model 19

1969
Model 22

Clipper (1958–early 1960s)

Clipper Manufacturing Company • Fort Worth, Texas

The Clipper Manufacturing Company introduced the boxy 15-foot Clipperette, 17-foot Nomad, and 21-foot Sunchaser to trailer dealers in 1958. All models had double-floor insulation, double-wall construction, and stop and direction lights. The 1959 13-foot Clipper Sportster could fit in a garage, and had a step-down floor and a roof rack. You could write, wire or call collect for more information.

1958 Clipper Nomad

While the name evokes images of the streamlined Clippers made by Airstream, Curtis Wright, and Silver Streak, the models made by Clipper Manufacturing bore little resemblance to those aircraft-style trailers. A jutting pointed brow was a feature of trailers in the Clipper lineup.

1959
Sportster

Coachmen (1964–present)

Coachmen Industries, Inc. • Middlebury, Indiana

Coachmen Industries, Inc. was a full-line manufacturer of RV products and accessories, including travel trailers, truck campers, and motor homes. Ads emphasized its coaches' glue-and-screw construction, family-planned interiors, superb tow ability, perfect livability, and membership in the fun-filled Coachmen Caravan.

1964
Cadet

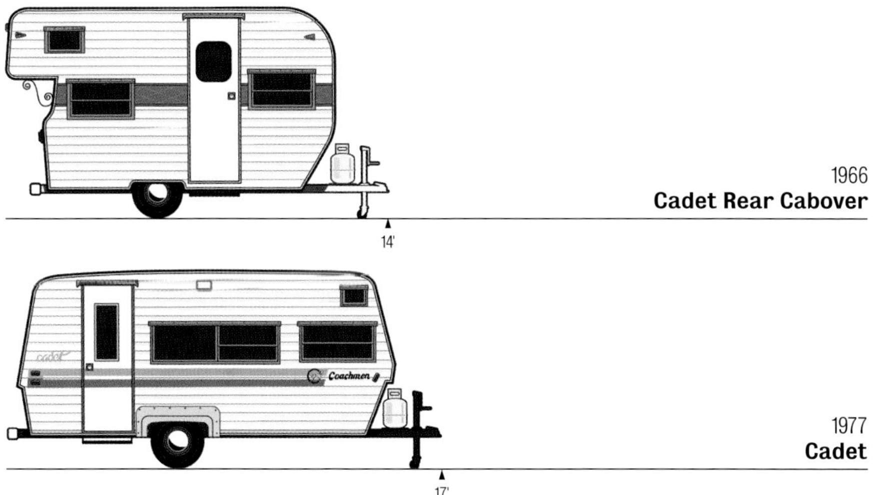

1966
Cadet Rear Cabover

1977
Cadet

Comanche (1958–early 1970s)

Comanche • Elkhart, Indiana

There's little evidence to be found about the manufacturer of this vacation trailer brand. We do know that the Comanche canned ham tribe of trailers ranged from 12 to 25 feet and included truck campers. The 1966 16-foot model sold for $1,193 FOB Elkhart, had a door with an eight-louver jalousie window, and a body with a straight bottom edge.

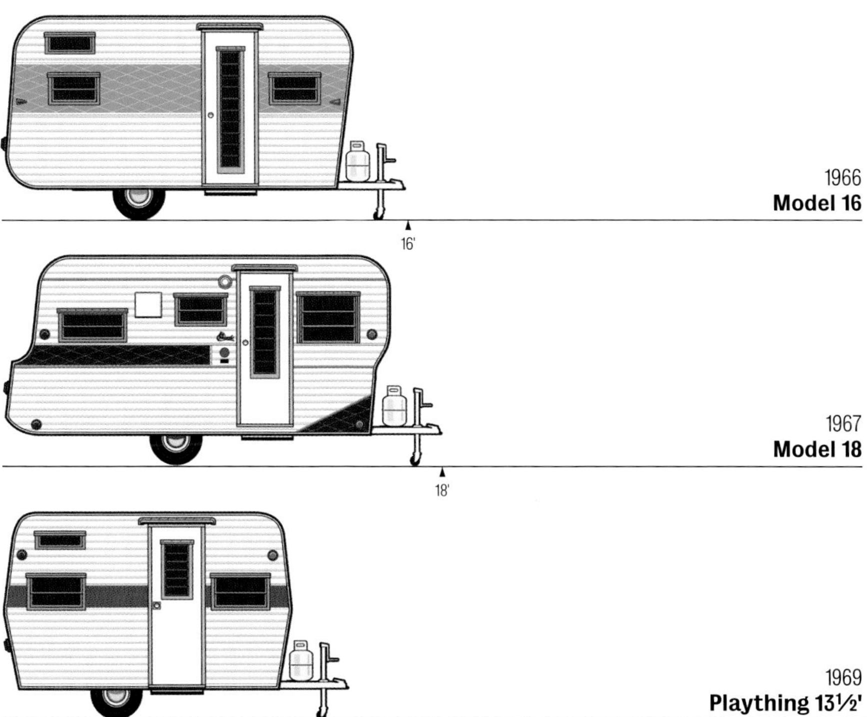

1966
Model 16

1967
Model 18

1969
Plaything 13½'

Comet (1947–81)

Comet Trailer Manufacturing Company • Wichita, Kansas / Comet Mobilehomes • Coffeyville, Kansas

Comet Mobilhomes, founded in a hangar, was likely named to honor the first aircraft built in Wichita and the national airspeed record holder of 1917, the Cessna Comet. Models were offered from 16-foot vacation trailers to the travel trailer–sized 28-foot Constellation. By the mid-1970s the Comet name traveled on park models, truck campers, and fifth wheels throughout the Midwest.

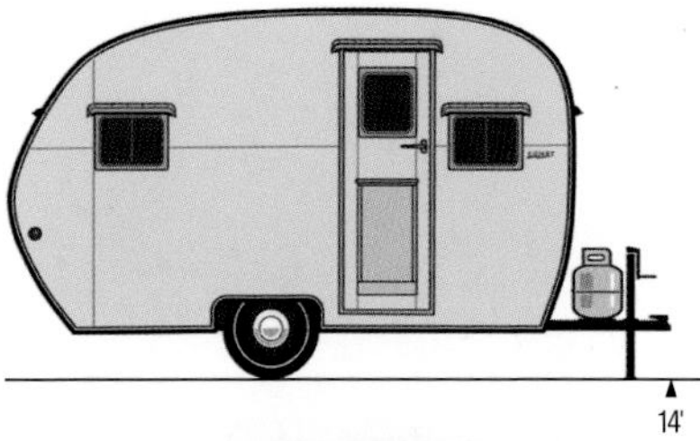

1953
Model 14 Deluxe

14'

1956
Model 16

16'

1962
Model 161

16'

Compact Jr. (1968–74)

Hunter Structures • Chatsworth, California

The fiberglass Compact Jr. was so light, 960 pounds with a 75-pound tongue weight, that a Volkswagen Beetle could tow it. The garageable 13-foot trailer had a "Tele-Top" roof that gave it 6 feet 9 inches of headroom. A rear-door design allowed room for a six-seat dinette that converted into a king-size bed. The larger Compact II model had a water heater, gas heater, toilet, and three-way refrigerator.

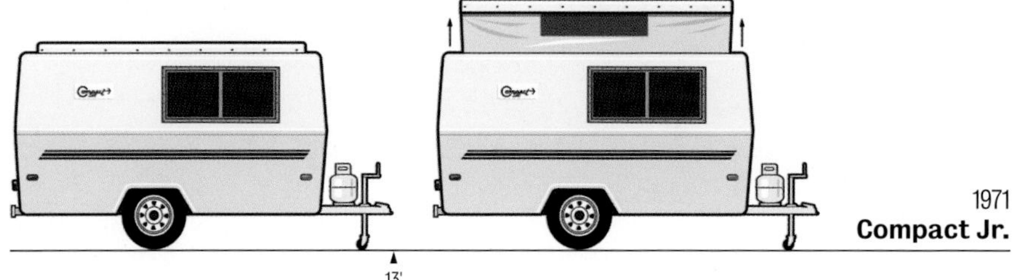

1971
Compact Jr.

13'

Corvette (1957–59)

Sterling Trailer Coach Company • El Monte, California

The Corvette brand of canned ham trailers, only sold in the 11 western states, boasted of more than 10,000 satisfied users in 1958. Vacation trailer–equipped models were offered in 14-, 15-, 16-, and 18-foot lengths. The Corvette 18 had 10 opening windows, four louver windows, a Marvel ice machine–electric refrigerator, a Princess range, and an exterior in three-color automotive paint.

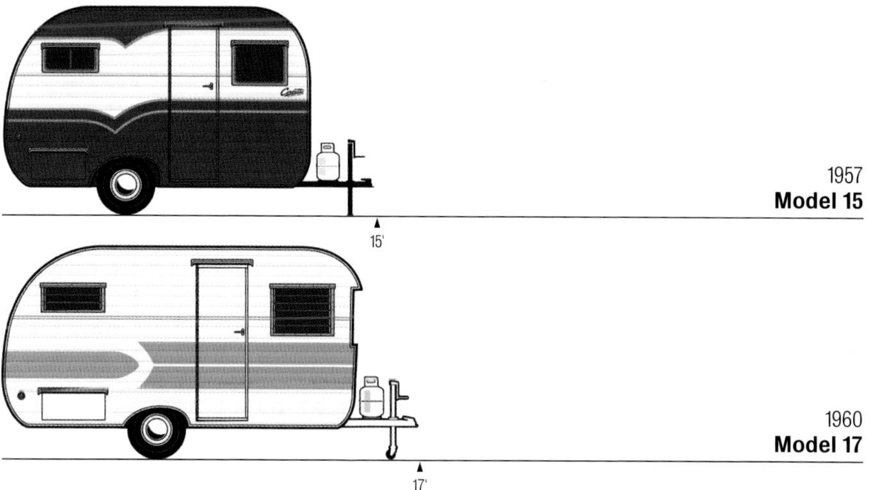

Cozy Cruiser (1950–52)

Cozy Cruiser

Cozy Cruiser Trailer Company • Los Angeles, California

Shasta Industries made their first foray into the vacation trailer market with the Cozy Cruiser branded Model 1400 canned ham. It had a double bed, convertible dinette, and a Pullman-type berth that allowed it to sleep five. Ads at the time stated the manufacturer as Cozy Cruiser Trailer Company, while the trailer's badge read the Cozy Cottage Trailer Company.

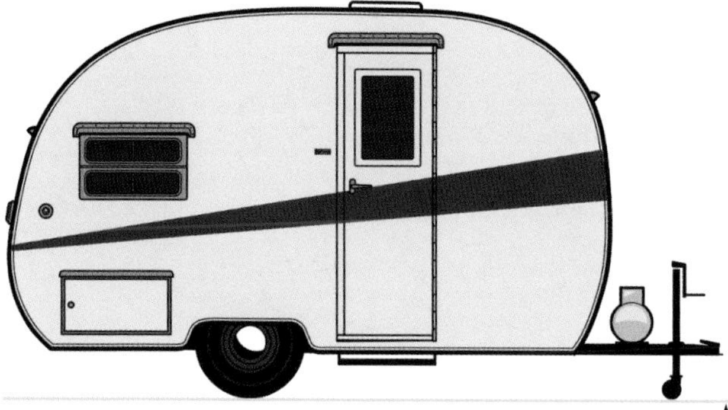

1952 Cozy Cruiser Model 1400

The Model 1400 is a predecessor to the 1954 Shasta Model 1400 (see page 241). They share the same body shape, doors, and windows. Although the Cozy Cruiser had a smooth aluminum skin, it's easy to see how its red stripe morphed into the painted bottom of the Shasta version.

Cree (1945–92)

Cree Coaches, Inc. • Marcellus, Michigan

Cree Coaches, founded by Howard Cree in 1945, built a modified truck camper. Trailers were added to the line in the early 1950s. Models from the 1960s had aluminum exteriors, two-tone baked-on enamel, and frost-free windows. Model names were based on a trailer's length until 1971, after which units had names like Teepee, Tomahawk, and Track Scout. That naming convention was gone by 1974.

18'

1960
Model 18

13'

1963
Model 13 Step Down

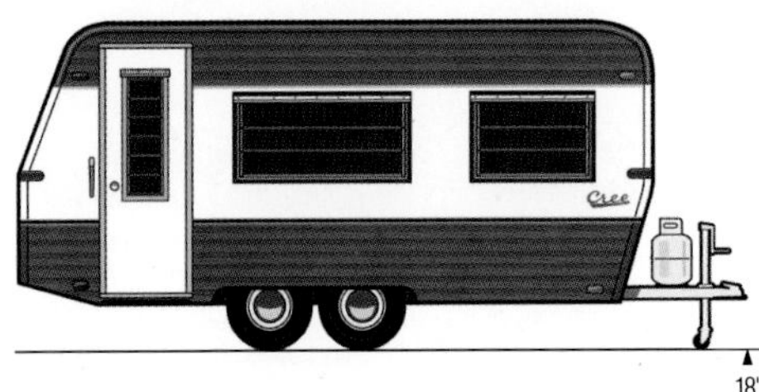

18'

1972
Teepee Tandem

Crown (1949–55)

Made for Al Rose, the Trailer King • El Monte / Palm Springs, California

The Crown was made exclusively for Al Rose, the "Trailer King." His trailer dealership sold thousands of the Crown 14 canned hams in the early 1950s. It had a smooth aluminum exterior and sporty-shaped wheel wells. Basic features included wood cabinets with latching doors, an icebox, stove, and sink. The dinette seated four and converted to a bed.

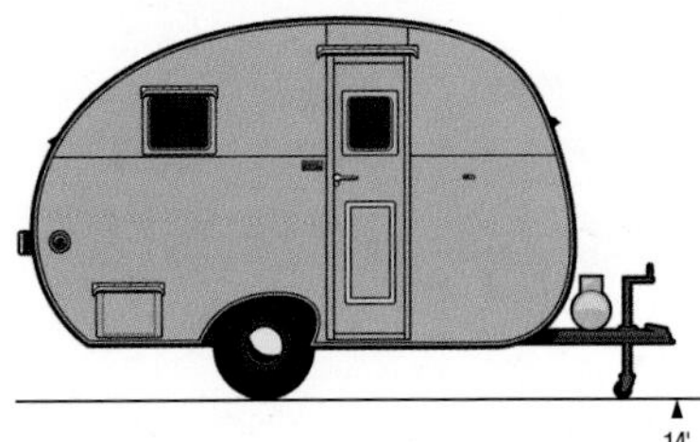

14'

1950
Model 14

D

DeVille TRAILERS

Early models display common graphics in either black, blue, or brown with double yellow ribbons underneath

Early '60s models feature an arched roof and bird-like crest detail on the back of the body

DeVille (1954–71)

Catolac Corporation • El Monte, California

The Catolac Corporation was incorporated in 1954. If the similar pronunciation to "Cadillac" wasn't enough to make a connection to the Cadillac DeVille automobile in their customer's minds, then Catolac's magazine ads shouting that DeVille trailers were "the Cadillac of Travel Trailers" left no doubt.

DeVille Travel Trailers shared the quality construction, finishing touches, and a price tag associated with the luxury brand. They came with a one-year manufacturer's warranty and were built to California building codes. The bold three-tone exteriors on the earlier models caught the eyes of many buyers then and collectors today. And the price, while high for trailers of this type, was a long-term value.

The names of their models display a Francophile bent. There was the Legionnaire (15 feet), the Algerian (16 feet), the Corsican (17 feet), the Tunisian (21 feet), the Moroccan (23 feet), and the Sultan (32 feet). In 1958, Catolac dropped their naming conventions in favor of delineating their trailers by length only. Most owners simply call their Catolac trailer, whatever its length, a DeVille.

They were made through the early 1970s.

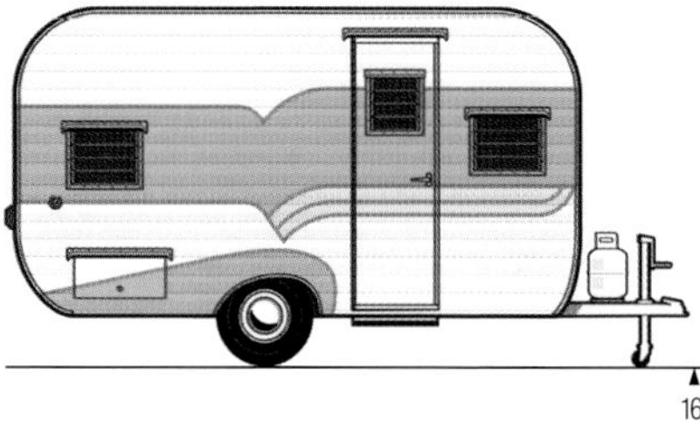

1956
Algerian

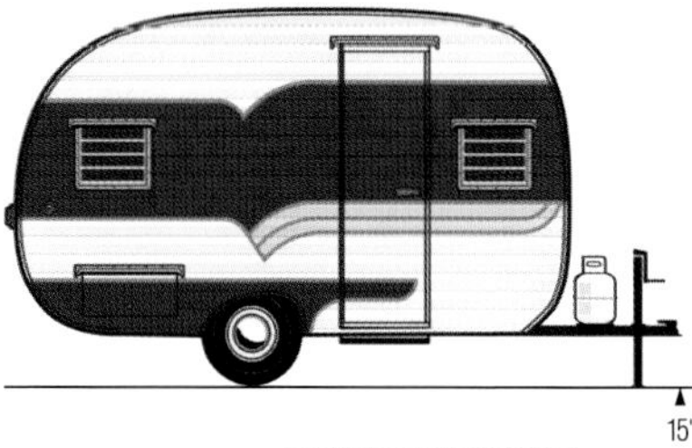

16'

1958
Legionnaire

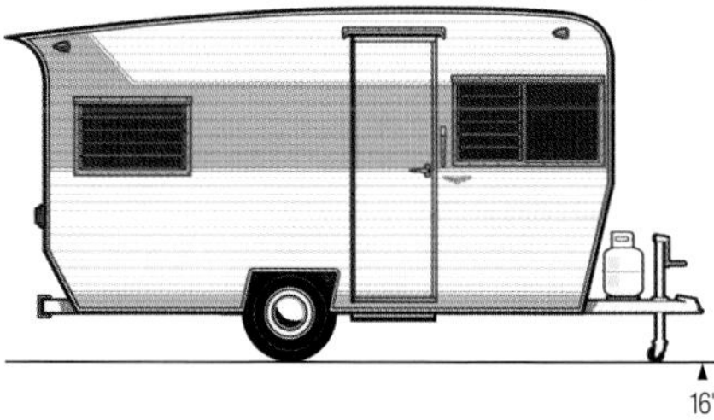

15'

1963
Model 16

16'

Aladdin's Lamp

The story of Aladdin's lamp is given a twist in this 1958 DeVille ad that depicts a Legionnaire trailer appearing from a magic lantern, instead of a wish-granting genie. Other trailers in this telling include the Corsican, Algerian, and Moroccan.

The link to Aladdin's lamp is a bit mysterious, but the folk tale supposedly took place in an untold part of the Middle East.

Dalton (mid-1950s–1961)

Dalton Trailer Company • El Monte, California

A Dalton canned ham–style trailer is a classic 1950s trailer. It had an aluminum exterior with two-tone paint in a bold wraparound design. The trailer's kitchen was outfitted with a stove, a hand water pump sink, and a dinette with a front picture window. In the evening, butane lights gave a Dalton's birch interior a warm glow. Larger models came with showers and toilets.

16'

1957 Dalton Model 16

The canned ham shape and painted graphics of the Dalton 16-footers were very similar to the 1957–58 Cardinal 16s (see page 85), which were also built in El Monte.

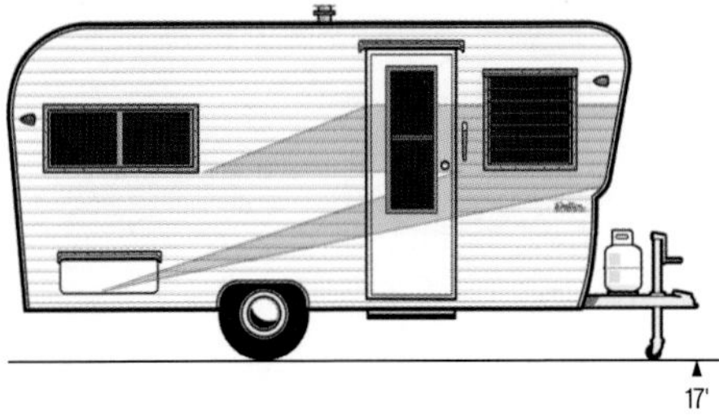

17'

1960
Model 17

Davron (Cricket) (1967–69)

Davron Trav'ler, Inc. • Bristol / Elkhart, Indiana

The Cricket trailer made the unassailable claim to be the "jumpin'est little trailer you've ever seen . . ." The sharp, compact 12- and 14-foot models were attractive to sportsmen and the occasional camper or traveler. They could sleep four, and had a large dinette and plenty of storage space for gear. The kitchen faced front, and had a two-burner stove and an icebox.

12'

1967
Cricket 12'

DeCamp (mid- to late 1960s)

DeCamp Homes Inc. • Elkhart, Indiana

The body style of DeCamp vacation trailers shared common characteristics with many other brands made in Elkhart, Indiana, during the 1960s. DeCamps were modified canned hams, and had jalousie windows and a straight-edged bottom. What makes the 1965–66 models stand out is a turquoise band on their sides with matching turquoise-colored sink, stove, hood, and icebox.

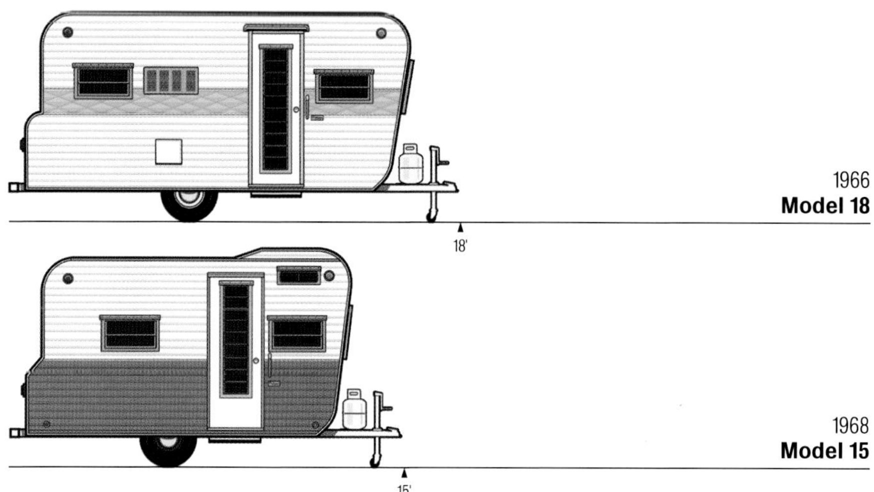

1966
Model 18

1968
Model 15

Detroiter (1947–mid-1960s)

Detroiter Coach Company • Detroit, Michigan

The motor city's own Detroiter trailers hit the road after World War II. The original units served as aluminum-sided affordable housing for returning vets and displaced war workers. Larger park models built for families soon followed. The 1956 Sportsman was the company's first vacation-sized trailer. The 13-foot trailer had a pointed aluminum exterior, birch interior, and a jalousie window in its door.

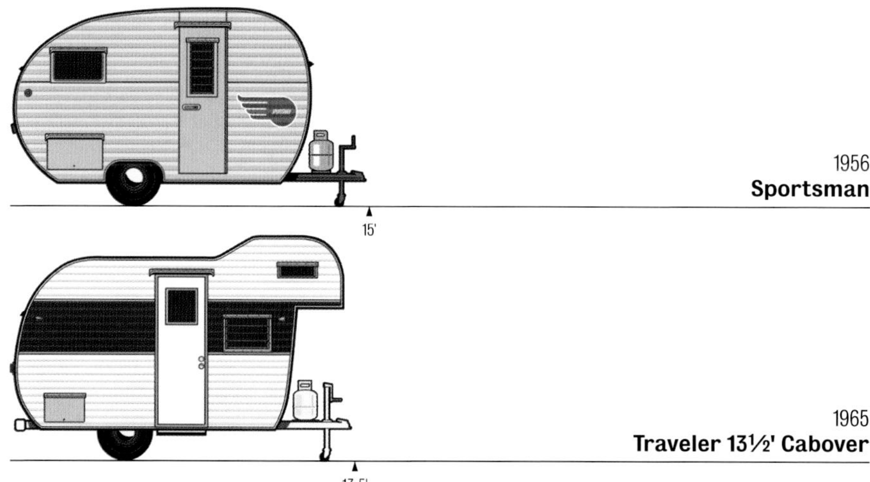

1956
Sportsman

1965
Traveler 13½' Cabover

Driftwood (1963–69)

Driftwood Homes Corporation • Elkhart, Indiana

The Southern California surf culture of beach parties, surf music, and bikinis was at high tide across the United States in the mid-1960s. So it seems natural that Driftwood vacation trailers of the era included handles like Surfer, Cruiser, and Beachcomber. The 18- to 26-foot Driftwood line came standard with brand materials, equipment, and appliances.

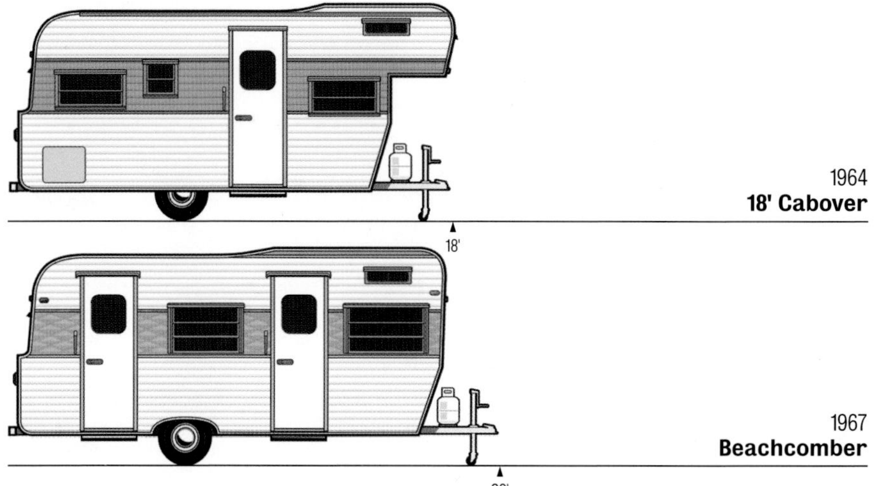

E

Post-1940 models had a bread loaf shape with skirted sides over their wheels

Early 1950s models had porthole windows in their doors

Elcar (1936–late 1960s)

Elcar Coach Company • Elkhart, Indiana

In 1936, the Elcar Coach Company began production of "trailerized homes" in a former motor car factory. The Elkhart Carriage and Motor Car Company had made Elcar automobiles in Elkhart since 1915, and before that, in different corporate incarnations, horseless carriages and buggies.

The pre–World War II Elcars were rounded bread loaf–style models that came sheathed in leatherette, Masonite, or steel exteriors. They were meant for extended travel or living on the road in economical comfort.

Elcar-brand post–World War II canned ham trailers were surfaced with Kimpreg, a resin-infused plywood that resisted moisture, decay, and temperature changes. Elcar aimed for efficiency, comfort, and easy housekeeping for newly married couples. By the early 1950s the brand shed its wooden skin and was covered in 22-gauge cold-rolled aluminum with a horizontal color stripe.

Soon thereafter the Elcar brand, adapting to the changing needs of growing families, stopped building trailers and began manufacturing mobile homes. The Elcar brand lived on through the late 1960s.

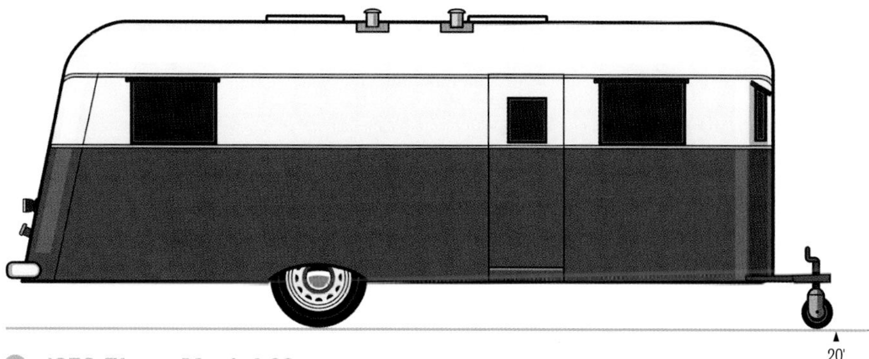

1938 Elcar Model 69

The Model 69 shared many of the same attributes as one of its brethren trailer lines of the day: the Covered Wagon (see page 86). It had similar wheel wells, doors, windows, and roofline.

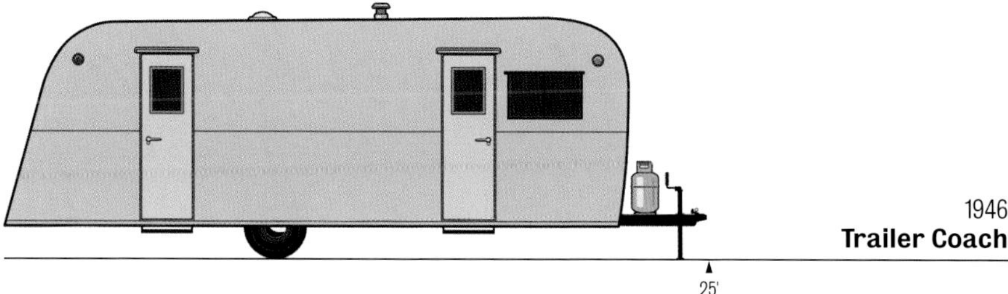

1946
Trailer Coach

The Elcar automobile, introduced in 1915, was made by the Elkhart Carriage and Motor Car Company. The company went on to build ambulances for the army during World War II and then became a popular choice for taxi cab companies in Chicago and New York. Elcar automobiles were produced until 1931, but the name lived on in Elcar trailers until the late 1960s.

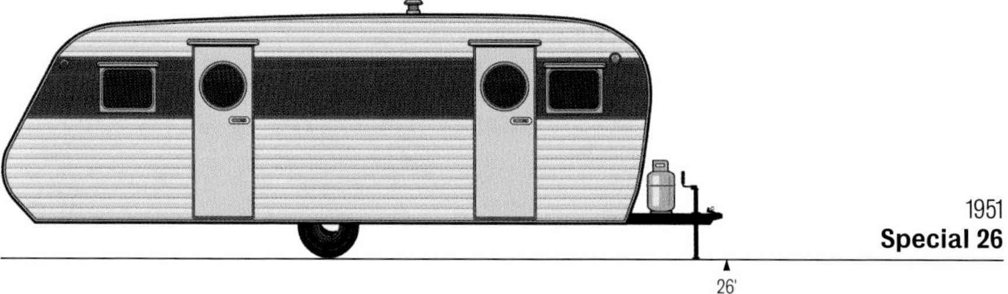

1951
Special 26

EASY TRAVLER

Easy Travler (1958–60)

Easy Travler Mfg. • Elkhart, Indiana

The Easy Travler brand took off in 1958 with the 12-foot Scamper. It was a low-cost, 940-pound, garageable canned ham with a step-down floor and small tires. The brand entered the jet age with its introduction of "jet designing" on their 1959 models. The Explorer 1 had little wind resistance, was garage height, and had the outline of a jet painted across its side.

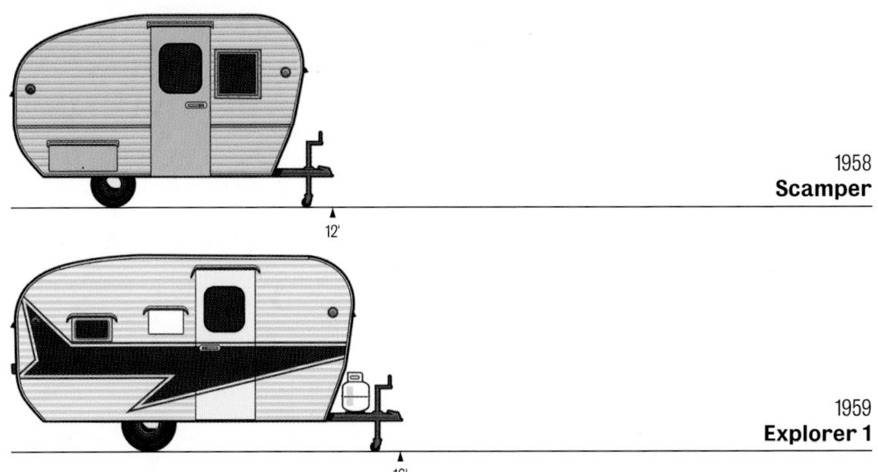

El Rey

El Rey (1955–late 1950s)

El Rey Trailer Company • El Monte, California

Originally titled Airlight, the brand changed its name to El Rey in 1955. All-aluminum models using aircraft construction techniques were presented in 15-, 19-, 23-, and 27-foot lengths. Advertised as both affordable and "one of the World's Greatest travel trailers," options included a choice of floor plans and interior furnishings, butane lights, a butane refrigerator, a water tank, and a pump.

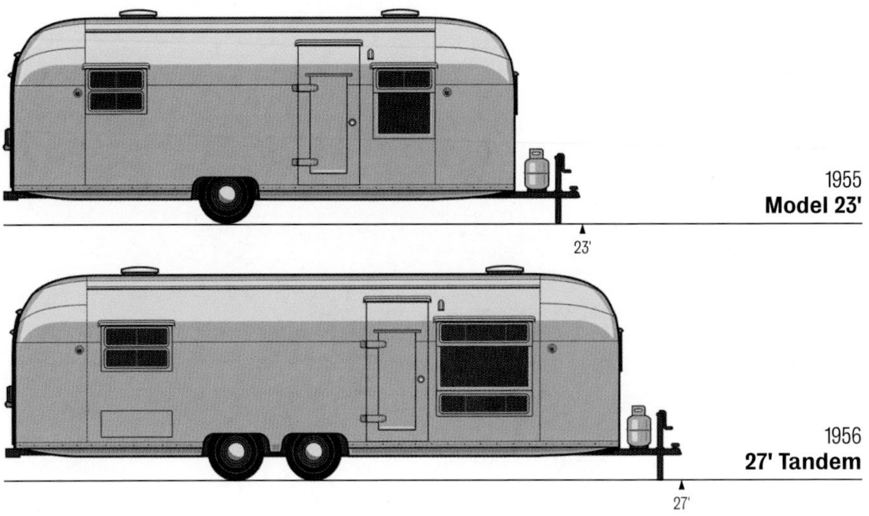

Empire (1950–60)

Empire Trailers, Inc. • El Monte, California

The first Empire canned ham was a 15-foot model with an aluminum-ridged skin, birch-paneled interior, and modest amenities. By the mid-1950s the travel trailer line was painted white with a wave of color across the lower body. In a 1958 ad, Empire claimed that its now luxurious Traveler, Loafer, and Aristocrat trailers were "built for miles and years of carefree roaming."

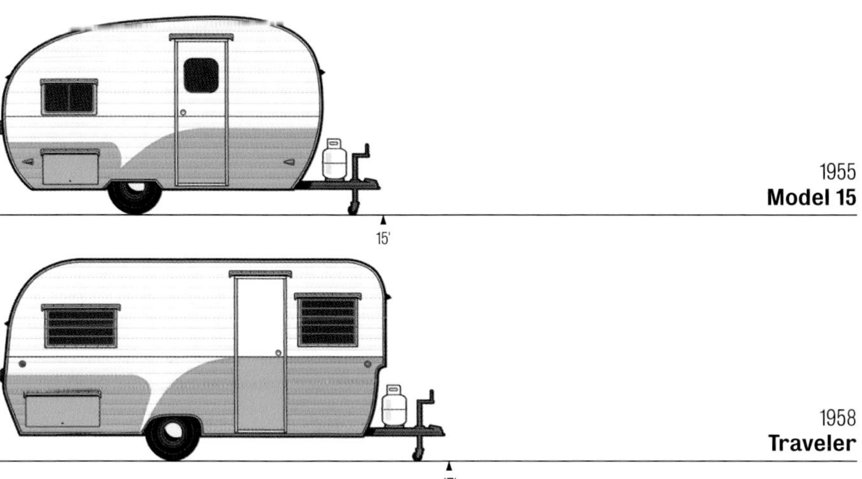

EXCEL

Excel (1966–97)

Excel Trailer Company • North Hollywood / Sun Valley, California

The Excel Trailer Company arrived in Hollywood determined to prove that they made the West's finest, most towable and comfortable travel trailers. The 20-foot Excel Side Dinette with a rear entrance was their most popular model in the mid-1960s. Extra details like a porch light, a battery clock, a skylight vent in the bathroom, a front awning, and back-up lights were a hit with buyers.

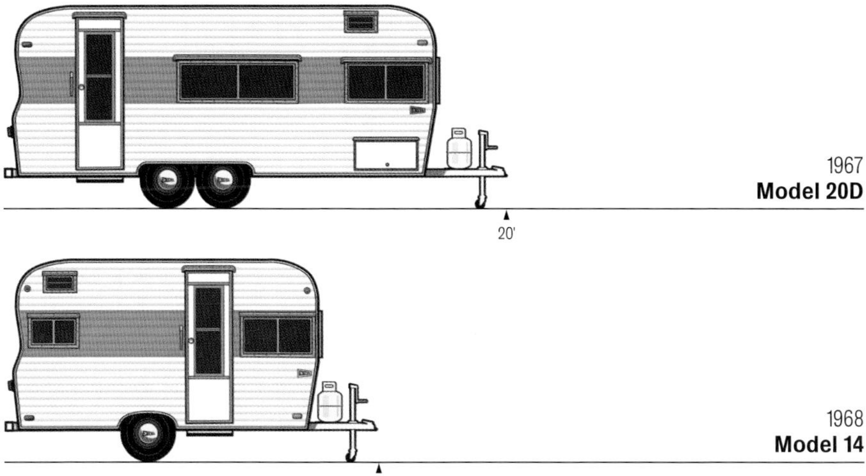

1956 Airstream Bubble MICHAEL AND AEDAN HAWORTH

1972 Airstream Safari MARY AND BOB GROSHONG-ELLIOTT

1955 Airstream 18' JANET MOSSMAN

1947 Aero Flite JAYNE BAROCELA

1950 Airfloat LEWIS PULS

1955 Airlight ERIC MENARD

1967 Aladdin Sultan's Castle NANCY HAMILTON

1955 Aloha RENE PERRET

1965 Aloha CHAD AND ALI WYKHUIS

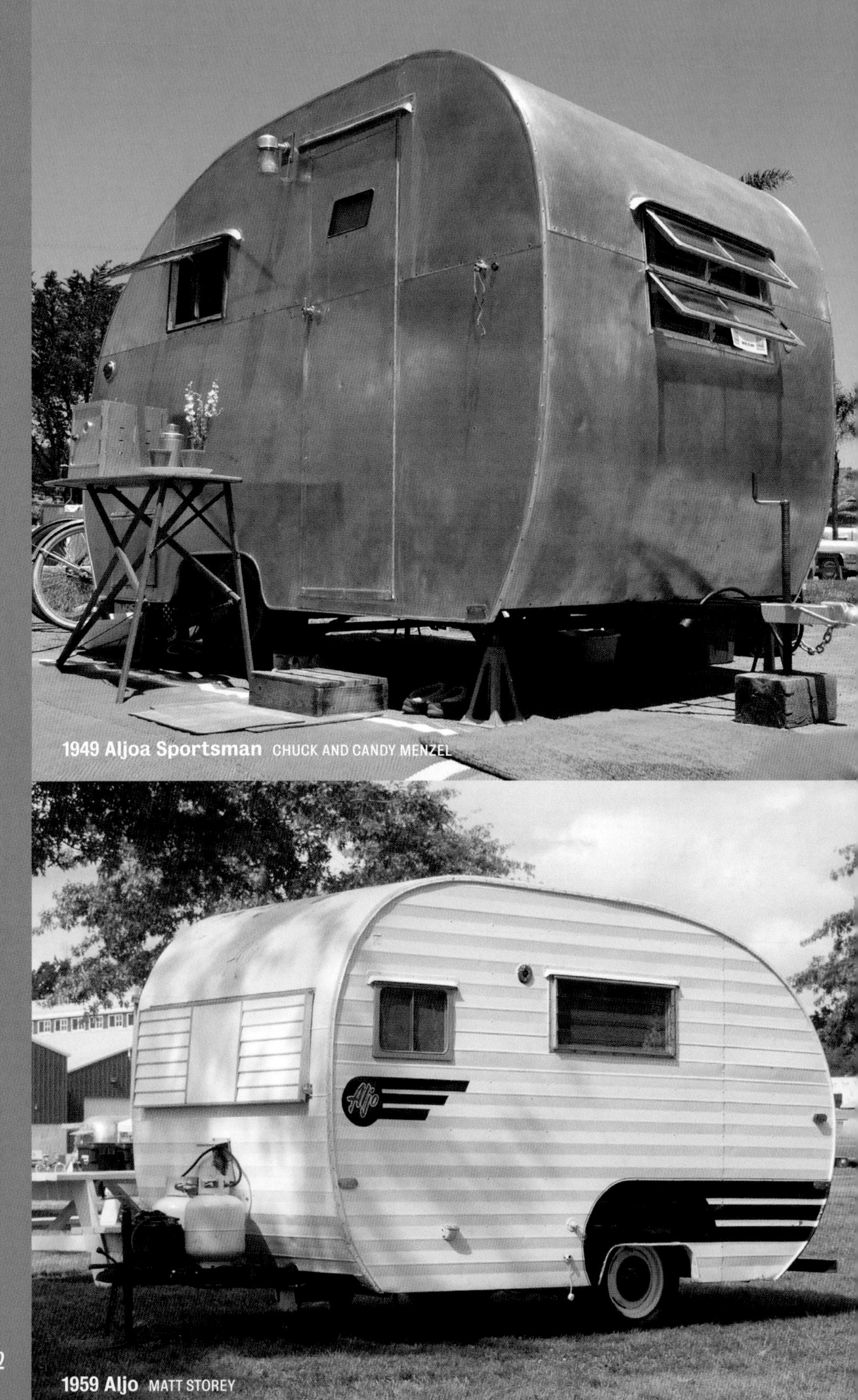

1949 Aljoa Sportsman CHUCK AND CANDY MENZEL

1959 Aljo MATT STOREY

1955 Aljoa Sportsman DAVE AND KAREN GEHRING

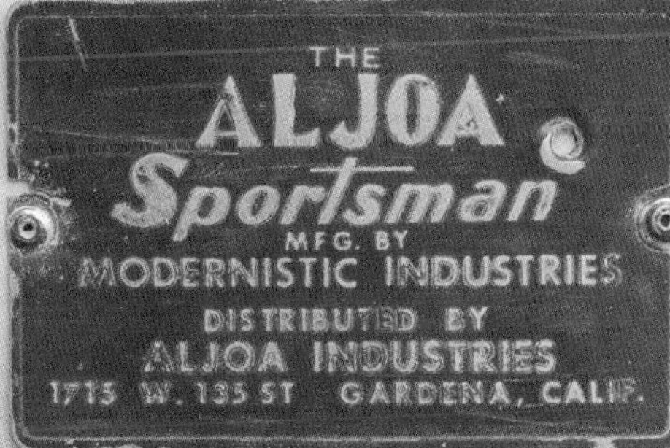

1950 Aljoa Sportsman TIM AND PAM HAWORTH

1978 Argosy TIM AND BETSY MEEHAN

1965 Arrow Little Chief ROBERT DOUGLAS

1957 Arrowhead JEFF AND NANCI HILL

1969 Avion CINDY AND RIC RISTOW

1967 Banner ROBERT DOUGLAS

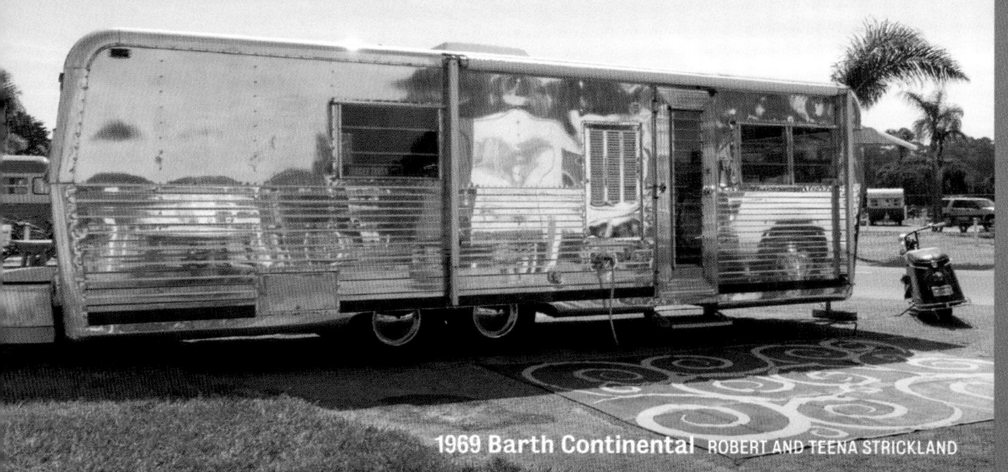

1969 Barth Continental ROBERT AND TEENA STRICKLAND

1960 Aristocrat Li'l Loafer RYAN HUFF

1967 Aristocrat Lo-Liner MARK DAVIS

Hi Liner

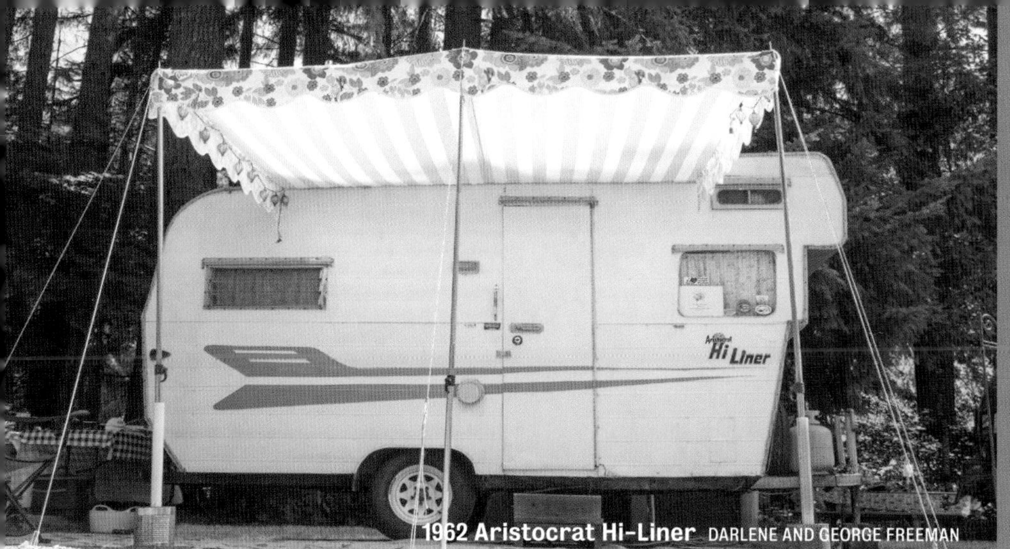

1962 Aristocrat Hi-Liner DARLENE AND GEORGE FREEMAN

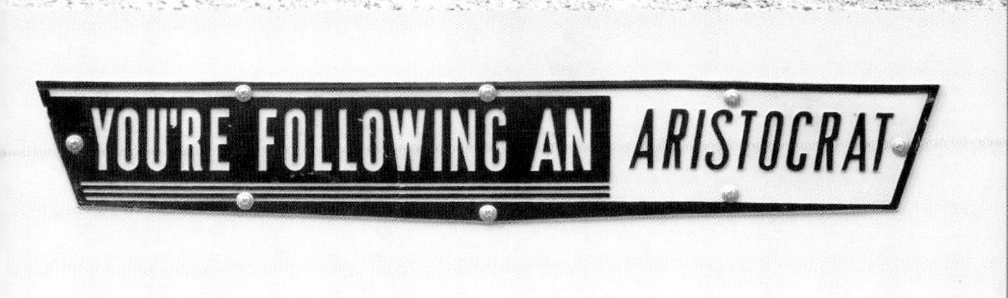

YOU'RE FOLLOWING AN ARISTOCRAT

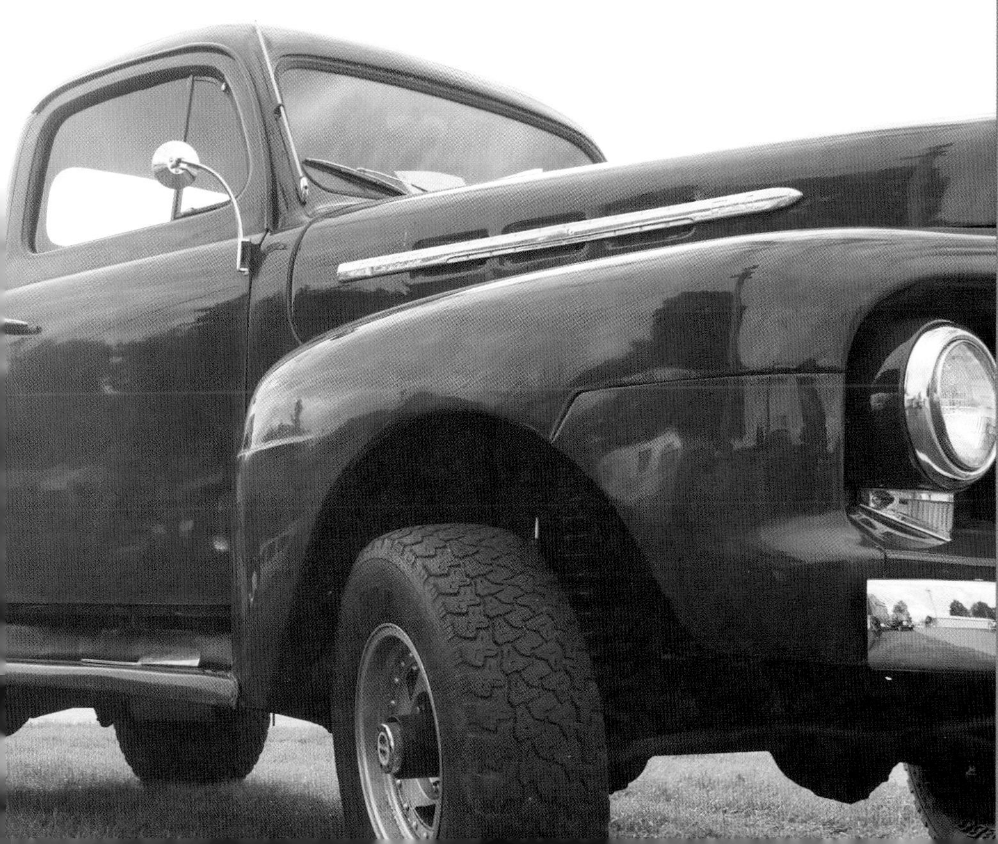

1975 Boler DALE AND TERESA HORTON

1963 Bee Line Hornet DOUG AND SUE OWEN

1964 Bee Line Queen Bee DENISE GODFREY AND NIELS KROP

1955 Beemer KATHLEEN ROSE

1973 Bell DANA MURRAY

1953 Bellwood Vacationer BILL AND BECCA INGRAM

1948 Boles-Aero KEVIN AND SHANNALEE PHILLIPS, ZEEK (DOG)

1947 Boles-Aero SHAWN AND CARRIE GRAY

1963 Boles-Aero PAUL AND JILL MCFARLIN

1935 Bowlus Road Chief CON AND CAROL OAMEK

1936 Bowlus Deluxe Road Chief VINCE MARTINICO

1936 Bowlus Papoose BOBBY GREEN

1956 Benroy BOB REINKE

1956 Cardinal Deluxe HEIDI MITCHELL

1966 Cardinal Love Bird AMY CHARRON

1963 Century DEBBIE BROWNING

1958 Corvette AMY COOPER

1936 Covered Wagon DANIEL AND BERNIE DONOVAN

1946 Curtis Wright Model 1 DAL SMILIE

1946 Curtis Wright Model 2 VINTAGE TRAILER SUPPLY, INC.

1948 Curtis Wright Model 5 Clipper DAVE AND LORI WHITE

1968 DeCamp ROBERT DOUGLAS

1957 DeVille Legionnaire TOM AND SUE BAILEY

1955 Empire JAYNE BAROCELA

F

Pre-1964 models had a canned ham body style, many with skirted sides covering the wheels

Post-1965 models often incorporated a round molded edging between the sides and roof

FAN (1954–86)

FAN Coach Company, Inc. • Wakarusa / LaGrange, Indiana

Franklin A. Newcomer founded the FAN Coach Company in 1954, using his initials for the company's name. The first FAN trailers were built in Wakarusa, Indiana, a small farm community just south of the home to many trailer manufacturers and the RV/MH Hall of Fame: Elkhart.

Over the next 40 years FAN grew into a complete family of trailers for travelers, campers, and sportsmen, and from basic to self-contained luxury models. The company prided itself on using the best materials to build trailers that would last for years.

While the shape of a FAN trailer evolved, like many other manufacturers, from the canned ham style of the late '50s to the more boxy look of the late '60s, they still could lay claim to originating many popular interior arrangements, including the super-center frame and the hideaway bunk.

The company faltered after being sold to W. R. Grace and Company in 1970. Coachmen Industries eventually bought FAN in 1978. The line was discontinued in the mid-1980s. Franklin A. Newcomer was inducted into the RV/MH Hall of Fame in 1996.

1955
Rambler
15'

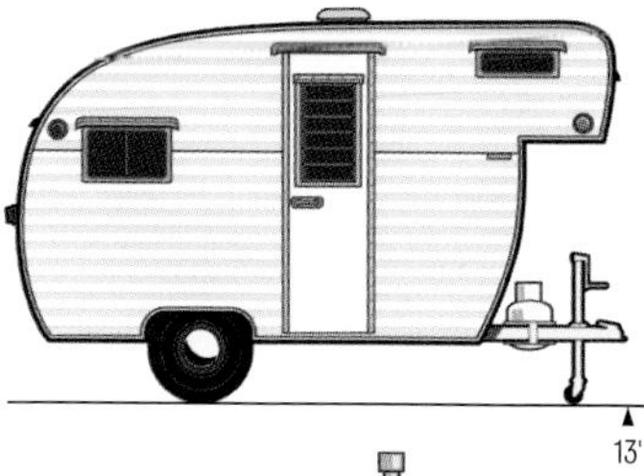

1962
Traveler
13'

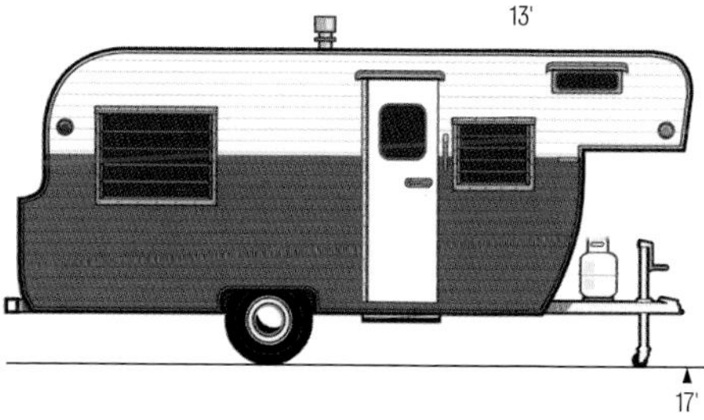

1962
Fantasy
17'

20'

1966 FAN Luxury Liner

A top-of-the-line model, the self-contained Luxury Liner had a unique wrap-over body molding. A rear-door layout allowed space for a centrally located dinette and a large front bedroom with bunk.

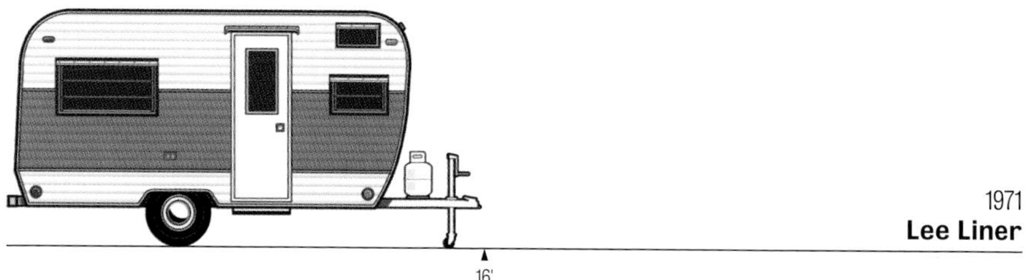

A small canned ham, Fireball was originally a model under the Starfire brand name

The 1960-64 models feature a Fireball graphic streaking across the trailer's body

Fireball / Starfire (1955–92)

Kurmann Trailer Manufacturing Company • San Fernando, California

The Kurmann Trailer Manufacturing Company launched Starfire trailers in 1955. By the end of 1956 it had burned out, and the Fireball line formed. The first trailer with the Fireball name was a lightweight 13-foot model with a 48-inch innerspring mattress, a Modernaire stove, and a gravity water tank.

In 1957 the Soviet Union sent *Sputnik 1* into orbit, and the Space Age began. By the time 1959 came around, Fireball trailers landed with names like Meteor, Martian, Mercurian, and Palomar. The Super Meteor, Jupiter, Rocket, Explorer, and Constellation arrived by the early '60s.

In 1962, Fireball trailers led a caravan that started at their factory in San Fernando and ended with a rendezvous at the Seattle World's Fair, where they explored the imagined future of science and technology in the twenty-first century.

When the Fireball brand retired in 1992, it left behind an inspiring line of trailers, fifth wheels, and Class C motor homes.

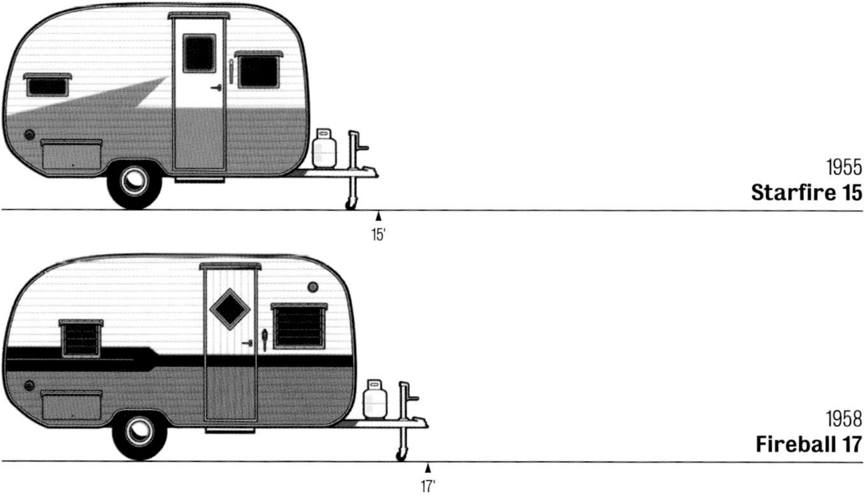

Starfire/Fireball

Both Kurmann trailer brands appeared to come from outer space in the mid-1950s.

The Starfire brand logo with its small constellation of stars streaking across the night sky first came into view on their trailers in 1955, then quickly faded away.

In 1956 the new Fireball brand logo replaced stars with a meteorite shower that burned its way across the same design and into trailer history.

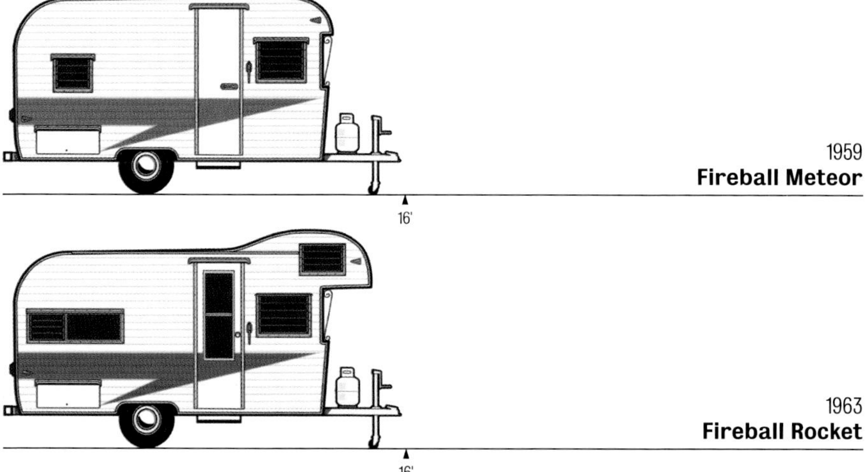

Fleetwood

Compact canned ham with a bare aluminum body and swooping painted graphics (early 1950s)

Square-bodied trailers sporting various brand names included Terry, Prowler, and Wilderness (1960–1970s)

Fleetwood (1950–2008)

Fleetwood Enterprises, Inc. • Riverside, California

Building a trailer was a favorite pastime in post–World War II America. Plans were available in magazines like *Popular Mechanics* and by mail order. John C. Crean, the founder of Fleetwood Enterprises, Inc., built one for himself. A Riverside, California, trailer dealer saw Crean's work and asked him to make more.

Crean built the first trailer with the Fleetwood name badge in 1950. The Fleetwood Sporter, a small canned ham trailer, became the progenitor to a vast family of trailers, fifth wheels, mobile homes, motor homes, and manufactured housing.

The company grew through the 1950s by manufacturing mobile homes; then in 1964 it added Terry trailers to the extended family. By the early 1970s, Fleetwood had created the Prowler, Taurus, and Wilderness brands. Each one offered different layouts and amenities depending on their intended owner.

John C. Crean was honored with an induction into the RV/MH Hall of Fame in 1985. Fleetwood Enterprises closed up shop in 2008. Heartland RV, a subsidiary of Thor Industries, Inc., currently owns and manufactures the Mallard, Wilderness, and Prowler lines.

1950 Fleetwood Model 12 Sporter

Fleetwood's first production model, built for lovers of the great outdoors, was a weekend or vacation coach. It had a convertible dinette, center galley, and rear bedroom with an upper bunk.

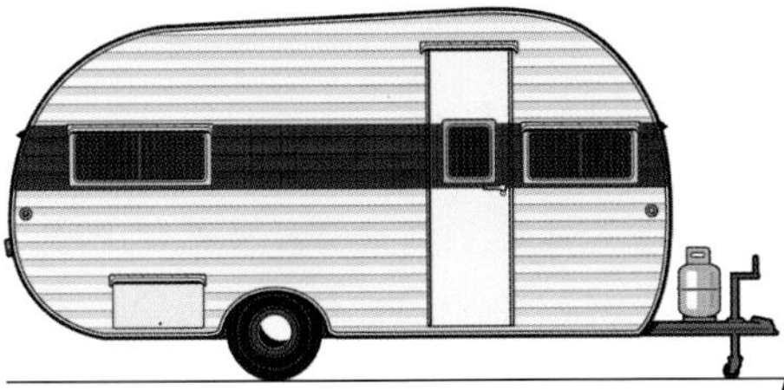

18'

1951
Model 18

10'

1953
Model 10

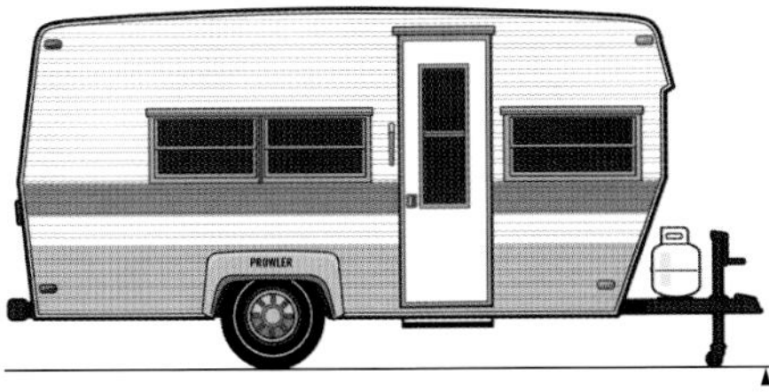

17'

1973
Prowler

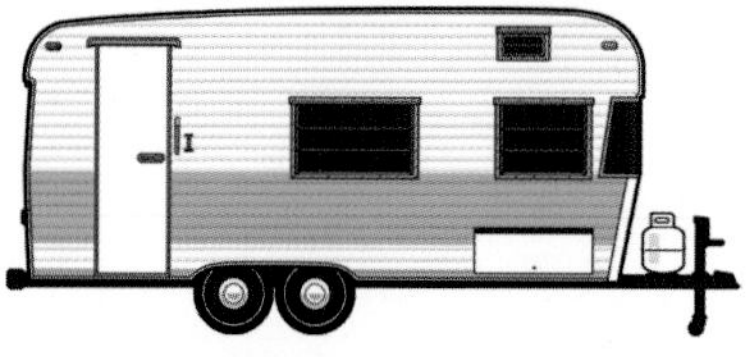

Terry Coach Industries, established in 1953, became a well-known manufacturer of well-built vacation and travel trailers. It was acquired by Fleetwood Enterprises in 1964. Terrys continued to be produced until the 2009 model year. (See page 262.)

FLEETWOOD FAMILY TREE of VINTAGE BRANDS

Mallard Coach Corporation was founded in 1952. They built a complete line of trailers through the 1992 model year. Fleetwood went on to make them until 2009. The brand is presently nested under the wings of Heartland Recreational Vehicles. (See page 184.)

Fleetwood began crafting Prowler travel trailers for the 1967 model year; by 1973 it added fifth wheels to the golden-hued lineup. The brand was sold in 2009 to, and is currently made by, Heartland Recreational Vehicles. (See page 207.)

WILDERNESS

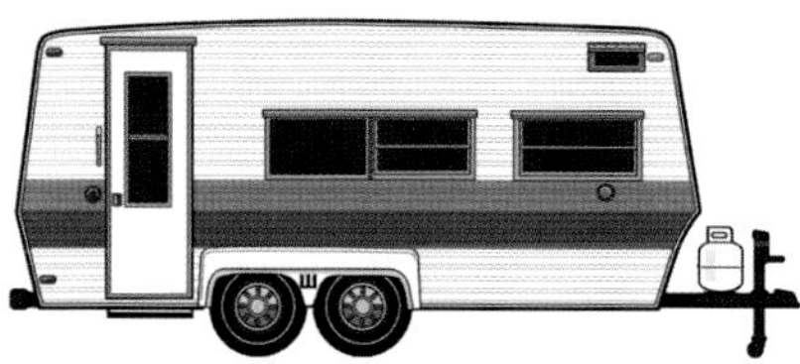

Wilderness travel trailers, swathed in a green palette, were added to the Fleetwood line in 1972. They added fifth wheels in 1973. Fleetwood made their last Wilderness trailer in 2009. Heartland Recreational Vehicles manufactures them today. (See page 286.)

Fleetwood added the Taurus name to their growing family of brands in 1973. The travel trailers and fifth wheels were all self-contained models. They were a short-lived line. They joined the Terry line after the 1980 model year.

AVION

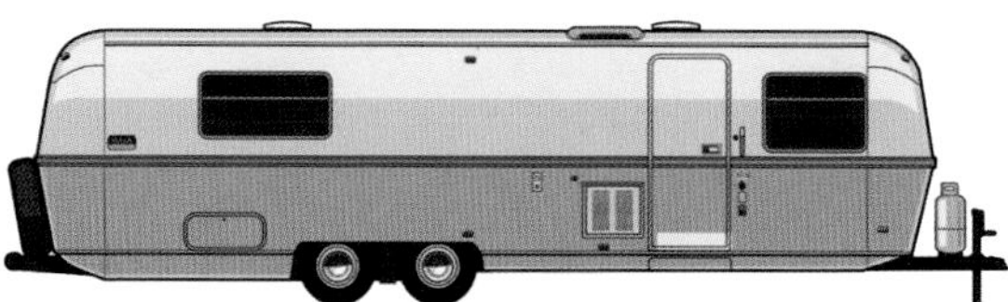

Avion Coach Corporation built aircraft-style trailers and campers from 1955 until 1976. The company was bought by Fleetwood in 1976. The streamlined aluminum trailers were replaced in 1991 with models built with more common materials and a more common shape. The brand retired from service in 2002. (See page 58.)

Fiber Stream

Fiber Stream (1975–86)

Fiber Stream Company • San Diego, California

The Fiber Stream Company made a 16-foot, lightweight, molded fiberglass trailer. The boxy trailers sported dual axles and a roof with rounded corners. Thin, colored pinstripes wrapped around its midsection and sometimes its lower body. It had a bathroom with a shower, a dinette that converted into a king-sized bed, and a kitchen.

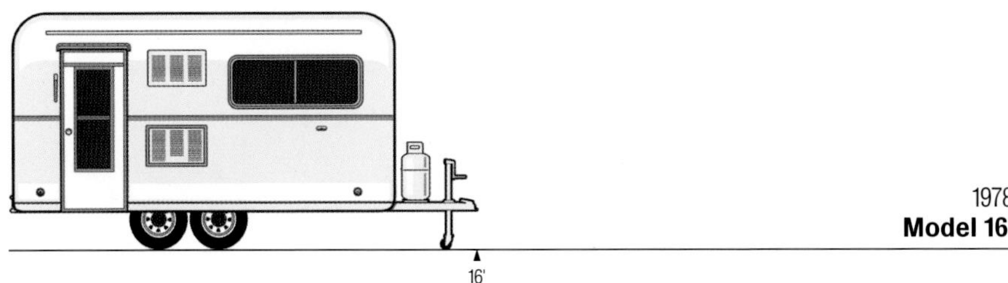

1978
Model 16'

Field and Stream

Field and Stream (mid-1950s–early 1980s)

Vacation Industries, Inc. • Redondo Beach, California

Several manufacturers made the modestly priced Field and Stream brand of vacation trailers over its lifetime. Midway Engineering Co. created some of its most notable models in the early 1960s. The popular Model 17, with its front picture windows, pointed sill, and roofline, inspired the line's design throughout the decade.

1957
Model 14D

● 1962 Field and Stream Model 17

While in name Field and Stream trailers appealed to the gritty outdoorsman, the design of the 1962 Model 17 had a lot in common with the high-styled Holiday House (see page 150). It has the same general body shape, color pattern, and front protrusions. Differences include a flat roofline, a bump-out rear end, and straight-cornered front windows.

Fleetwing (mid-1940s–1988)

Fleetwing Mobile Homes, Inc. • Wakarusa, Indiana

Fleetwing vacation trailer ads described them as being "pretty as a bird and light as a feather." They ranged from 12 to 18 feet in length and carried names like Wren, Chickadee, Sunbird, Thrush, Lark, Falcon, and Eagle. The Fleetwing brand grew in the 1970s with the addition of fifth wheels, motor homes, and truck campers to the line.

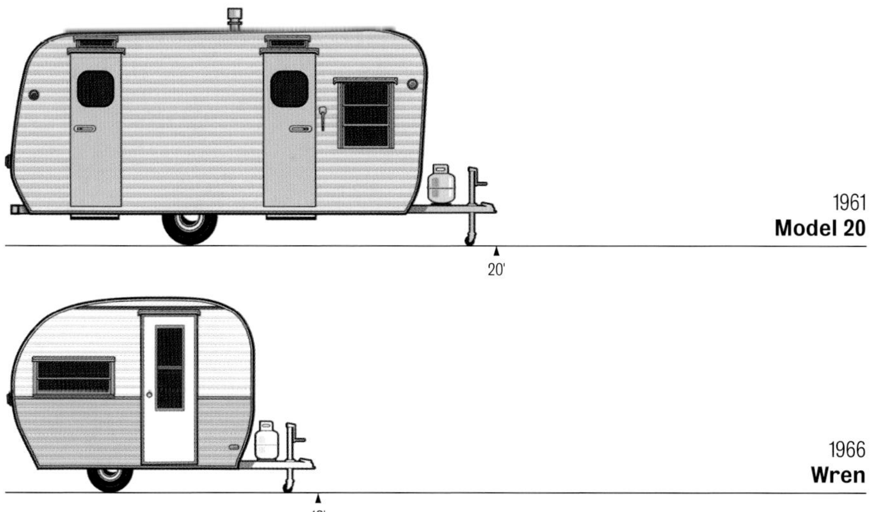

Forester

Forester (1958–79)

Forest City Industries, Inc. • Forest City, Iowa

In 1958, the founders of Forest City Industries, Inc. took their newfound knowledge of trailer building at Modernistic Industries of Iowa, makers of Aljo trailers, and created the Forester trailer line. Throughout its lifespan, Forester offered vacation trailers with the latest features of the day, like color-keyed interiors, cabovers, and low-silhouette models.

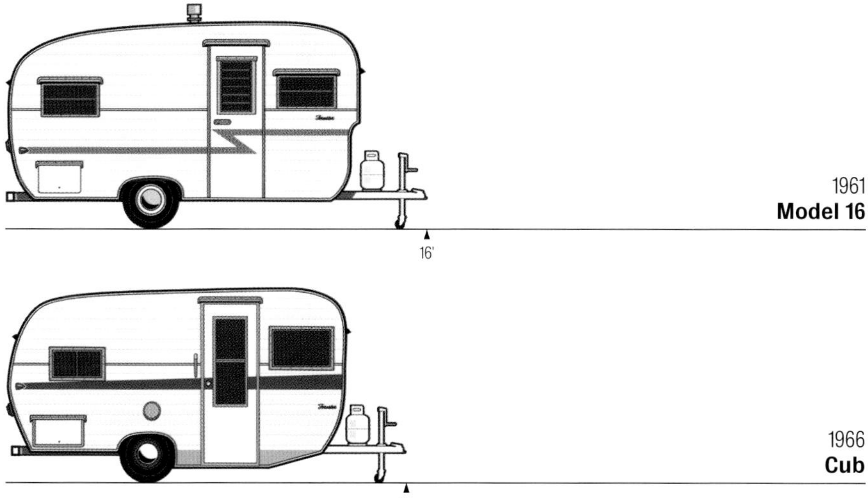

Franklin

Franklin (1945–2008)

Franklin Coach Company • Nappanee, Indiana

The Franklin Coach Company built travel trailers in a wide variety of sizes, interior plans, and price ranges. Franklin models throughout the 1960s displayed Gold Seal construction and Bonded Travel Equipment emblems as evidence of their high quality. The line included an extended family of mobile homes, trailers, tent campers, motor homes, and truck campers.

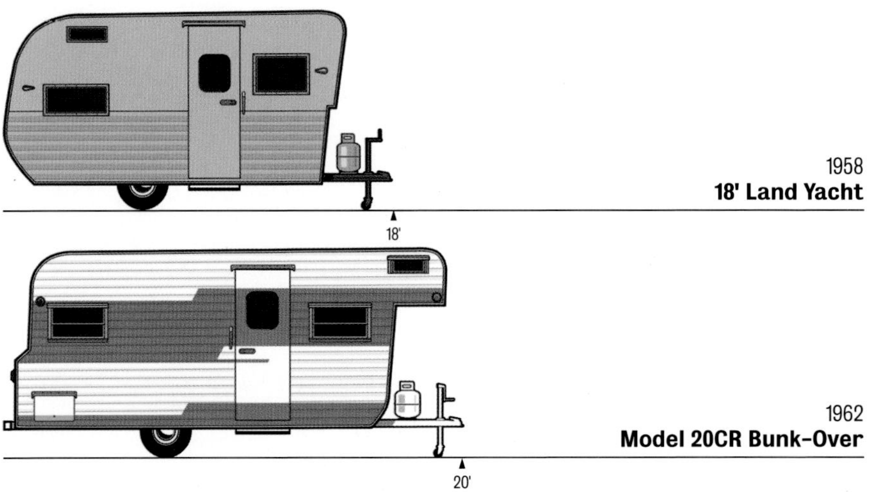

1958
18' Land Yacht

1962
Model 20CR Bunk-Over

Frolic (1963–mid-1970s)

Frolic Homes, Inc. • Elkhart, Indiana

The popular-priced line of Frolic vacation trailers was fully insulated, had all metal frames, and a prefinished two-tone aluminum skin with a one-piece roof as standard equipment. The 18-foot Sun Seeker had a marine stool, shower, and sewer hose bumper. It had an atypical set of two exterior doors with screen doors for increased airflow in the summer.

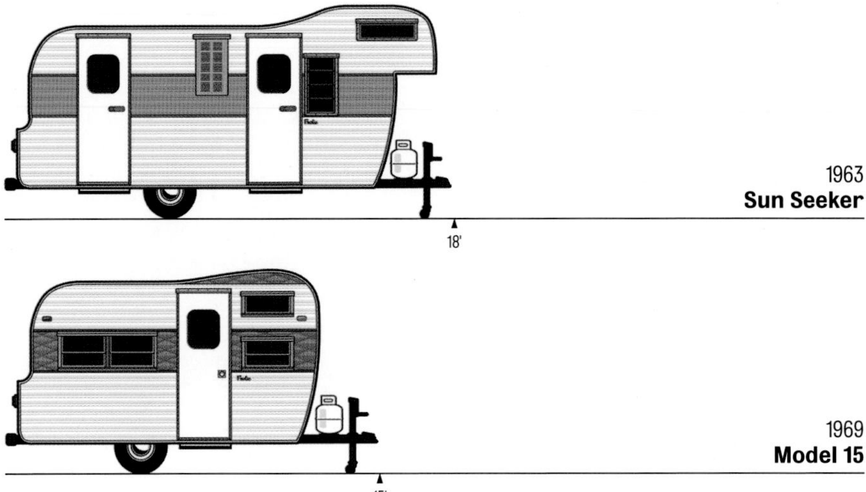

1963
Sun Seeker

1969
Model 15

G

GO Tag-A-Long

MFG. IN WASHINGTONVILLE, OH.

Canned ham–like body with bold horizontal stripe and rounded door window

Low-profile, angled wheel well cutouts and a slight bump-out in trunk area

Go Tag–A–Long (1964–88)

Go Tag–A–Long Manufacturing, Inc. • Washingtonville, Ohio

Go Tag-A-Long Manufacturing, Inc. was a small family business founded in 1964 by Joseph S. Dusi. Its trailers were distributed in 28 states east of the Mississippi River. Go-Tag-A-Longs stood out for their quality construction and lower prices when compared to competitive brands. Costs were kept down by forgoing an on-the-road sales team, instead marketing themselves to dealers through direct mail and at trade shows.

The line presented both the rounded corners of a canned ham and the elongated shape of a bread loaf–style trailer, and the trailers' look changed little over their lifespan. They had an aluminum skin with a galvanized steel roof, an electrical hookup for air conditioning, and a bump-out trunk. The 14-foot models could sleep two, but their most popular trailers were longer, self-contained models with room for up to six people.

The Go-Tag-A-Long owners club, the Tagaliers, gave members the opportunity to camp at Trailerville on Go-Tag-A-Long Lake in Unity, Ohio. Production ended in 1988, but the lake and the campground (now called the Flying Finn Family Campground) are still open for trailers, pop-ups and RVs only.

14'

1968 Go Tag-A-Long Model 14

The rounded square body shape, trunk bump-out, and signature turquoise stripe were features shared by every model in the lineup from longest to shortest. Remarkable in their consistency, Go Tag-A-Longs remained virtually unchanged until the mid-1970s, when new color tones were introduced to keep in step with the era.

1971
Model 16

16'

1971
Model 18

18'

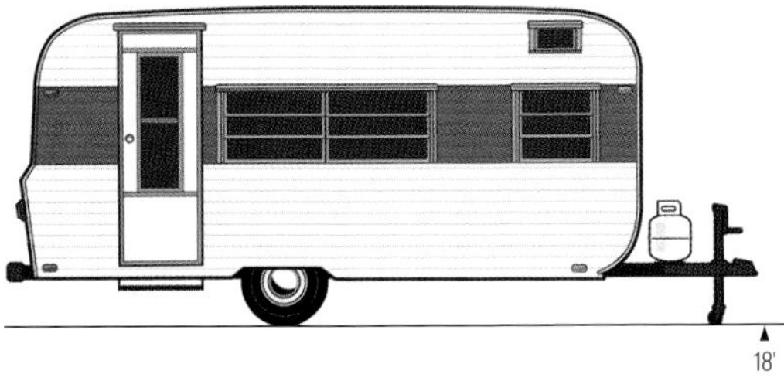

1975
Model 18

18'

Garwood (1958–59) / Garway (1960s)

Garwood Homes, Inc. / Garway Homes, Inc. • Elkhart, Indiana

Garwood vacation trailers were built in 1958–59. In 1960 the company and its trailer line changed their name to Garway. The Garway line of canned ham models advertised its trailers as fitting any budget and offering as much comfort as an average home. Garways could also take rough roads in stride and came in a range of popular sizes.

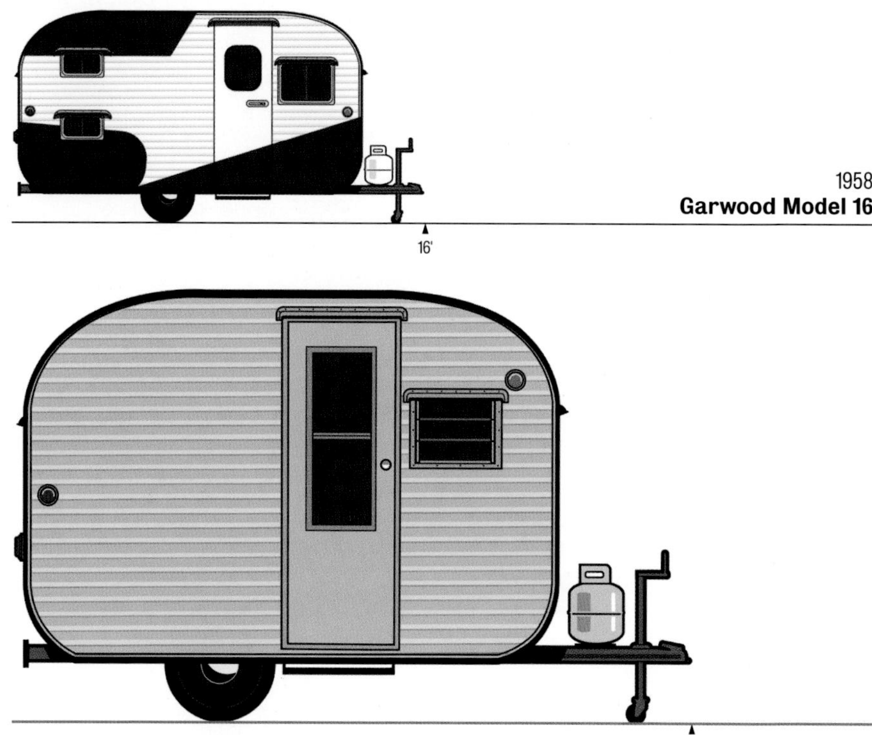

1958
Garwood Model 16

1961 Garway Model 13

Priced with the most price-conscious buyer in mind, the Garway Model 13 was a basic travel trailer with the minimum of amenities. It had an unpainted aluminum body, small jalousie windows, and little ornamentation.

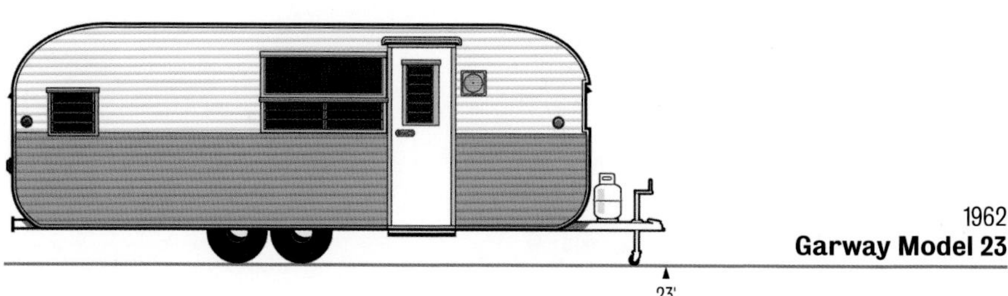

1962
Garway Model 23

Glider (1932–late 1950s)

Glider Trailer Company • Chicago, Illinois

Glider apartment-sized trailers were meant for extended travel or temporary housing. They were a low-cost option for defense workers seeking a home-like environment during World War II and permanent shelter for many displaced citizens after the war. In 1950, Gliders were given a design makeover so they were roomy enough to raise a family.

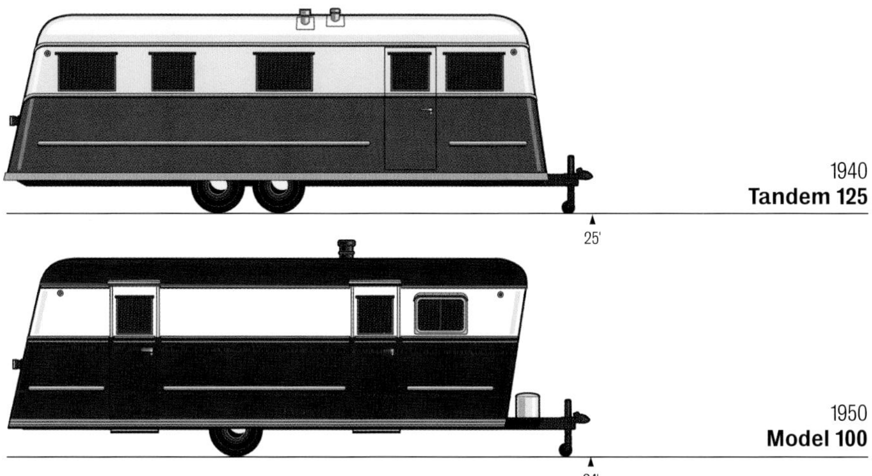

1940
Tandem 125

1950
Model 100

Go-Lite (1961–79)

Herzig Manufacturing Company / Go-Lite Campers, Inc. • Fremont, Nebraska

The original Go-Lite name appeared on the Herzig Manufacturing Company's Alumalite line of vacation trailers. The 1961 canned ham–style 15-foot and 16-foot Go-Lite models had aluminum exteriors and an oak interior. A large arrow graphic painted across their upper side bodies pointed them down the road.

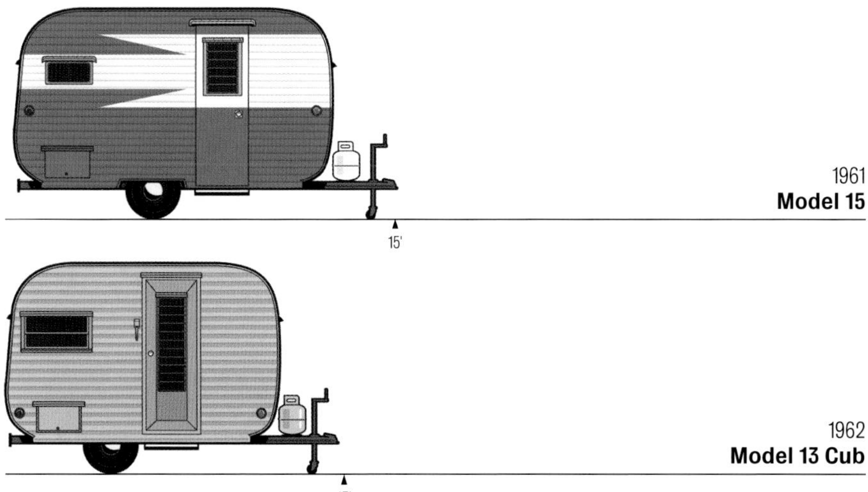

1961
Model 15

1962
Model 13 Cub

GREAT WESTERN CORP.

Great Western (1947–48)

Great Western Corporation • Los Gatos, California

Great Westerns only *seemed* to be spaceworthy vehicles. They were in fact trailers constructed of aircraft aluminum and featured louvers around the front window that allowed filtered air to enter the otherwise sealed unit. A roof with a raised tail increased the interior height and light. Around five are known to have been made.

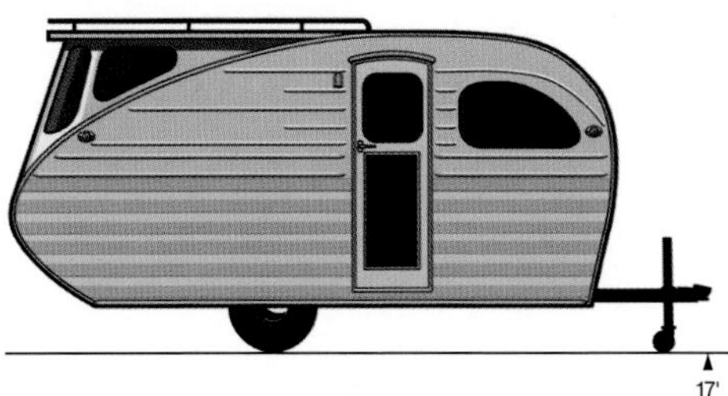

1947
Great Western

1947 Great Western

A Great Western is rumored to have appeared in *The Big Clock,* a 1948 film noir starring Ray Milland, Maureen O'Sullivan, and Charles Laughton. Director John Farrow bought the trailer after filming. Frederick C. Hoffman patented designs for both Great Western trailers and their longer lookalikes, Aero Flite trailers (see page 32).

H

A classic canned ham with a rounded body and flat sides

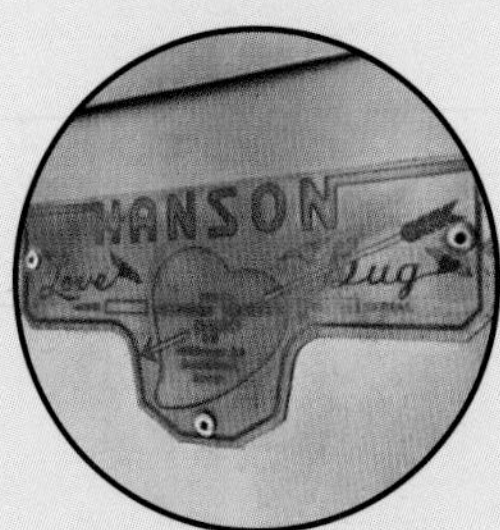

Distinctive Love Bug badge to the right of the door

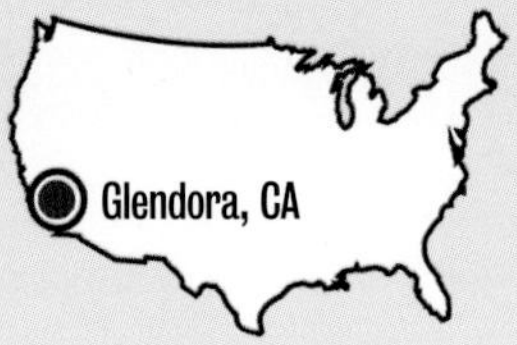

Hanson (1948–58)

Hanson Trailer Sales • Glendora, California

Henry M. Hanson Sr. showed his business savvy when he built the Hanson Love Bug factory just off Route 66 in Glendora, California, in 1948. Thousands of potential customers traveled the celebrated cross-country route every day. A huge Hanson Trailer Sales sign that shouted out the world's lowest prices, small down payments, and five-year financing gave drivers a reason to pull into the sales lot.

Love Bugs were built with first-time trailer buyers in mind. They were aluminum-sided canned ham–style trailers from 10 to 20 feet long, just the right size for a young family. Factory-direct pricing and sales promotions kept the production line busy. *So* busy that Love Bugs were essentially made to order and customizable.

Larger models were called "custom coaches" and ranged from 22 to 37 feet long. In 1958, Hanson stopped making trailers and contracted the Kenskill Trailer Corporation to finish about two years' worth of back-ordered Love Bugs. He went on to start the Automated Metals Corporation. Aluminum trailers built in the 1950s and '60s have a 75 percent chance of using metal from his company.

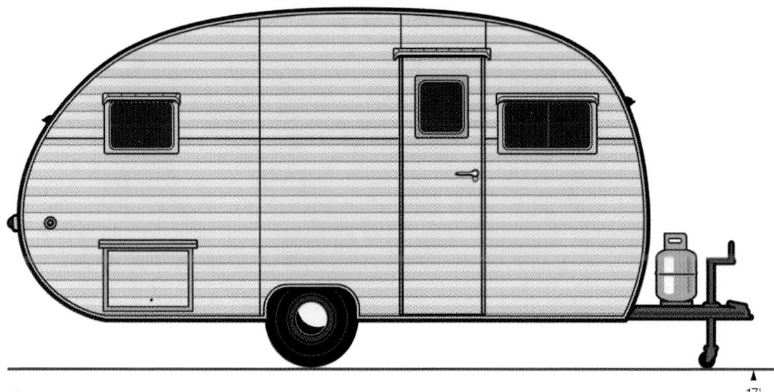

1952 Hanson Love Bug Model 17

The lightweight and easy-to-tow Model 17 was the embodiment of a canned ham trailer. It had a rounded body with a curved front and tail, an unpainted aluminum skin, and essential amenities.

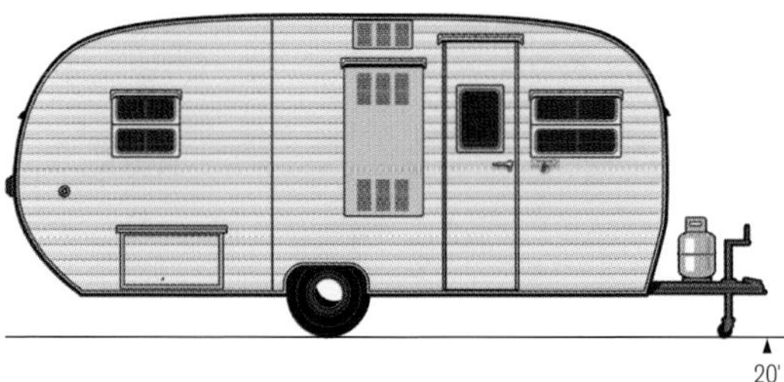

1954
Model 20

1957
Model 10

Hanson Love Bug Factory, 1951

A line of 1951 Hanson Love Bugs illustrates their manufacturing evolution. The trailer closest to the factory needs an aluminum skin, door, and windows. The trailer at the head of the line is complete, hitched, and ready for the customer. All Love Bugs were uniquely insured for falling aircraft since the Glendora, California, factory and sales lot shared the property with Hanson's private airfield.

Showy plexiglass wraparound front windows

Angled bare aluminum and painted side panels with a painted band dividing the lower and upper body

Holiday House (1960–61)

Holiday House, Inc. • Medford, Oregon

In the late 1950s, skilled workers at the Harry & David company in Medford, Oregon, kept busy from August to December picking, packing, and mailing fruit baskets filled with Royal Riviera pears, but during the offseason they were idle and many left town.

To solve this problem, company president David Holmes Jr. came up with the idea to have his employees build trailers during the offseason. Holmes's new Holiday House travel trailers were wood framed and had an aluminum skin, but they were worthy of the "space age" moniker. In 1960 and 1961, less than 200 units were manufactured. Production ceased in January 1962.

The pièce de résistance of the line is the Geographic, an ultrafuturistic luxury coach with an all-fiberglass body. Between 4 and 11 were made, but with an out-of-this-world price tag of $8,495, only the floor model sold. Three are known to exist: the restored floor model is currently in France. Flyte Camp, located in Bend, Oregon, restored a Geographic and then sold it to an undisclosed buyer. Casey Kielbasa, nearly a decade after spotting one in Utah, bought it in 2019. It is now part of the Gulley Collection. What became of the others remains a mystery.

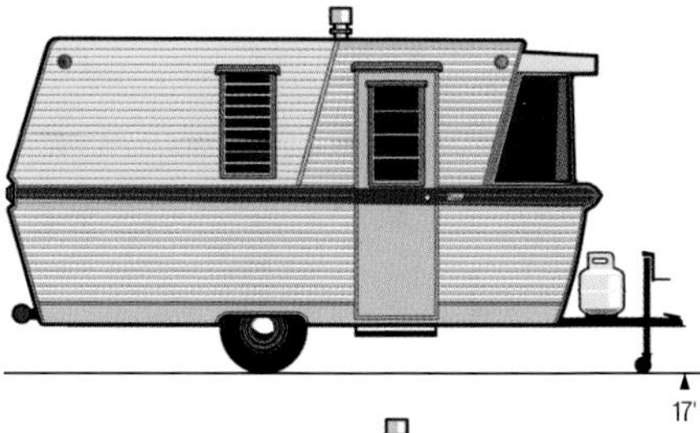

17'

1960
Model 17

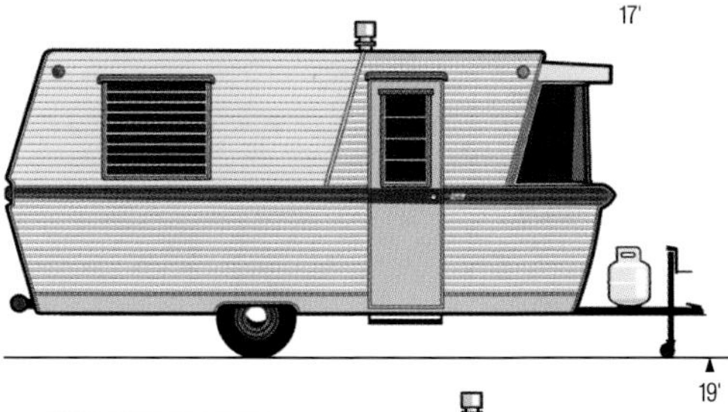

19'

1960
Model 19

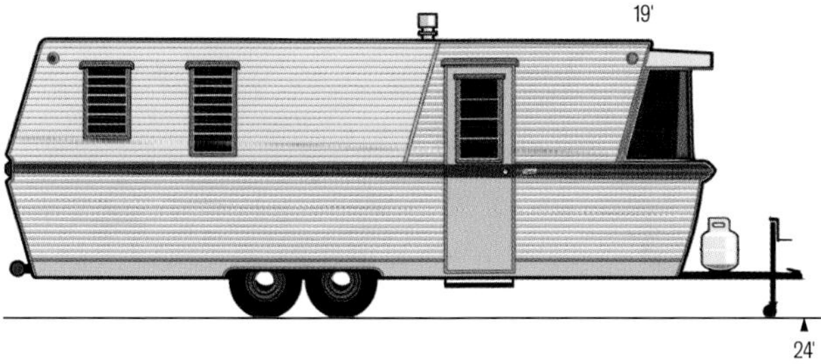

24'

1961
Model 24

Googie Style

The bright logo and geometric ornamentation of the Holiday House are excellent examples of the modern futurist style known as Googie—atomic and space age design infused with a heady mix of prosperity and optimism.

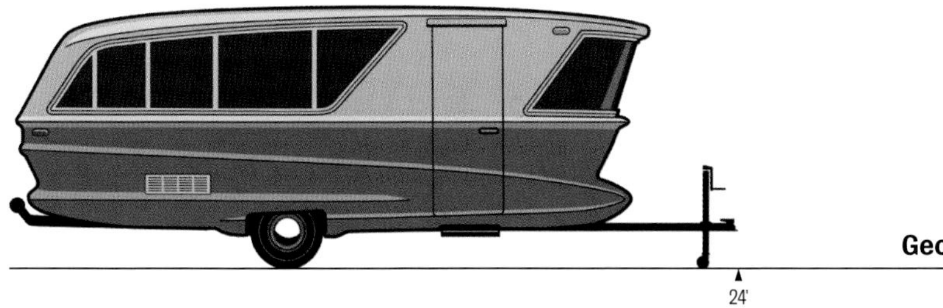

24'

1961
Model X Geographic

1950s-early '60s models were canned ham–like trailers with skirted sides covering the wheels

Post-1964 models had a rounded-off roofline and sported a bold diamond aluminum stripe and emblem

Holiday Rambler (1953–present)

Holiday Rambler Corporation • Wakarusa, Indiana

Richard Klingler founded the Holiday Rambler Corporation in 1953 in the small town of Wakarusa, Indiana. And like the town, where he built trailer parts in a chicken coop and assembled them outdoors, the first Holiday Rambler travel trailers were modestly sized and outfitted. They were aimed to please hunters and fishermen who needed a basic camping trailer.

Holiday Ramblers were the first trailers that offered built-in refrigerators, toilets with holding tanks, and an aluminum frame known as "Aluma Frame." Two more Holiday lines emerged in the 1960s. The Holiday Vacationer line satisfied those with modest budgets, while the Holiday Trav'ler line was constructed using a wood frame and was medium priced.

Arriving in the 1973 model year, the Royal Holiday was the ultimate in luxury on wheels, completely self-contained, and built for year-round use. It came in a choice of gold, green, or orange color schemes. Standard features included shag carpet, an eight-track tape stereo system, and a 12-inch Sony television with an antenna.

The Holiday Rambler's nameplate has survived over six decades and multiple owners, and has adorned campers, motor homes, and fifth wheels.

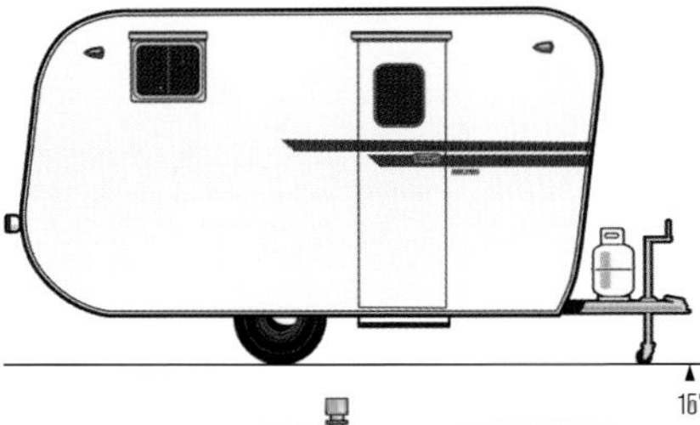

1954
Rambler 15'

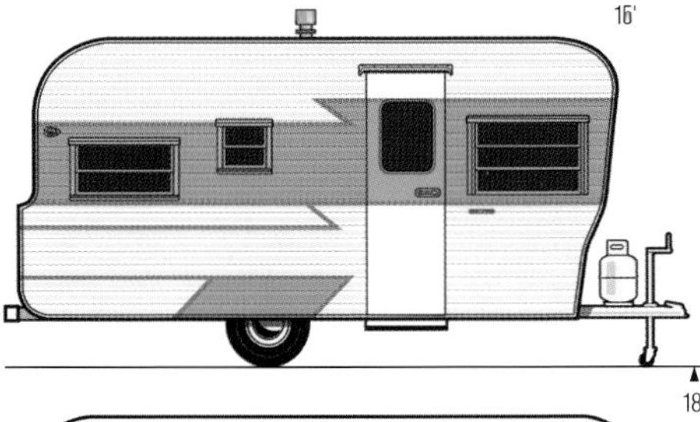

16'

1962
Rambler 17½'

18'

1967
Vacationer

19'

The Holiday Rambler Band

Holiday Ramblers from the mid-1960s to early 1970s are easily recognized by a quilted diamond band and stamped emblem along their sides. The USA-shaped logo and color-keyed stripe distinctively branded the Holiday Rambler, Vacationer, and Trav'ler lines. On later models the diamond pattern evolved into various other stripe treatments.

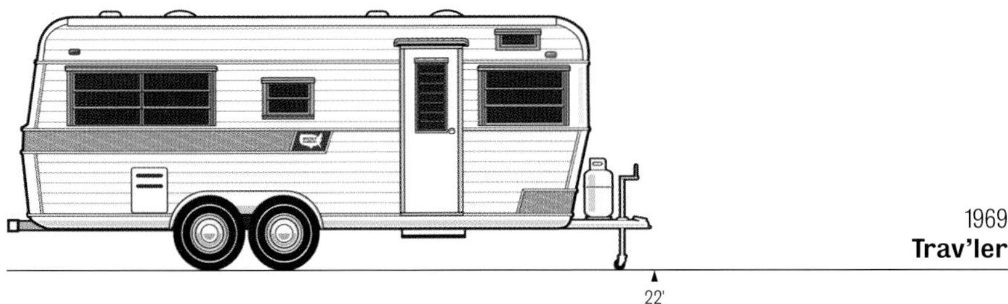

1969
Trav'ler

22'

Hayes (mid-1930s–early 1940s)

Hayes Manufacturing Corporation • Grand Rapids, Michigan

During the slow years of the Great Depression, the Hayes Manufacturing Corporation took their expertise in building automobile bodies and applied it to trailers. The all-steel Hayes bread loaf–style "motor homes" were welded into one rigid piece, soundproofed, and rust protected.

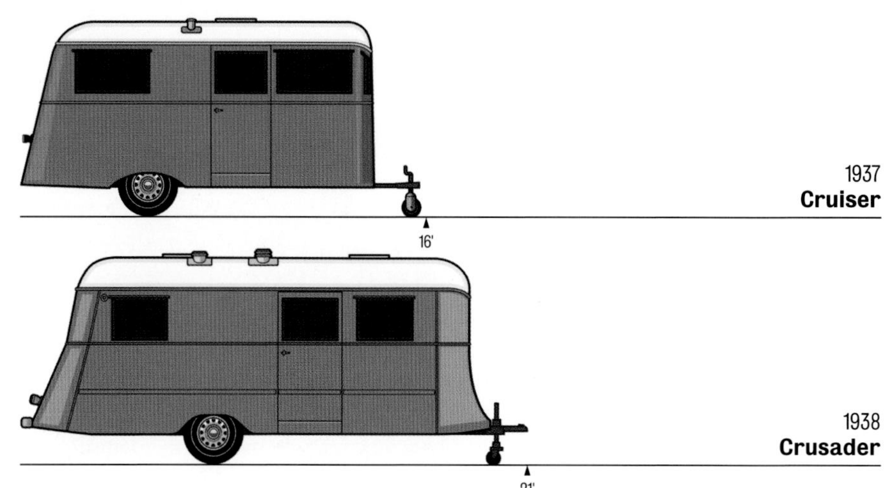

1937
Cruiser

1938
Crusader

Hiawatha

Hiawatha (1952–early 1970s)

Hiawatha Mobile Homes • Ironwood, Michigan

Hiawatha was a regional trailer manufacturer that brought together a powerful line of RV products that included vacation trailers, mobile homes, and truck campers. In the early 1970s the company ceased trailer manufacturing and went on to sell RV parts and materials to DIYers who had the know-how to build their own camper, topper, or trailer.

● 1955 Hiawatha 12

The Hiawatha 12 was an economical vacation trailer that was equipped with the exclusive Hagstrom folding couch/bunk bed: a full-sized 54-inch bed with a 44-inch upper bunk that converted to a daytime couch. It had ample room to store bedding for four, a block tile floor, a birch interior, and an all-aluminum exterior.

Hi–Lo (1955–present)

Snyder Trailer Company / Hi-Lo Trailer Company, Inc. • Butler, Ohio

Hi-Lo trailers could be adjusted up for camping and down for traveling. Their low profile allowed for stable towing and saved on fuel. They could go anywhere a tow vehicle could go, including the garage. When raised to full height they offered plenty of headroom and all the amenities of the day.

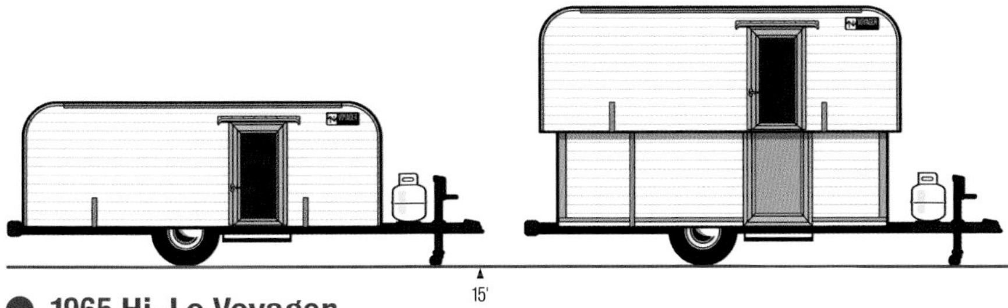

1965 Hi–Lo Voyager

The Voyager in its lowered, or "travel," position (left) was a little over 5 feet tall. The trailer was raised by using a hand crank or an optional electric motor. The Voyager at its full height (right) had over 6 feet of headroom.

Holly (mid-1950s–early 1960s)

Holly Coach Company • Holly, Michigan

The Holly line of trailers were built for travel or year-round living on the road. Four models came in popular lengths, from 17-foot vacation trailers to 29-foot coaches. Holly coaches had "more floor space without sacrificing needed storage space and other built-in conveniences that appeal to housewives."

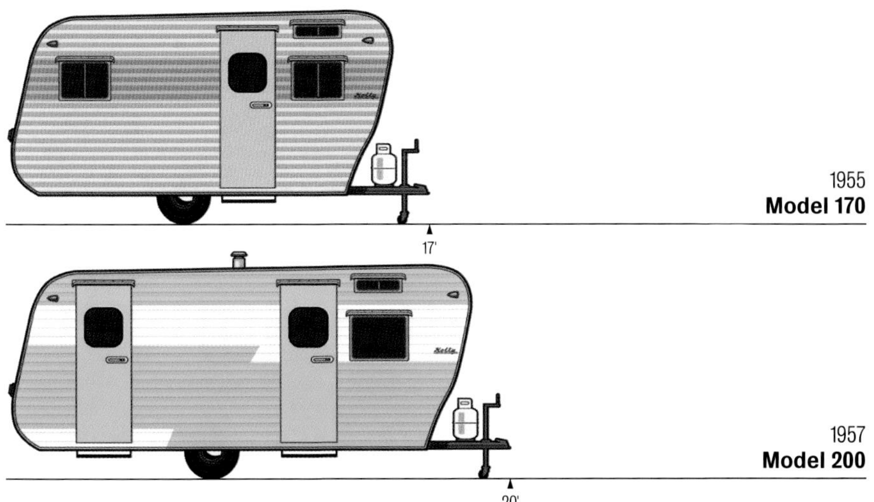

1955
Model 170

1957
Model 200

Honorbuilt (early 1950s–mid-1970s)

Honorbuilt Trailer Manufacturing Company • Lakeview, California

The Romer line of vacation trailers was lightweight, inexpensive, and "built for modern high-speed roads or the toughest pioneer trail." They came in 15-, 16-, and 24-foot editions. Deluxe models came with a toilet and shower. The Romer brand appeared on trailers, truck campers, and motor homes.

1957 Honorbuilt Romer 15

The Romer 15 was a basic canned ham–style trailer. It had an all-aluminum exterior with a two-tone enamel paint design. The birch interior had electric or butane lights. It had space to sleep five campers, a convertible dinette, and extra upper cabinetry in the kitchen.

Hummingbird (1955–56)

Hummingbird • Southern California

The Hummingbird trailer brand flitted in and out of existence and left little information behind. The manufacturer's name cannot be traced with any authority, although it appears to have been made in Southern California. It's likely that Hummingbirds sold factory direct to an allied trailer dealer.

1956
Model 16'

Ideal (1948–82)

Ideal Industries, Inc. • El Monte, California / Ideal of Idaho, Inc. • Caldwell, Idaho

Ideal Industries, Inc., founded in 1948, flocked together with many other trailer manufacturers in Southern California. When they landed in the small farm town of El Monte, just 12 miles east of Los Angeles, they became part of a population explosion of people and industry. But it wasn't only El Monte that grew up fast; the whole country experienced a postwar boom.

Ideal park models were a "house beautiful" solution for young couples looking for a home. In fact, Ideal claimed that its whole family of trailers were for traveling or year-round living. The lady of the house was lured with amenities such as convenient TV shelves, roomy bathrooms, and well-planned kitchens with double sinks.

Many trailerites remember fun-filled family vacations and weekend trips in their Ideal trailer. They had excellent roadability, comfortable sleeping accommodations, ample kitchen and storage space, plus the larger models had bathrooms complete with a shower.

Ideal production facilities moved to Caldwell, Idaho, in 1978. They made trailers through the 1982 model year using Ideal of Idaho, Inc. as their company name.

The Ideal badge was affixed to the right of the door on models from 1952 to 1963

Most models presented a rounded roofline and large front window(s)

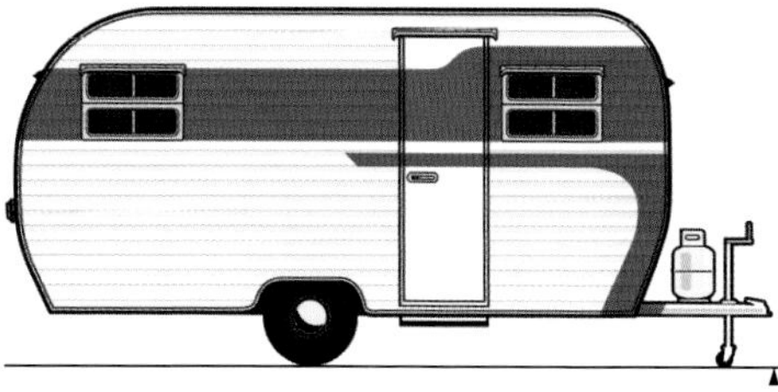

1954
Model 17

17'

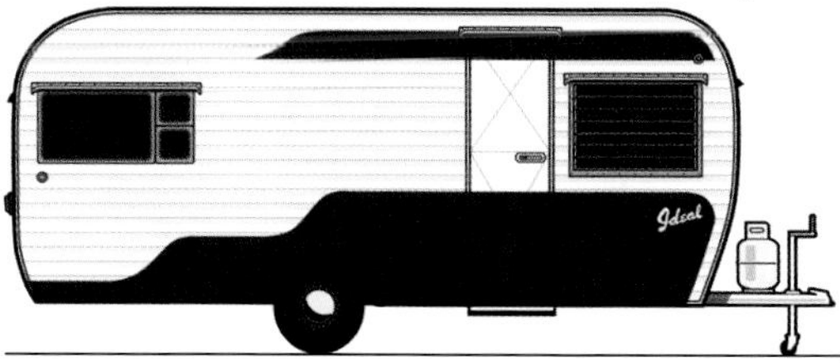

1955
Model 20

20'

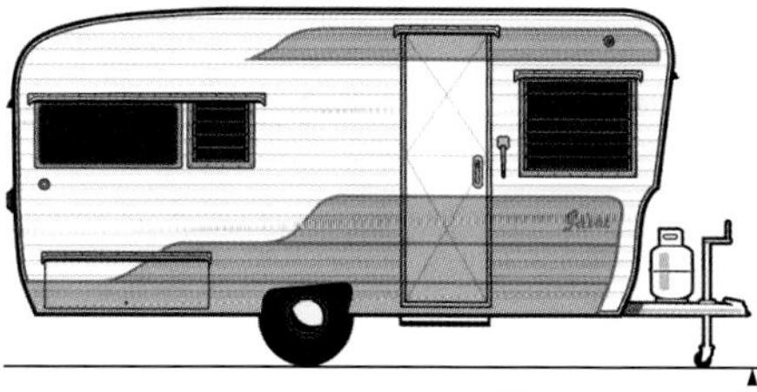

1958
Model 17

17'

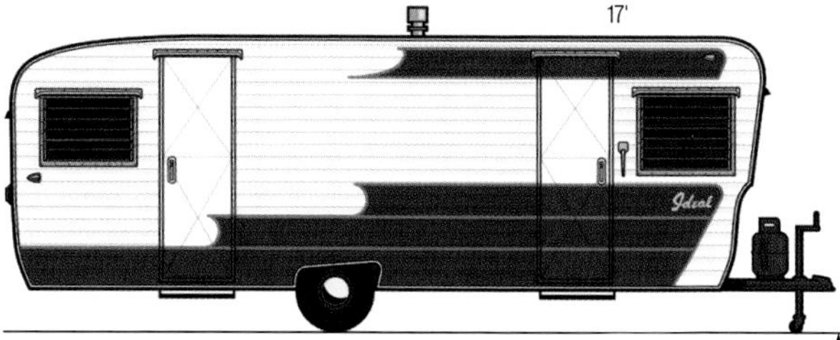

1959
Model 23

23'

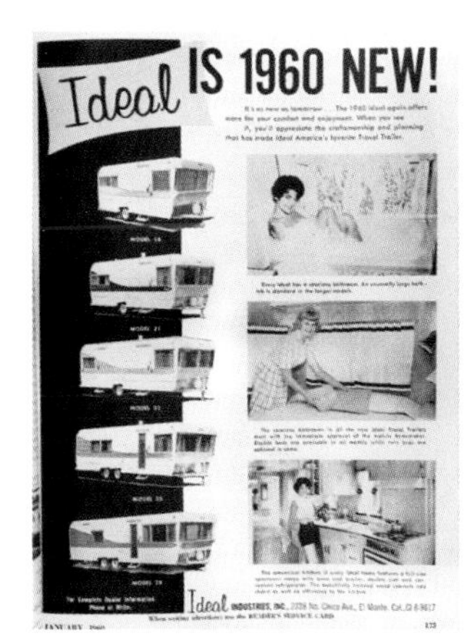

Ideal Is 1960 New!

This ad from 1960 shows the line of Ideal trailers, from the Model 18 to the Model 28. They all have full front windows, a protective metal band behind the hitch, and a jet-like graphic on their sides. Interiors featured bubble-bath-worthy tubs, easy-to-make beds, and coffee klatch–sized kitchens.

Ideal Wheel Wells

The 1958–71 model years displayed knife-edged wheel wells that seemed made to cut a trail down the road. Their angled shape contrasted with the otherwise rounded features of the trailer's body.

19.5'

1964
Model 195

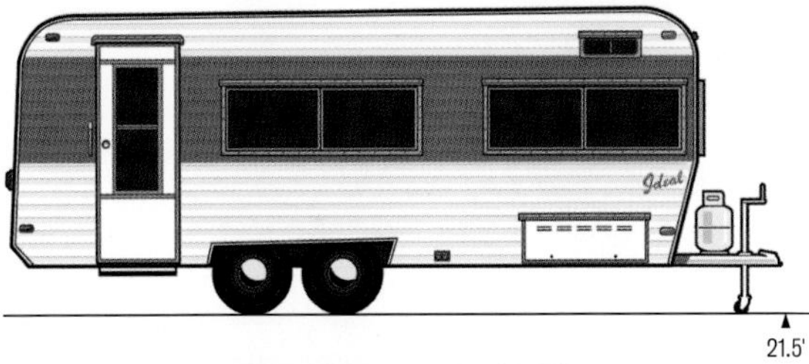

21.5'

1967
Model 215

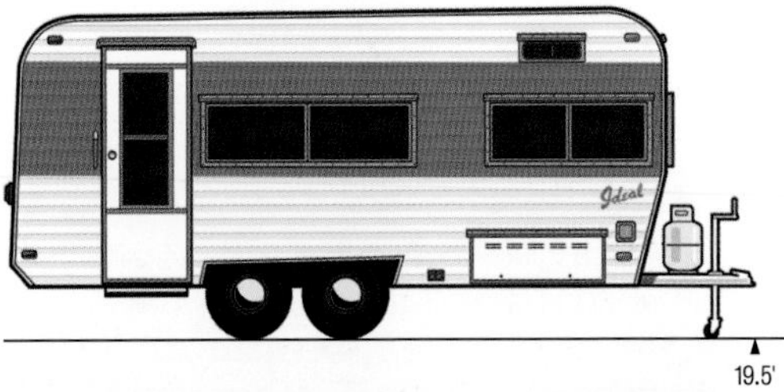

19.5'

1970
Model 19½

21.5'

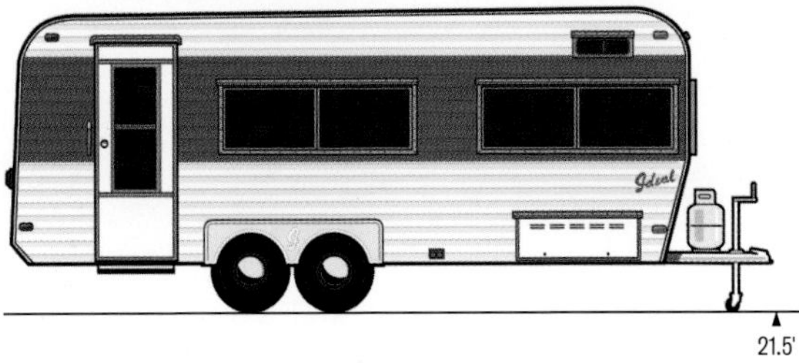

1972
Model 21½

J

Jewel

Canned ham body sporting a distinctive bump in profile under the front window

1954–59 models had a stair-step graphic that flowed down their sides

Jewel (1954–63)

Trailer Industries, Inc. • El Monte, California

Trailer Industries, Inc. created the Jewel brand during the height of trailer manufacturing in El Monte, California. In 1954 the Jewel logo first appeared on travel trailers 15, 17, and 21 feet in length. By the 1960s it would grace the 18-foot Windsor, the Model 25, and the 30-foot Imperial.

Jewel trailers were marketed as a smooth-towing and luxurious replacement for a motel room or apartment. They featured quality construction using No. 1 kiln-dried lumber, an exceptionally sturdy chassis, and midcentury design. Standard equipment included complete kitchens with a modern icebox, a full cookstove, generous cupboard space, and an oversized dinette.

Larger Jewels had more livable room than many mobile homes and were available in self-contained and utility-independent versions. It made them an attractive choice for young couples just starting out, workers moving from job to job, or retired folks hitting the road on cross-country trips.

A different company, Jewel Trailers Inc. of South El Monte, California, made the Jewel brand in its final year, 1963.

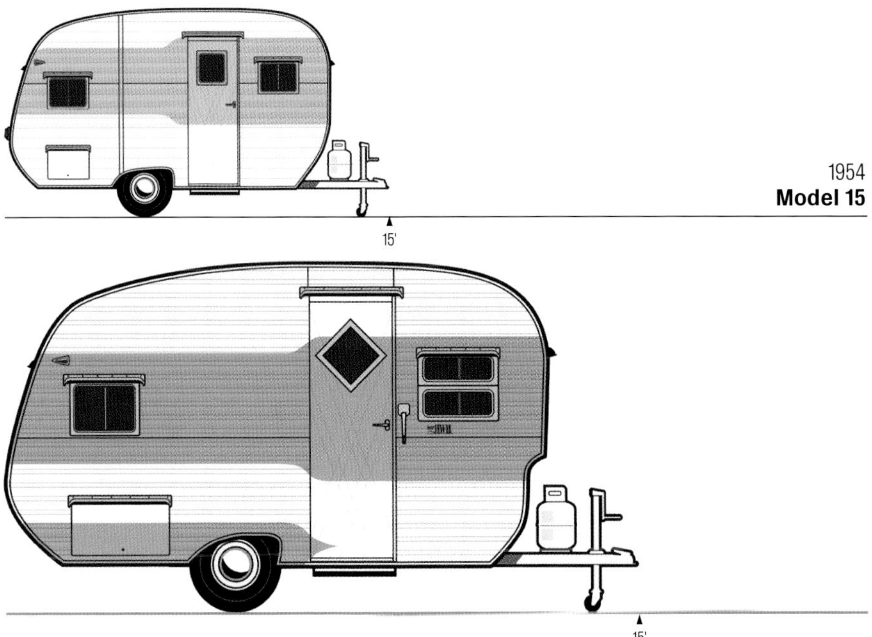

1957 Jewel Model 15

A "low, low price combined with quality" made the Model 15 shine. The most notable differences between it and its 1954 predecessor above is its diamond-shaped window, jutting front end, and a new band of color on its sides.

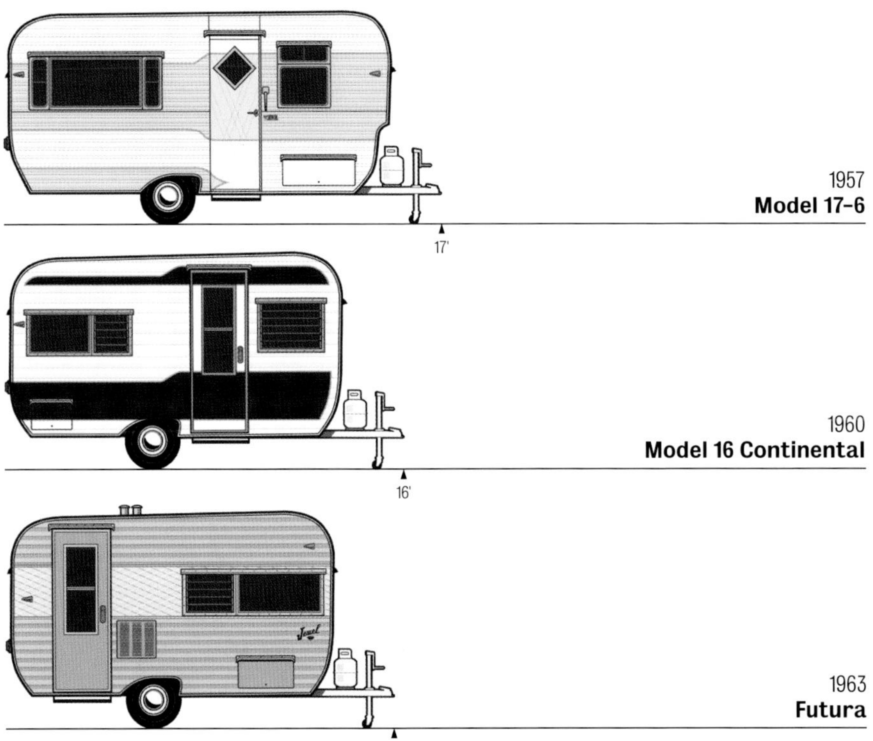

Jayco (1968–present)

Jayco, Inc. • Middlebury, Indiana

Lloyd Jay Bontrager patented his collapsible trailer, or pop-up camper, in 1967. In 1968 he founded Jayco and began making camping trailers. Jayco produced travel trailers, fifth wheels, and motor homes in the following decades. In 1994, Bontrager was inducted into the RV/MH Hall of Fame, followed by his sons William in 2008 and Derald in 2018.

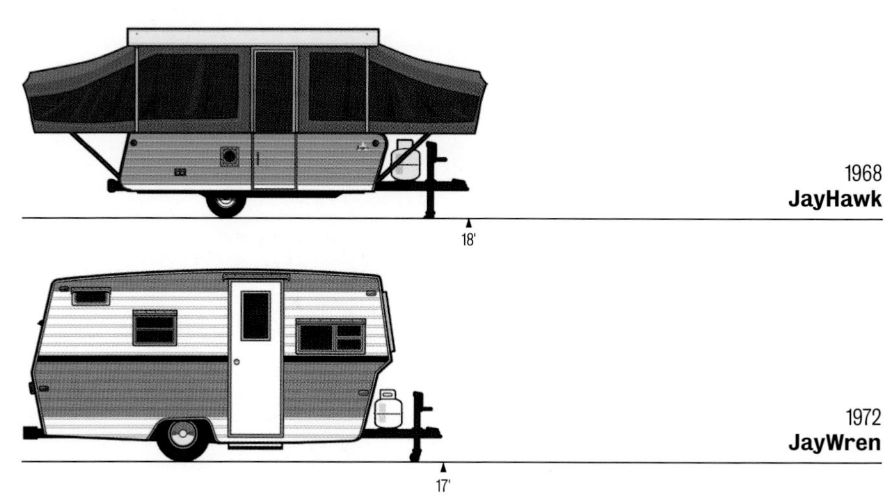

Jet (1964–mid-1970s)

Lofgren Manufacturing Company • Salt Lake City, Utah

A regional brand, Jet travel trailers were designed for maximum room and comfort. They were low priced but were marketed as being built with the finest of materials and fixtures. The mid-1960s models had color appliances that matched the decor, a rear gaucho, and top-grade tires.

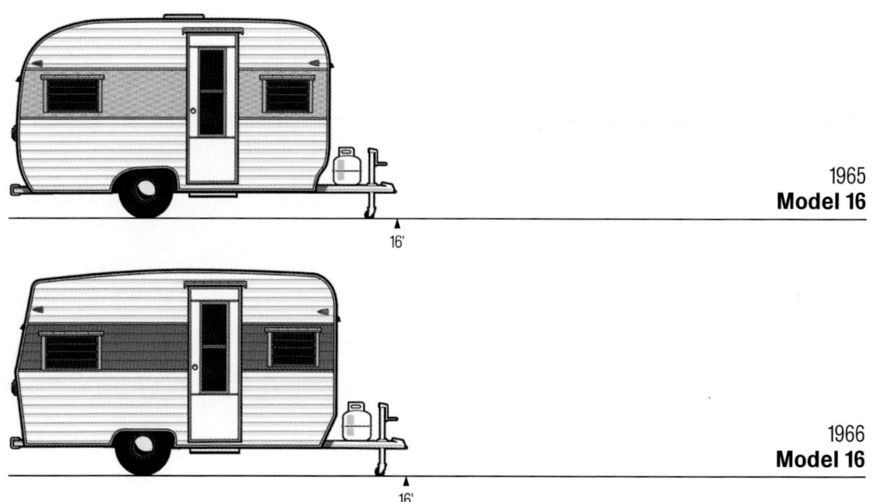

K

Ken-Craft (1955–75)

Ken-Craft Products, Inc. • North Hollywood / San Fernando, California / Upper Sandusky, Ohio

Bill Kennedy, the creator of the archetypal teardrop trailer, the Kenskill Kustom Kamper, launched Ken-Craft Products, Inc. into unknown waters with a molded fiberglass trailer in 1955. The first Ken-Crafts were 18-foot models that had no visible seams or joints and were resistant to salt air, salt water, and smog.

Ken-Craft chose to use fiberglass because it was lighter than aluminum and stronger than steel while providing superior insulation properties. The first Ken-Craft's roof, bow, stern, and side panels were bonded into a single unit that was as watertight as a ship at sea.

The interiors of Ken-Craft trailers came in a variety of floor plans, were decorated in the provincial style, and had well-appointed kitchens. They were designed to be a comfortable home away from home that required minimal maintenance to keep them shipshape.

By the mid-1960s, Ken-Craft Products, Inc., along with a half dozen other trailer companies, became subsidiaries of Midas International Corporation. Ken-Craft's last model year was 1975.

The first Ken-Crafts had a one-piece fiberglass body with a wave on its side

Canned ham body style with aluminum sides and a wrap-over fiberglass top

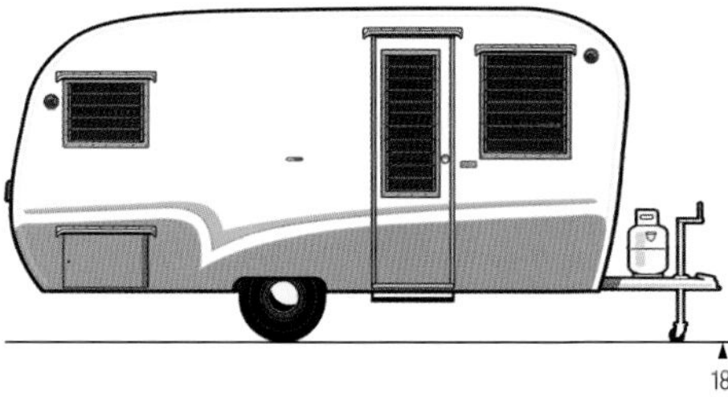

K

1955
Model 18

18'

1957
Model 17

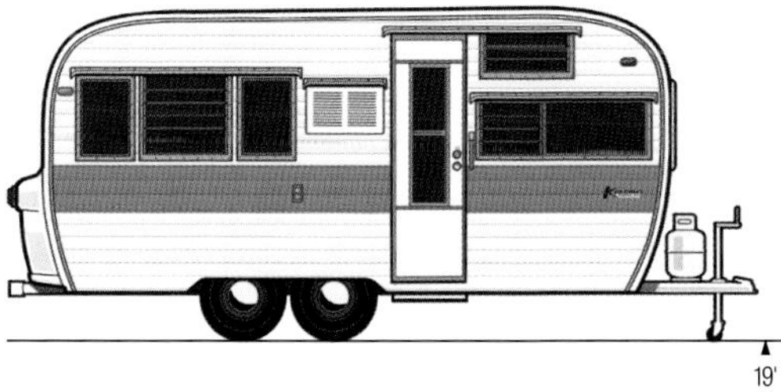

17'

1965
Model 190

19'

Molded Trunk

Mid-1960s models had a molded fiberglass tail section that wrapped around the rear end. It included a bump-out trunk with rounded taillight enclosures. The unique design made Ken-Craft trailers stand out from other brands and gave them more storage space.

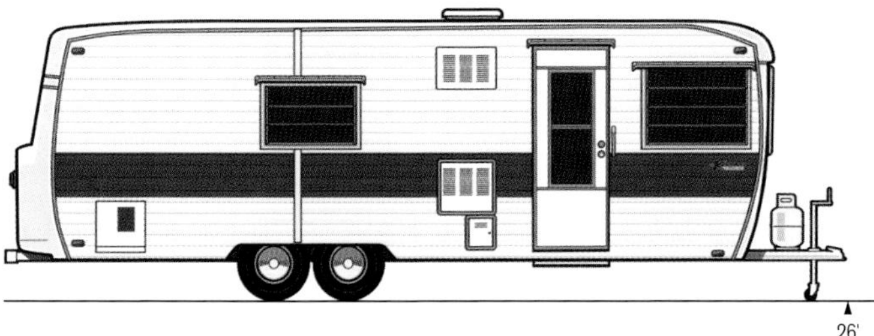

1975
Model 260

26'

1954–60 models had a thunderbolt design on their sides

In 1962, panoramic view windows were introduced on all models

Kenskill (1946–mid-1970s)

Kenskill Manufacturing Company • Burbank, California

Bill Kennedy and Jim Brunskill partnered to build the Ken-Skill Kustom Kamper in 1946. Kennedy built the iconic teardrop trailers and Brunskill put up the money. They parted ways a few years later: Kennedy went on to found Ken-Craft Products, Inc. and Brunskill formed the Kenskill Trailer Corporation.

Longer and longer trailers soon followed. The 1953 models included the 35-foot Cosmopolitan, a park model meant for long-term living. Kenskill advertisements made trailer life feel like home. Their list of features included a choice of salon or sectional divan living room, a bedroom with a Hollywood-style mattress, a complete bathroom, and three wardrobes—all in a 22-foot model.

They were built to the Trailer Coach Association construction standards, whose adoption was advocated for by Brunskill. By 1961, Kenskills became the largest-selling modern travel trailer in the West ("modern" meaning that they had bathroom facilities).

Kenskill sold its brand to Redman Industries, Inc. in 1965. They continued to be made through the mid-1970s. In 1972, Jim Brunskill was inducted into the RV/MH Hall of Fame.

1947 Kenskill Kustom Kamper

The aluminum-skinned Kustom Kamper teardrop trailer featured an all-aluminum galley, gravity feed water tank, and an innerspring mattress, all of which managed to fit within its 9 foot 6 inch length.

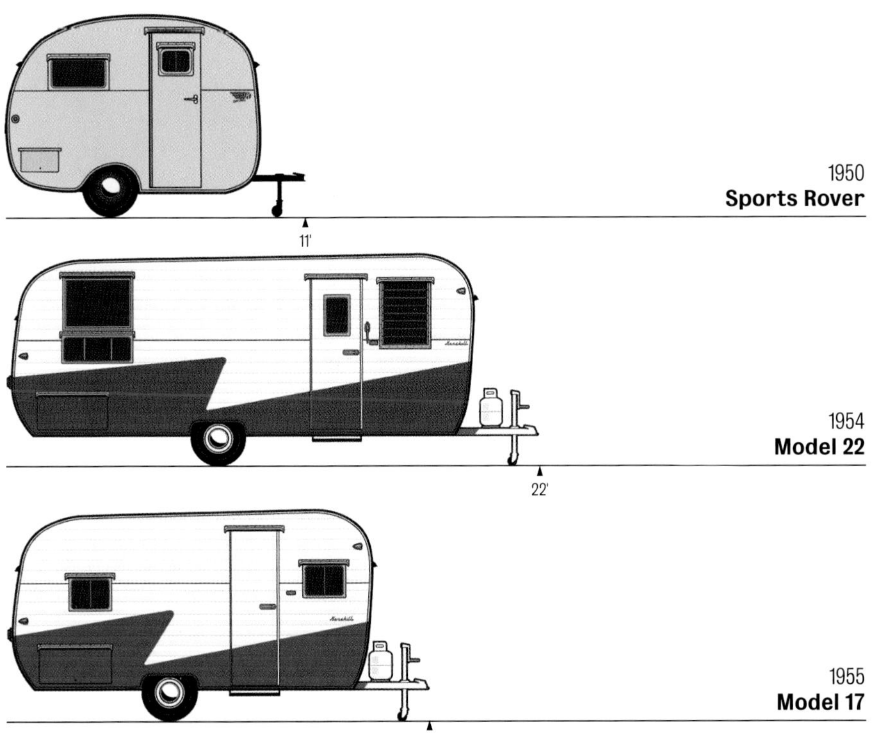

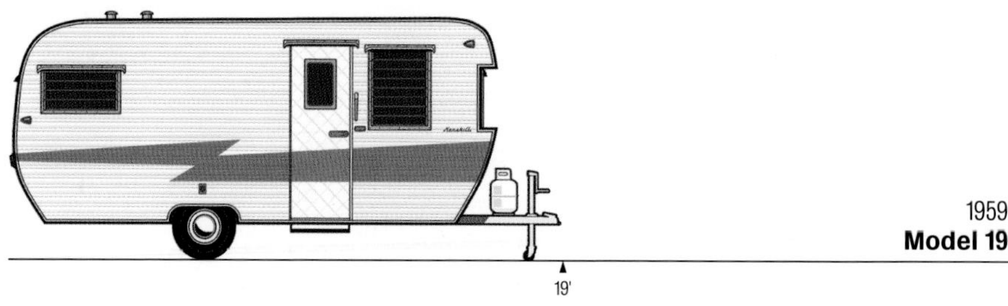

1959
Model 19

1960 Kenskill X-15½

Advertisements claimed that this "revolutionary" two-story model was the first of its kind, with enough sleeping space for a family with up to six children. The "upper Pullman," or cabover layouts became available on other models in 1961.

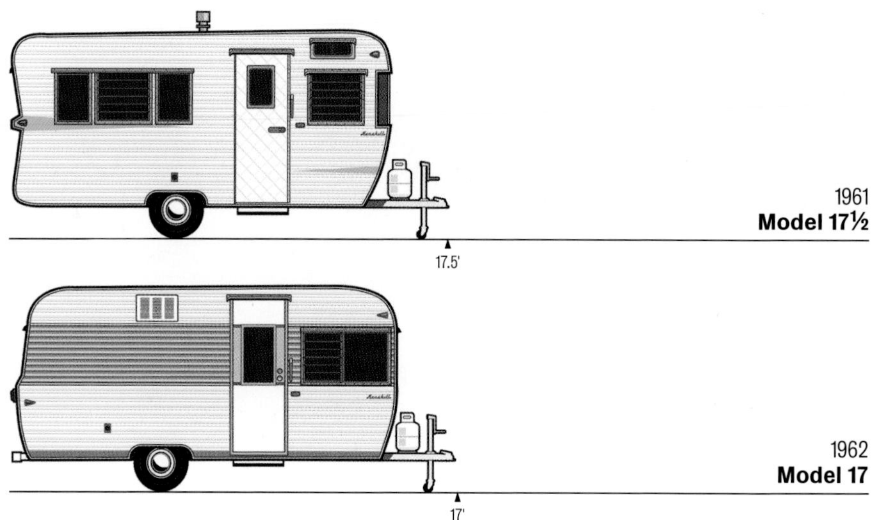

1961
Model 17½

1962
Model 17

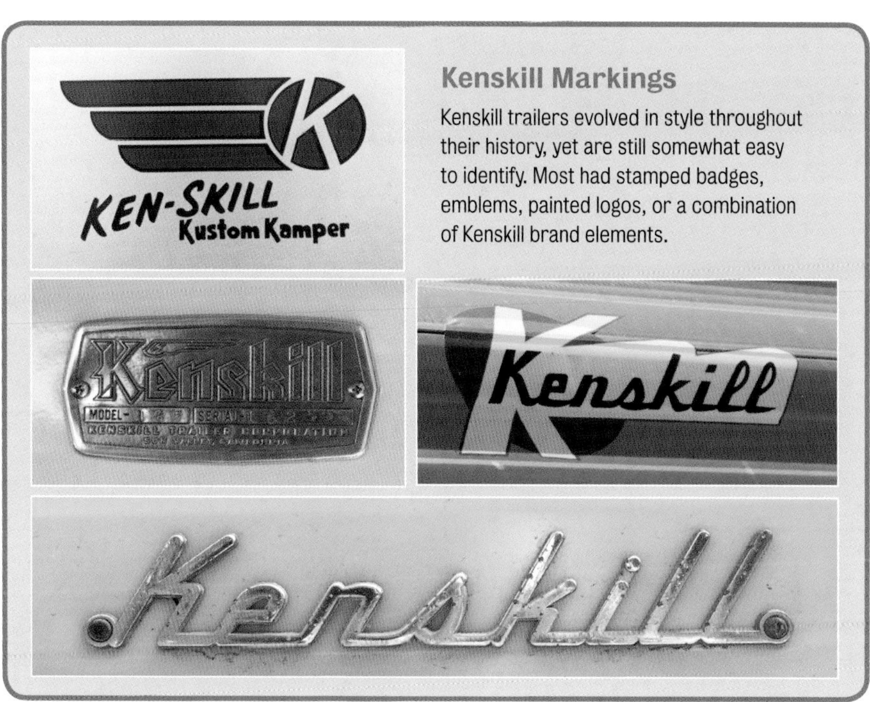

Kenskill Markings

Kenskill trailers evolved in style throughout their history, yet are still somewhat easy to identify. Most had stamped badges, emblems, painted logos, or a combination of Kenskill brand elements.

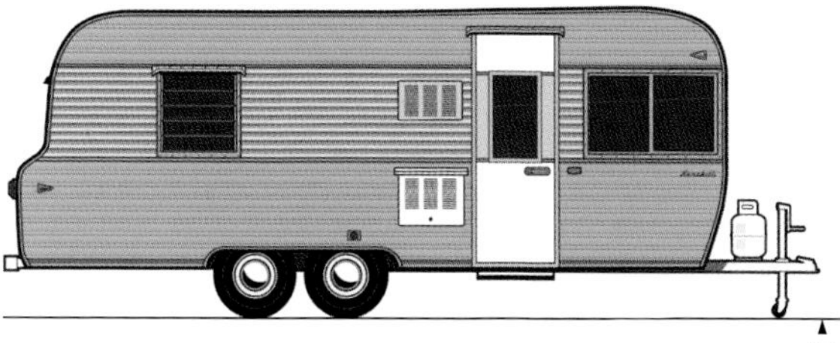

21'

1964
Model 21

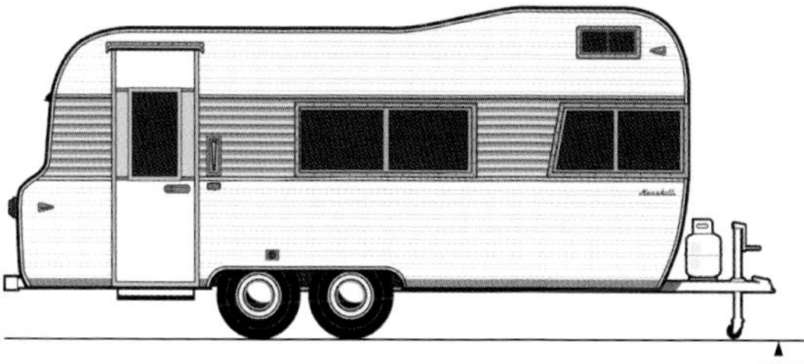

19.5'

1967
Model 19½

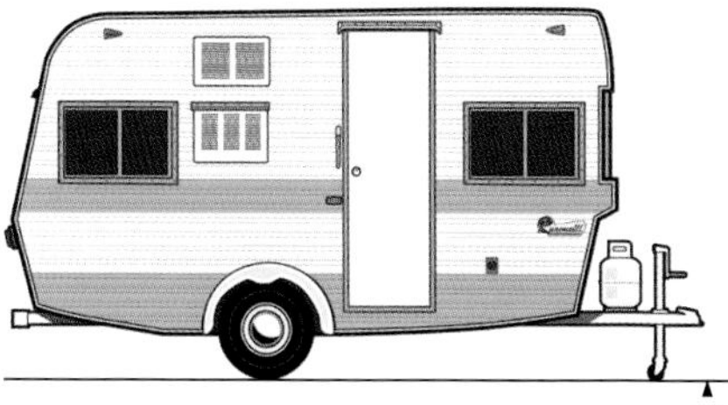

16'

1969
Karousell

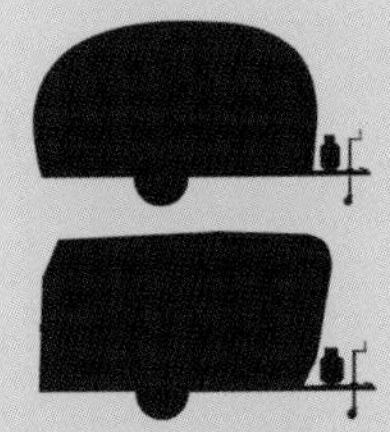

Teardrop- or canned ham–shaped with a curved band along the lower body (1940s–early 1950s)

In 1964, Kit introduced the square-shaped Kit Companion line

Kit (1945–2008)

Kit Manufacturing Company • Long Beach, California

Kit Manufacturing Company, founded in 1945 had a simple plan: make small teardrop trailer kits and sell them to do-it-yourself types to construct in their garages. That plan didn't last long. In 1946 the Kit Kamper hit the roadshow circuit.

Kit soon began building the Kit Companion trailer. Demand for their trailers soon exceeded production, and the company rapidly grew in both their manufacturing facilities and trailer styles. The popularly priced travel trailers were backed by a national publicity campaign in big-city newspapers, magazines like *Field and Stream,* and the *Queen for a Day* radio program. A park model, the Royal Chateau, even appeared in the Joan Caulfield and David Niven movie *The Lady Says No.*

By the 1950 model year, Kit added park models, mobile homes, and manufactured housing to their lineup. Truck campers and Class C motor homes followed in the 1960s.

Kit travel trailer production ended with the 2003 model year when the company was sold to Extreme RVs. Extreme RVs built them from 2004 to 2008. The name lives on at KIT HomeBuilders West, LLC, a manufactured housing company.

11'

1946
Kamper

Kit Beginnings

Kit began its successful run in 1946 with the introduction of a small teardrop trailer. Constructed with a unique combination of war-surplus aluminum and fiberglass fenders, the Kit Kamper debuted at a trade show in Hollywood, California.

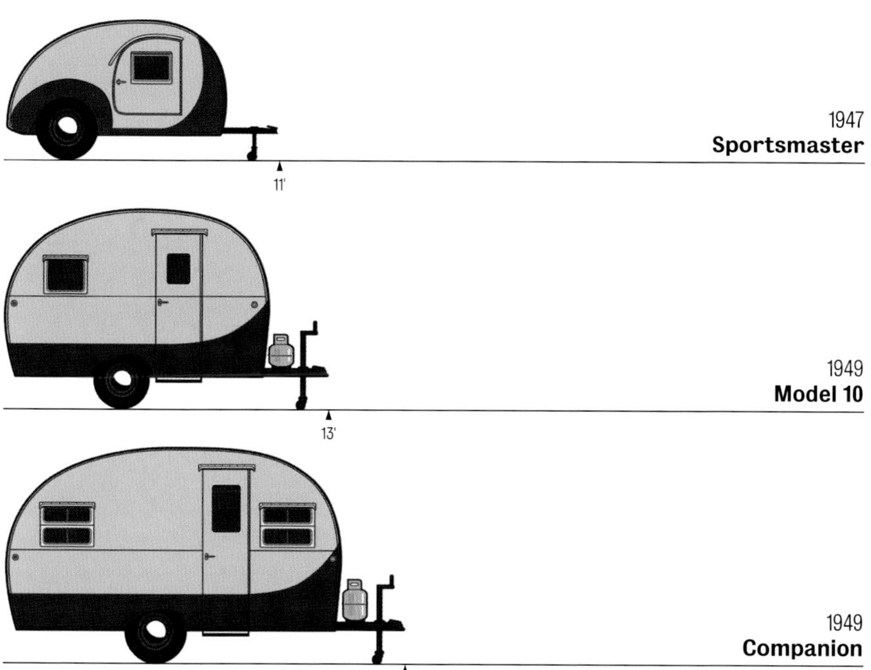

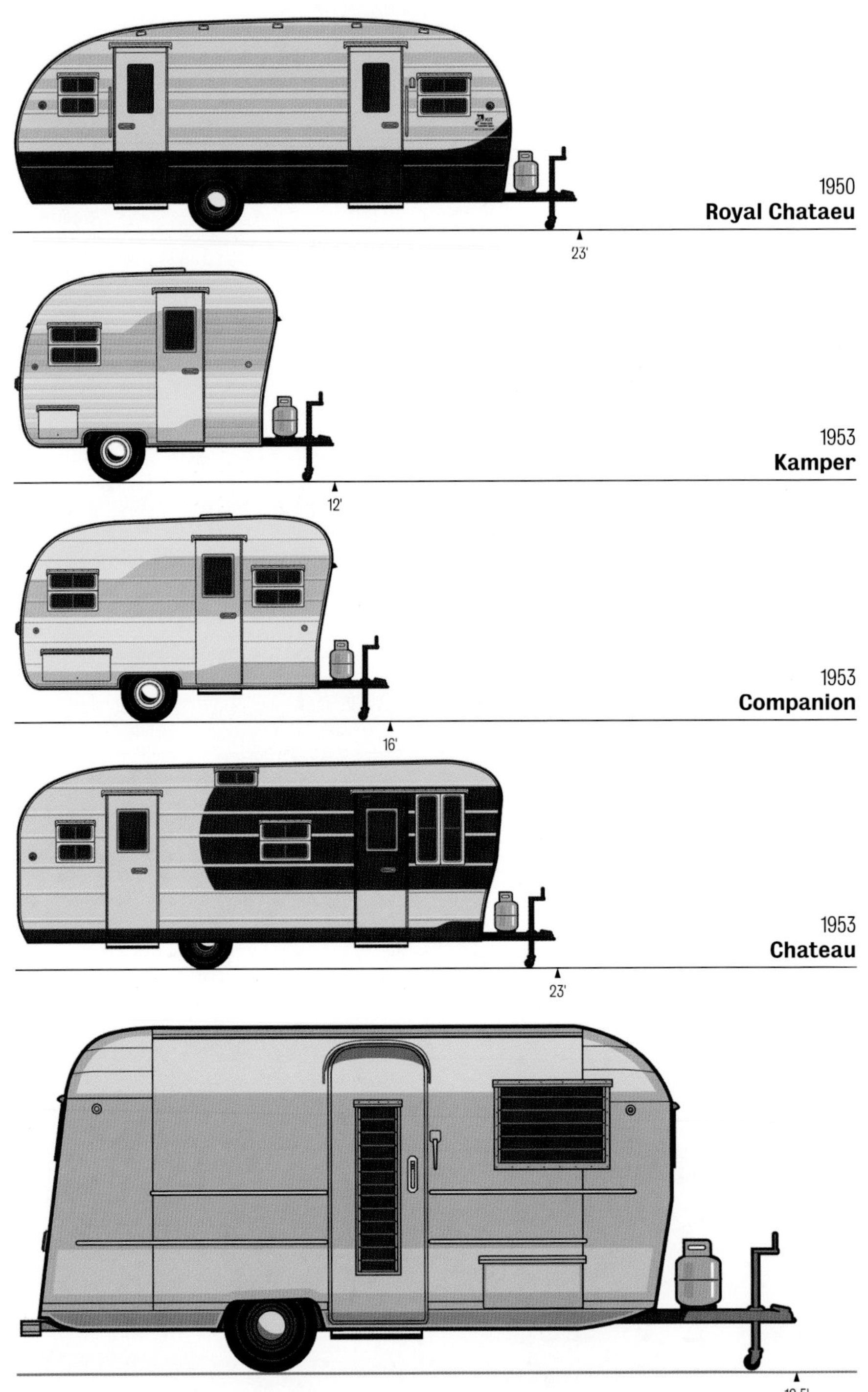

1957 Kit Jetstream 19

Kit briefly dipped their toes in the aircraft-style market by creating the Kit Jetstream Travel Trailer division in the late 1950s. Jetstreams were manufactured for only a couple of years and were designed with quality, luxury, and extra headroom in mind.

The Kit Companion Line

In 1964, Kit reintroduced the popular Companion travel trailers. Models ranged from 15 to 23 feet long. The Companion had luxurious appointments, outstanding strength, and road stamina. Kit also added the Companion Stowaway, following suit with other contemporaries like Aristocrat and Shasta in offering a low-profile, garageable model.

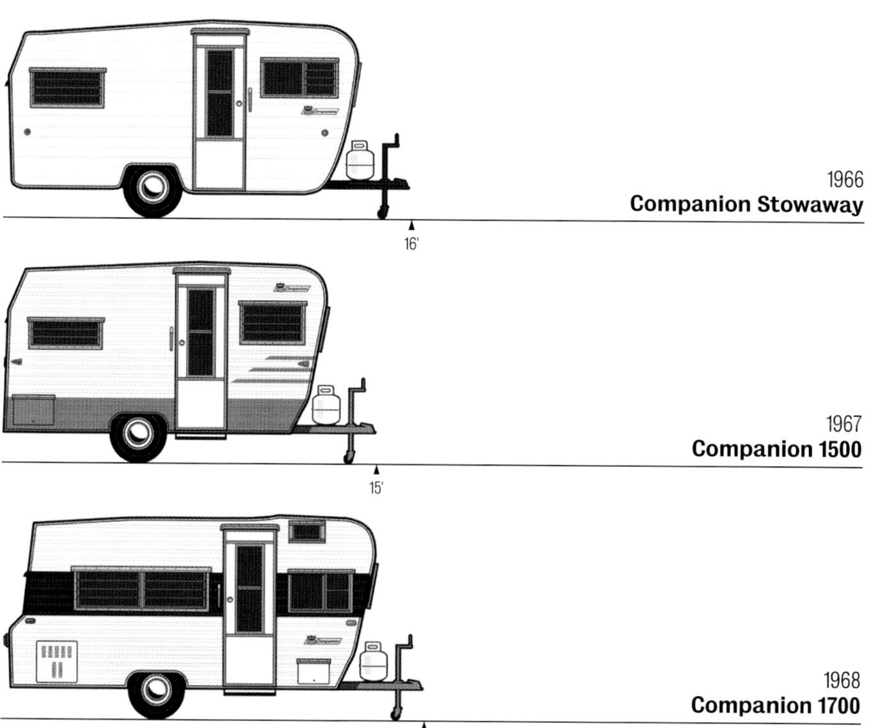

1966
Companion Stowaway

1967
Companion 1500

1968
Companion 1700

King (1952–early 1960s)

King Trailer Company, Inc. • Torrance, California

Walt King offered his factory-direct and custom-built trailers through newspaper ads and fairs. Model lengths spanned from 14½ to 24 feet. They came fully insulated, and had a birch interior and an aluminum exterior. In the late 1950s, King focused on truck campers and phased out trailer production.

16'

1952
Sportsman

Kom-Pak (1952–55)

Kom-Pak Trailers • Medford, Oregon

A fiberglass trailer with a removable roof that doubled as a boat, this unique model was molded to look like a 1953 Ford station wagon. When the boat was in use, on a nearby lake or river, a canvas top could be expanded to cover the sleeping area. Estimates suggest that fewer than 10 still exist.

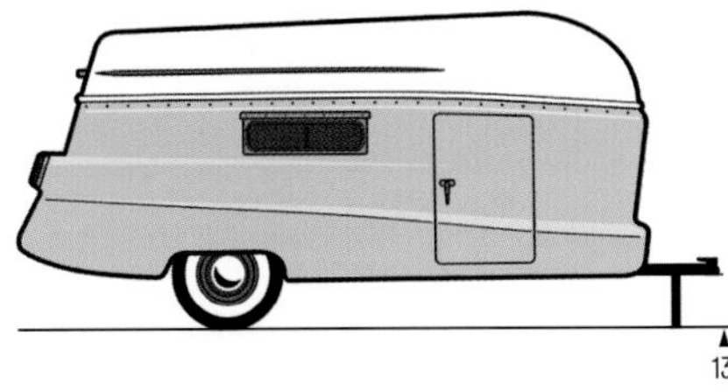

13'

1953
Kom-Pak

Kozy Coach (1931–early 1960s)

Kozy Coach Company • Kalamazoo, Michigan

The Kozy Coach Company built vacation trailers for over two decades. It added larger models during World War II and by the mid-1950s built mobile homes exclusively. The mid-1930s Kozy Coach is a classic bread loaf–style trailer. It came in three models: the Deluxe, Standard, and Junior.

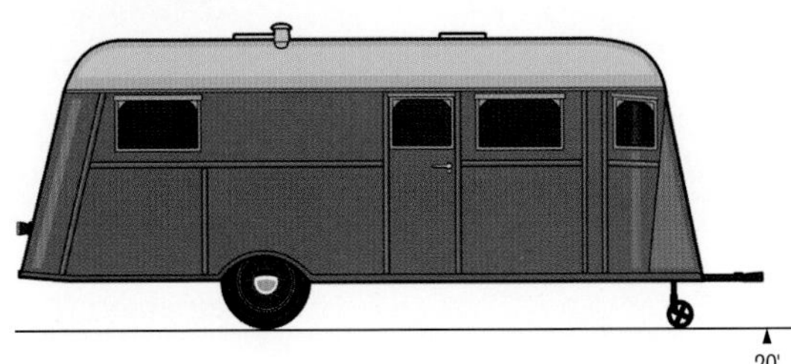

20'

1936
Deluxe

L

Little Gem BUILT BY SCHIEBOUT

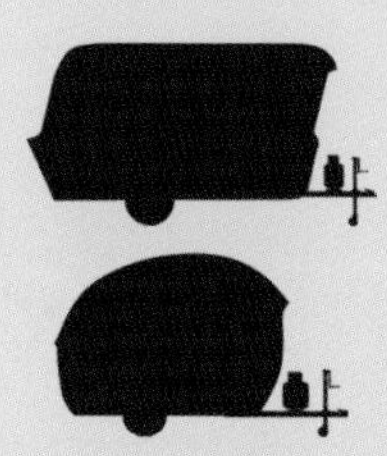

A flared tail and front window on Schiebout Manufacturing–made models (1947–65)

A diminutive lady bug–shaped body distinguishes the aptly named Bugg model

Little Gem / Gem (1947–75)

Schiebout Manufacturing Co. / Gem Industries, Inc. • Grand Rapids, Michigan

Herman Schiebout, at the age of 24, founded the Schiebout Manufacturing Co. and over the next few decades built his company into a regional manufacturer of vacation trailers.

The original Little Gems were a common style of canned hams. They had rounded bodies covered in a flat, unpainted aluminum skin. By the early 1960s the line, while still built using standard construction techniques, had evolved into uniquely shaped trailers that sparkled in primary colors.

In 1966, Schiebout reorganized the company into a corporation and renamed it Gem Industries. The new Gems were built using "Alum-A-Arch" construction and had rounded tops on their front and tail. They carried names like Telstar, Golden Jewel, and Dia Star.

Herman Schiebout was 55 years old when he was struck by a falling tree and died. After his death, his wife Dorothy and their daughters managed the company. They closed up shop in 1975.

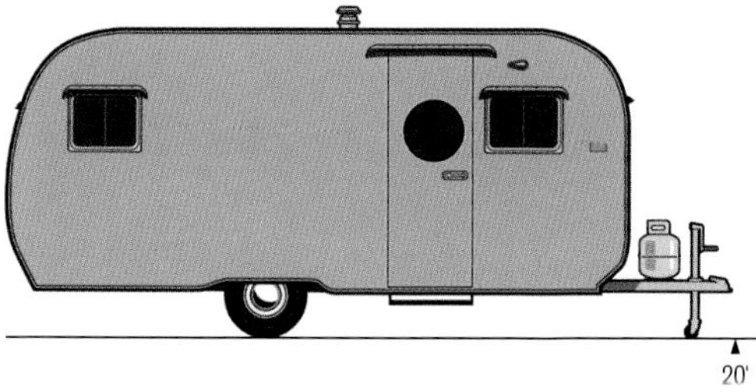

1954
Model 20

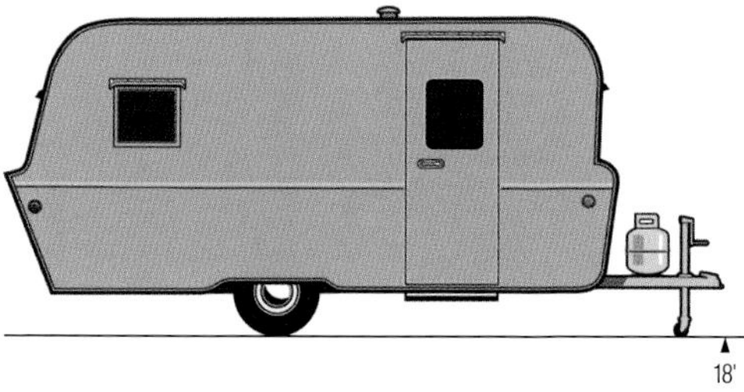

20'

1956
Model 18

18'

1962
Model 14

14'

12'

1963 Little Gem Bugg

Introduced in 1963, the Bugg is a compact ladybug-shaped trailer. It was listed at $795 for a standard model. With interior space at a premium, it featured a Murphy bed in its cozy cabin. Only a handful of Bugg models were made between 1963 and 1965.

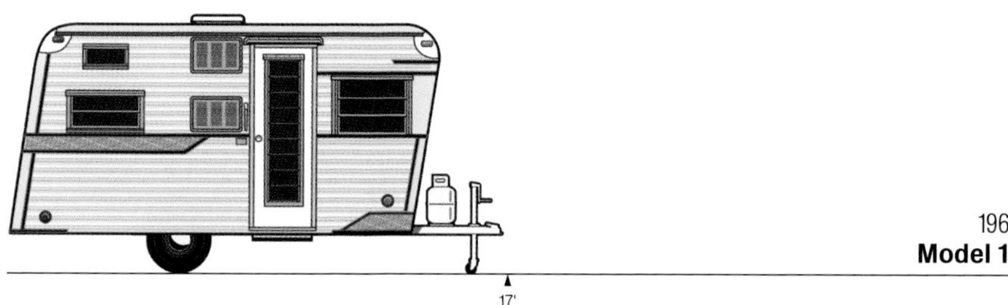

1968
Model 17

17'

LAKEWOOD
GARDENA, CALIF.

Lakewood (1954–early 1960s)

Lakewood Industries • Gardena / Artesia, California

The Lakewood brand of canned ham trailers had a one-piece capped roof, a two-tone automotive enamel exterior, and a high-gloss birch interior. Advertisements used Gardena, California, as their address, but some models had badges stamped "Artesia, California."

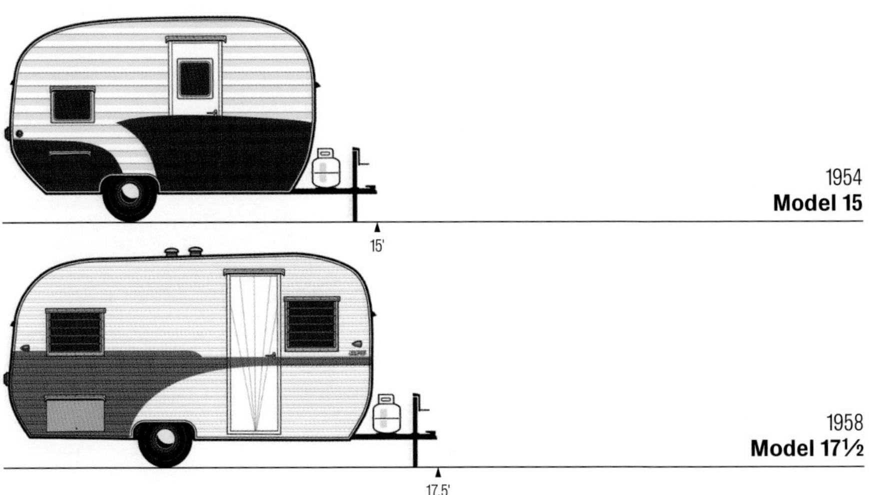

1954
Model 15

1958
Model 17½

LAYTON

Layton (1958–present)

Layton Homes Corporation / Skyline Corporation • Elkhart, Indiana

The original line of Layton trailers included models starting from the 11-foot Camper up to the 28-foot Ranch House. They were, claimed a dealer's classified ad, "Tops in Construction, Appearance and Economy." The Layton brand is still made today.

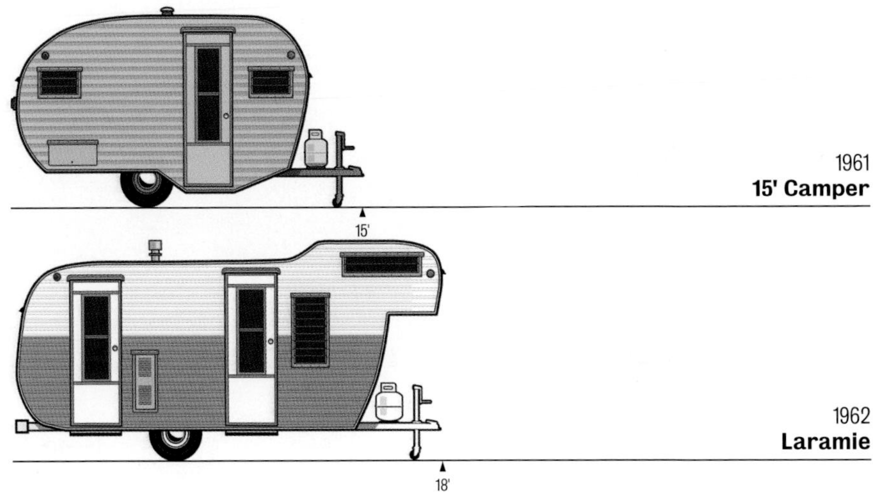

1961
15' Camper

1962
Laramie

Liberty (1941–mid-1950s)

Liberty Coach Company, Inc. • Bremen, Indiana

Liberty Coach Company was an offshoot of the Elcar Coach Company (see page 104). Their bread loaf–style coaches were marketed to World War II defense workers and later to families. They had an exclusive "three decker heated floor" and a ventilation system that moved warm air evenly throughout the trailer.

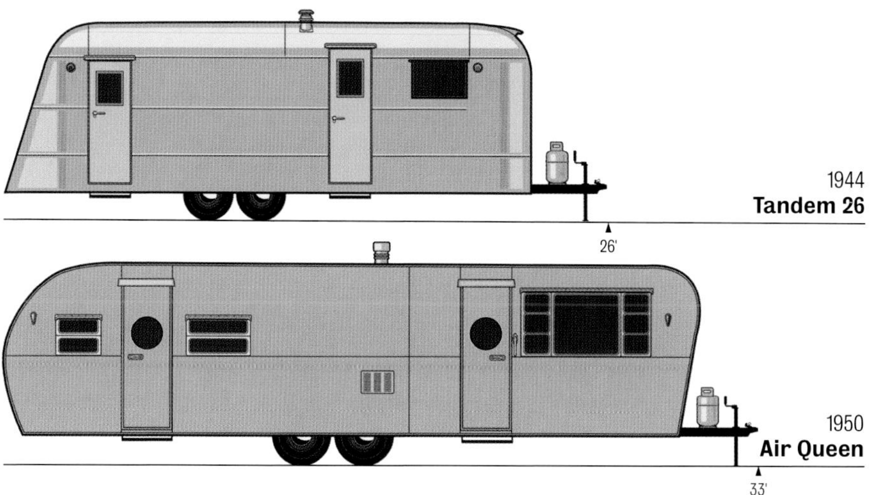

1944 **Tandem 26**

1950 **Air Queen**

Lighthouse (1937–mid-1950s)

Lighthouse Trailer Company • Chicago, Illinois

T. D. Thomas built his first trailer in his backyard in 1937; by the end of World War II the Lighthouse Trailer Company had delivered around 6,240 units to the US Army and US Navy. Over the next decade, the company made trailer homes in aircraft, bread loaf, and unique styles.

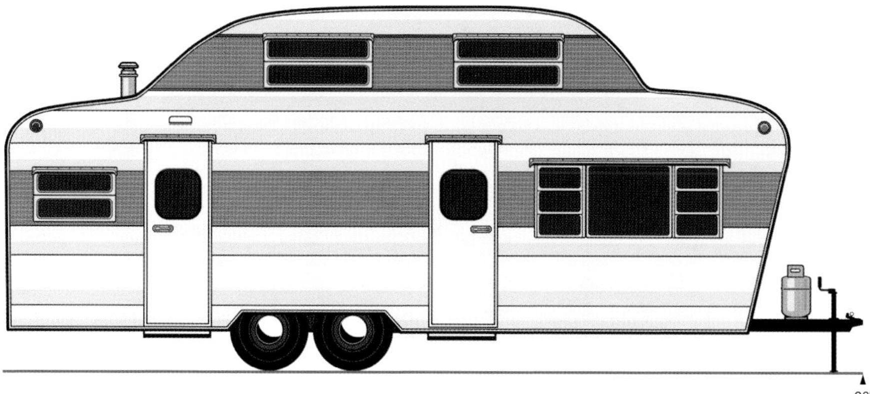

1953 Lighthouse DuPlex

The Lighthouse DuPlex was technically a trailer home, but it was built like a travel trailer "to go when and where you want." The double-decker design, at 11½ feet high, accommodated two upstairs bedrooms. Each bedroom had a double bed, a reading light, and a window.

LintzCraft (1947–55)

LintzCraft Trailer Manufacturing Company • Grand Ledge, Michigan

LintzCraft was a regional maker of canned ham trailers. They had a flat aluminum exterior with a painted band on their midsection, a birch-paneled interior, and an apartment-sized stove. Model names like Sportsking, Resorter, Mansion, and Homemaker represented their size and use.

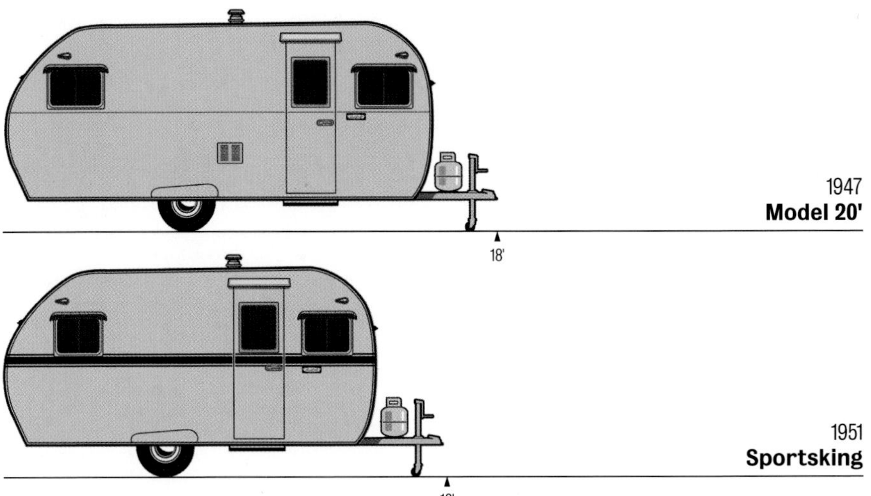

1947
Model 20'

1951
Sportsking

LITTLE CAESAR

Little Caesar (1946–65)

Sokolis Brothers Manufacturing Co. • Sebastopol, California

The typical Little Caesar, 13 feet long and under 7 feet high, was garageable. The unit was bolted together, and had walls made of ½ inch Douglas fir plywood and a smooth aluminum skin. Inside there was room for a double bed, icebox, sink, two-seat dinette, and propane stove.

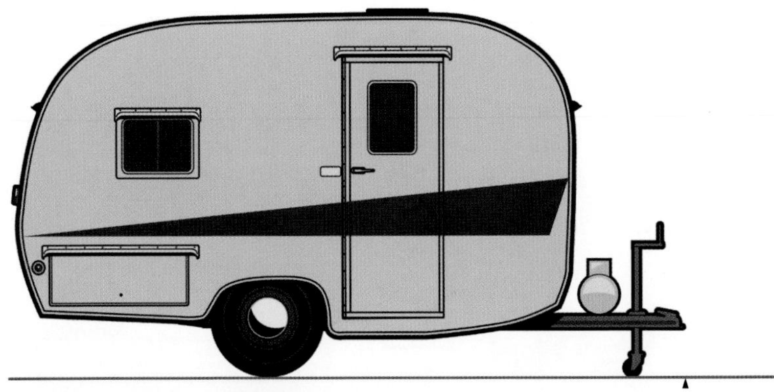

● 1950 Little Caesar

Many sportsmen in the early 1950s required a basic, light, and durable trailer. The highways were winding, the backroads were rough, and freeways were years away. The Little Caesar, like many canned hams of the day, met those requirements with ease.

M

Mallard

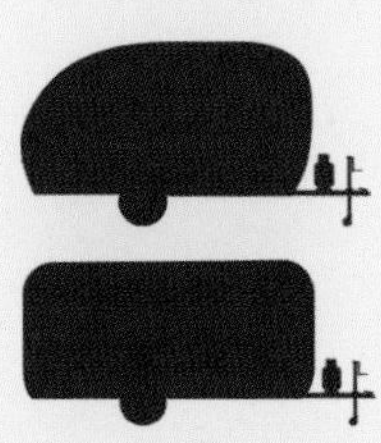

Canned ham shape with a bold, jagged stripe on models from 1954 to 1960

The first Mallard took flight across the side of the trailer line in 1961

Mallard (1952–present)

Mallard Coach Corporation • West Bend, Wisconsin

When the Mallard Coach Corporation was established in 1952 in West Bend, Wisconsin, it must have been a natural choice for its founder, Sylvester Hron, to name the company after the state's most abundant waterfowl. The state is home to over 15,000 lakes, outdoor recreation is popular and the male mallard duck is prized for its purple-blue and green plumage.

The company's first models were rugged canned ham trailers for sportsmen. A complete line of Mallard trailers soon followed with increasing lengths and amenities. By the mid-1960s the trailer line formed into the budget Duckling, the moderately priced Drake, and the elite Flight Leader models. The avian theme even migrated into Decoy and Canvasback tent campers and Drift Wing truck campers.

Motor homes, park models, and even snowmobiles were added and dropped during the 1960s and '70s. Mallard built a complete family of trailers through the 1992 model year. Fleetwood went on to make them until 2009. The brand is presently nested with Heartland Recreational Vehicles.

1953
Model 16

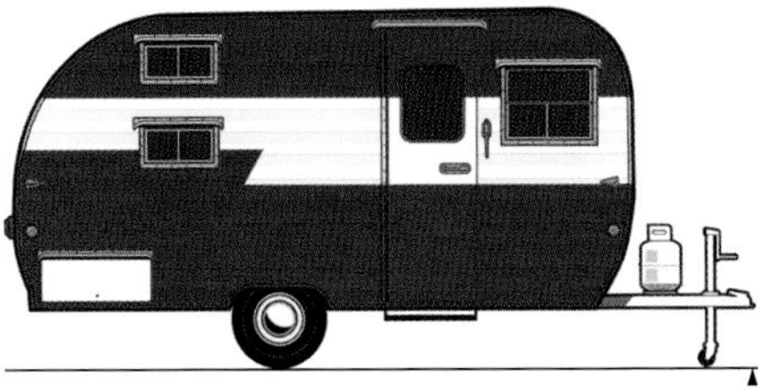

16'

1957
Model 17

17'

1961
Flight Leader

20'

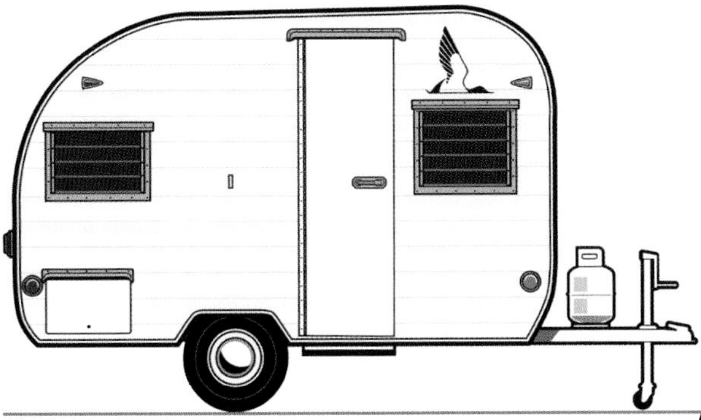

13.5'

1962 Mallard Duckling

The first Duckling landed in 1962. The economy model was light enough to pull behind a compact car, yet solidly built, practical, and stylish. There was room to fit six campers inside with the addition of optional canvas bunks. By 1967 the Duckling name was carried on a line of budget travel trailers from 13 to 16½ feet long.

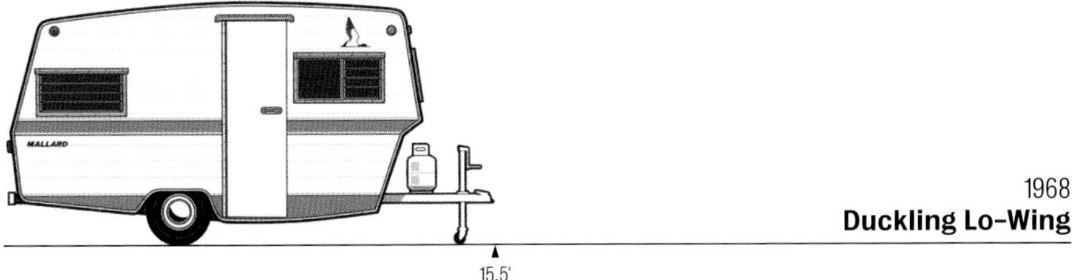

1968
Duckling Lo-Wing

15.5'

MOBILE SCOUT

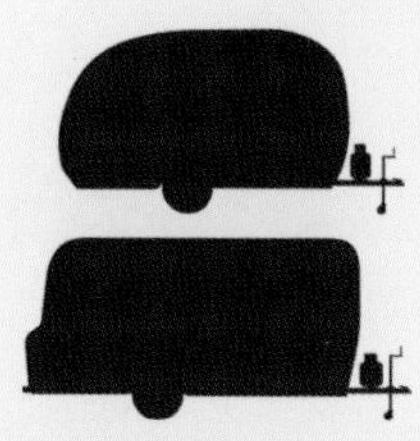

Mobile Scout (1955–2010)

Mobile Scout Manufacturing Corporation • Arlington, Texas / Denver, Pennsylvania

The United Mobile Home Company, later known as the Mobile Scout Manufacturing Corporation, was founded by William Dozer Thornton in 1955. The Arlington, Texas–based company made small vacation trailers.

Their first models, offered in 15- and 17-foot lengths, had an aluminum exterior and either a mahogany- or birch-paneled interior. By the early 1960s, Mobile Scout ads told the stories of famous western scouts like William Frederick "Buffalo Bill" Cody, Jim Bridger, and Albert Sieber. Buyers were encouraged to discover the West for themselves without the expense of motels and restaurants.

In 1966 the old canned ham–style Mobile Scouts gave way to longer models that added a shiny aluminum band and a trunk back. By the 1970s the Mobile Scout name appeared on fifth-wheel trailers, truck campers, and Class C motor homes.

The company was sold in the late 1970s. It went out of business in the early 1980s. The Mobile Scout name went missing until 1992, when William Dozer Thornton's son, Tom Thornton, began branding it on SunnyBrook trailers. It was last seen in 2010.

Canned ham body and diamond-shaped window in door (1958–64)

Models became longer and gained a trunk back after 1965

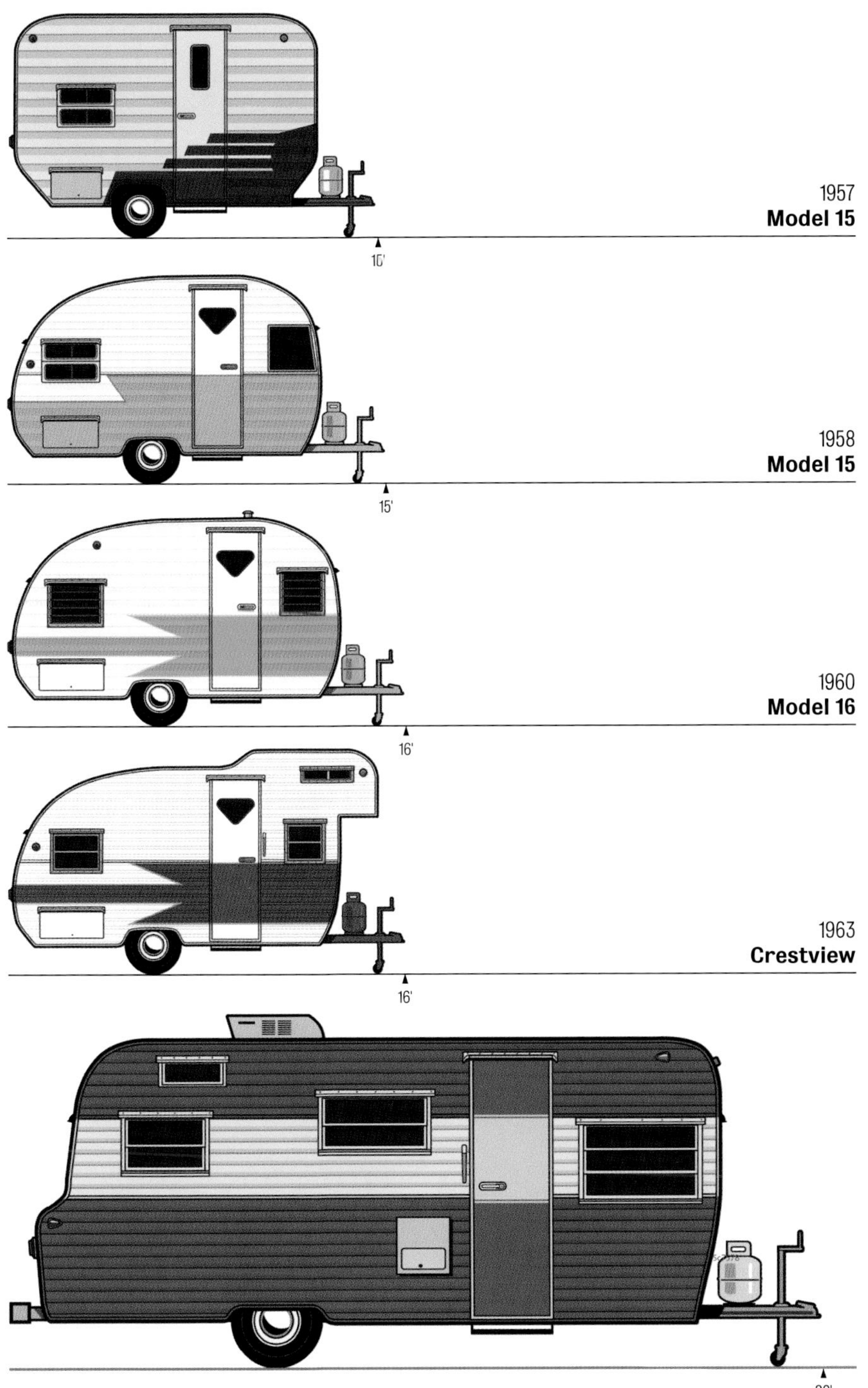

1966 Model 20 Self-Contained

Millions saw the most famous Mobile Scout, the 1966 Model 20, when it appeared in the Ford Motor Company's exhibit at the New York World's Fair. The Model 20 was self-contained, and among its unique features was a new electric sanitary system.

"M" System (1935–60)

"M" System Manufacturing Company • Vicksburg, Mississippi

Trailer coaches built by "M" System were a "home on wheels" that promised the freedom of the open road. They had space for large living rooms, a bedroom, apartment-sized appliances, and a compact bathroom. In the late 1950s, "M" System constructed single-wide mobile homes.

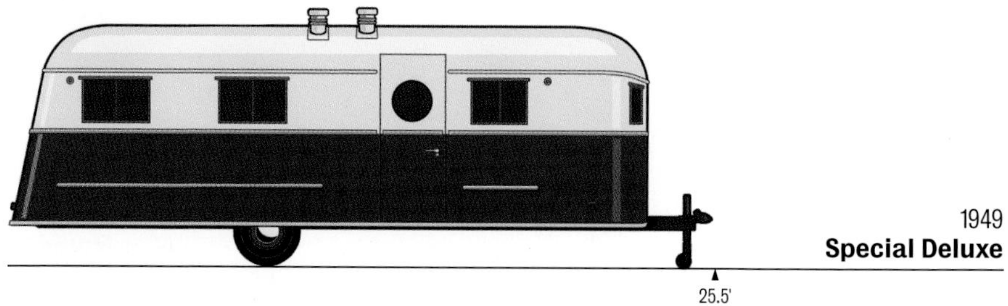

25.5'

1949
Special Deluxe

Main-Line (1947–49)

Main-Line Trailer Coach Company • Los Angeles, California

Main-Line was a short-lived line of trailers that came in three models: the Silver Lark, the Silver Lodger, and the Silver Liner. They were sheathed in smooth aluminum, and had pull-down windows and solid plywood walls. The units had no battery or water tank, but relied on shore power and a local water supply.

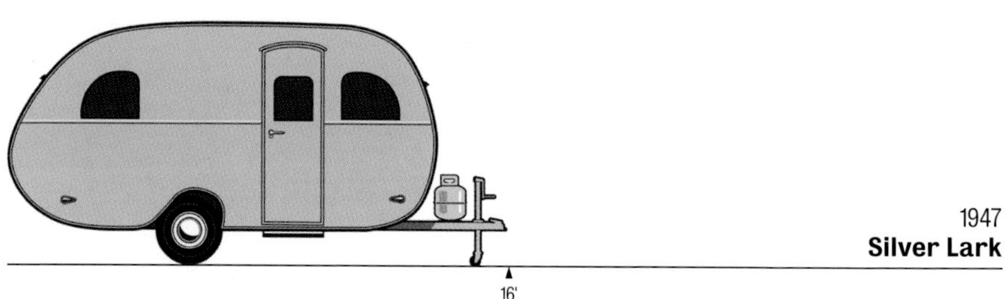

16'

1947
Silver Lark

Masterbilt (1934–mid-1950s)

Masterbilt Corporation • Glendale, California

A. R. Seaton was the architect, builder, and owner of Masterbilt. He was also a founder of the Trailer Coach Association of California in 1936. His trailer designs are best described as modified canned hams. Late 1940s models ranged in size from the 14-foot Tee-Pee to the 35-foot Super-Chief.

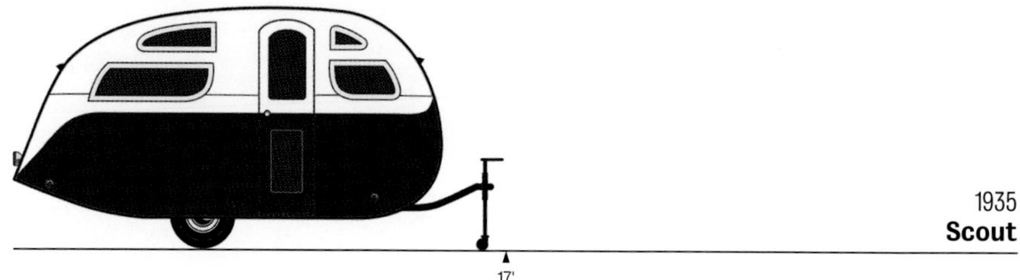

17'

1935
Scout

Mercury (1954–59)

Birtle Manufacturing Company • El Monte, California

In 1954, Mercury was the only travel trailer brand made on an automobile-type assembly line. The Birtle Manufacturing Company initially produced 15-foot canned ham–style models using a standard layout, premade cabinets, and standard materials. The 18-foot deluxe version was introduced in 1957.

15'

1956
Model 15

Metzendorf (mid-1950s–early 1970s)

Metzendorf Trailer Manufacturing Co • West Farmington, Ohio

Metzendorf was a regional manufacturer of vacation trailers, which were constructed in a small factory that employed local Amish workers. They were sold as being "economical and compact." Several models had step-down floors and fit in a standard garage.

15'

1962
Model 15

MOBIL-GLIDE

Mobil-Glide (mid-1940s–early 1980s)

American Manufacturing Company • Culver City, California

The American Manufacturing Company made a whole family of trailer types and brands. In the 1940s the Mobil-Glide name appeared on a utility trailer and a bread loaf–style coach. The coach was made with an airplane-like structure and covered in smooth aluminum.

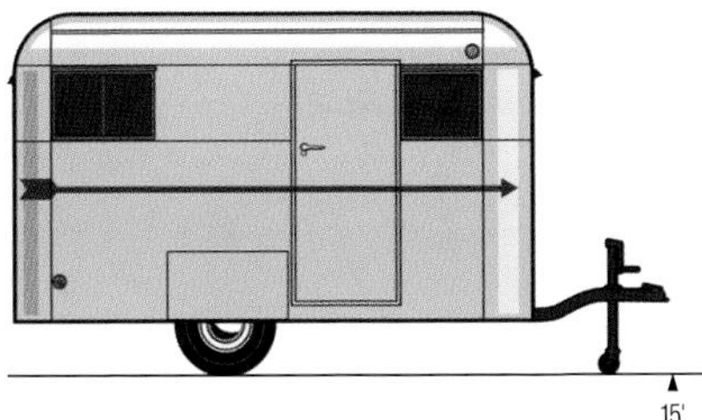

15'

1946
Globe-Trotter

Monitor (1963–91)

Monitor Coach Company, Inc. • Wakarusa, Indiana

Monitor trailers came in a wide variety of sizes, interior plans, and price ranges. The line included fifth wheels, motor homes, and truck campers. Monitor prided itself on offering "reliable and economical recreational vehicles that make traveling a pleasure."

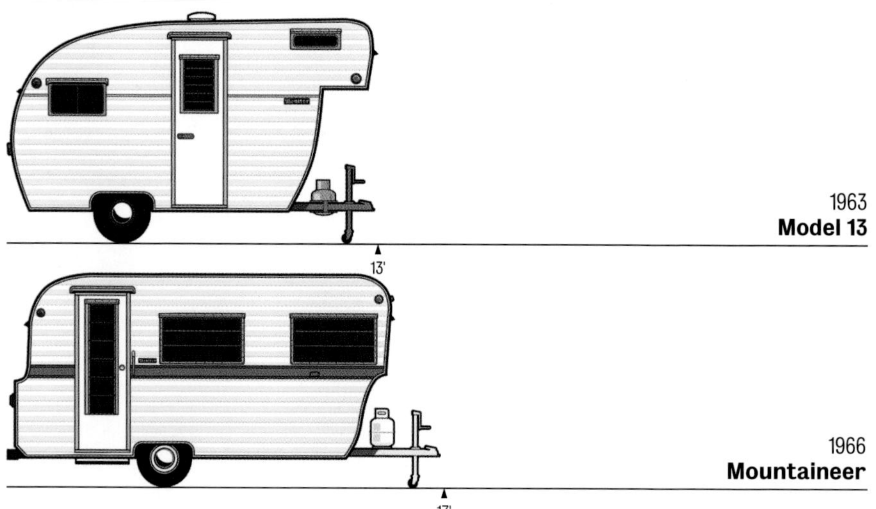

Mustang (1960–67)

Westward Coach Manufacturing Company, Inc. • Elkhart, Indiana

Westward Coach emblazoned their best trailers with the Mustang brand. In 1965, Westward sued the Ford Motor Company for unfairly using the Mustang trademark on the Mustang pony car and lost. Both 17-foot and 19-foot self-contained models were built, and had enough room to feed and bunk six.

1963 Mustang Penthouse

Mustang trailers not only capitalized on the name of their truck camper predecessors but also carried through the cabover feature. The distinctive swept-wing inclining roof had a rear area that could be used for a sun deck, storage, or even a photography platform.

N

Nomad

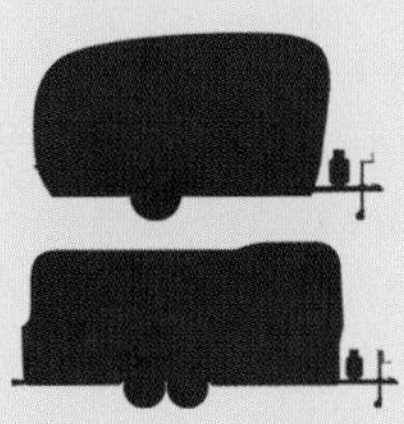

Nomad (1960–present)

Nomad Travel Trailers / Skyline Corporation • Elkhart, Indiana

When Skyline Corporation formed the Nomad Travel Trailers division in 1960 they brought "their know-how and quality craftsmanship mastered in the design and construction of mobile homes to the travel trailer field."

The Nomad brand's first trailers came in 16-, 19-, and 25-foot canned ham versions. They had a prefinished baked-enamel exterior, birch-paneled interior, and code plumbing, heating, and wiring. All models had custom drapes, a sofa bed, and a convertible dinette.

Reflecting trailer design trends of the mid-1960s, the line lost much of its round shape and gained a flatter front and rear. The new style allowed more interior room in the same length of trailer. By 1967, Nomads had grown so popular that the company claimed that "Someone, somewhere buys a new Nomad every hour of every day throughout the year."

Over its lifetime the Nomad line included trailers, fifth wheels, and park models. The brand was made until 2016.

1964–69 models had a front end that was pushed out at dinette height and a trunk

Models had an angular yet sleek shape in the 1970s that was similar to Prowler, Taurus, and Wilderness brands

1960
Model 16

1967 Nomad 19 SD (Side Dinette)

Trailer Life magazine's Livability Audits judged trailer layouts and found that rear-door models were generally more friendly and open than ones with conventionally located doors. In their April 1967 issue they declared the Nomad 19 SD had improved the rear-door model with several design changes, including a spacious side dinette.

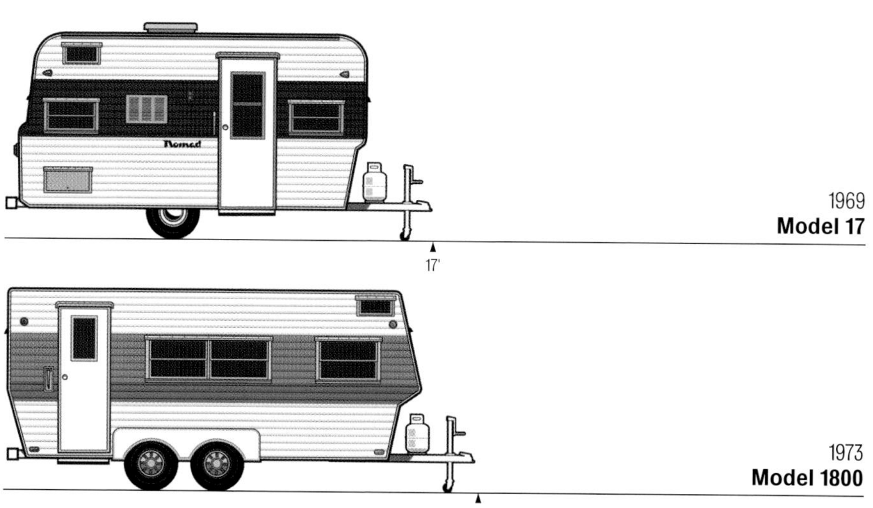

1969
Model 17

1973
Model 1800

Nashua (late 1940s–present)

Nashua Manufacturing Corporation • Nashua, Missouri

Before Nashua became a well-known brand of mobile homes, they specialized in building trailers. The low-priced trailers, made until the mid-1950s, came in sizes up to 27 feet long. The 15-foot Tour-It was a basic vacation trailer, while longer models were a "home on the road" for new trailer owners.

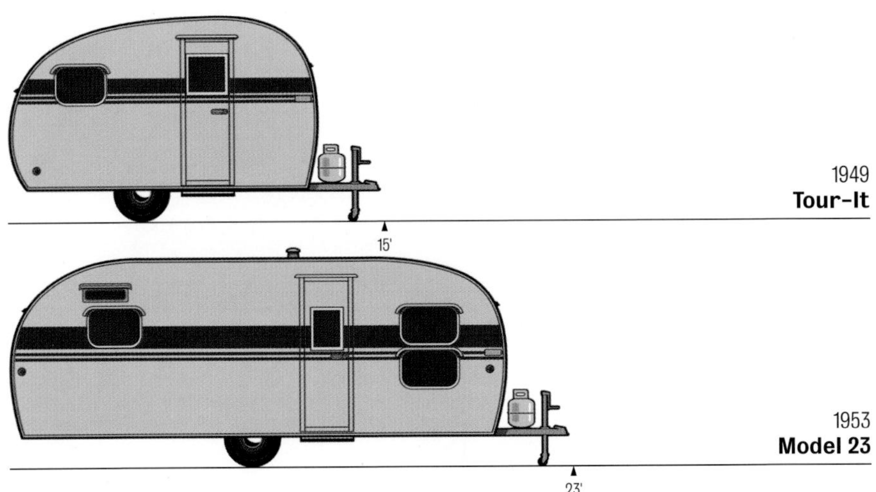

New Moon (1937–present)

Redman Trailer Company / New Moon Homes, Inc. • Alma, Michigan

In the late 1930s, Redman trailers were flat-sided aluminum models no more than 24 feet long. The company stopped making trailers for civilians during World War II and instead built trailers for the armed forces. After the war Redman made longer travel and park models.

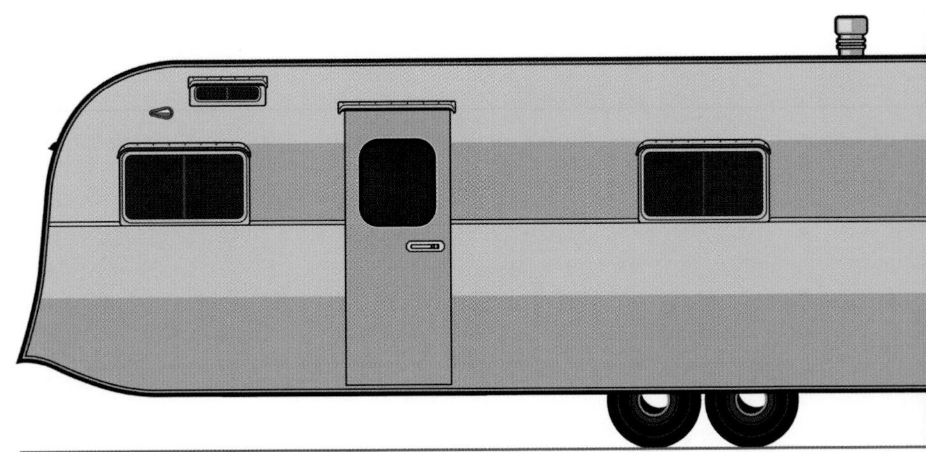

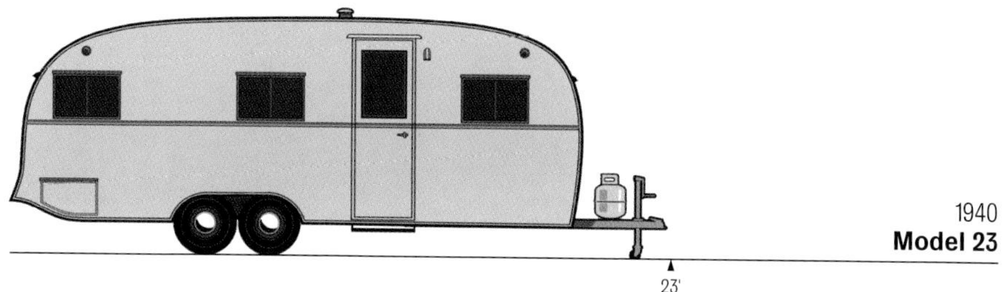

1940
Model 23

Norris (1966–74)

Norris Homes, Inc. • New Tazewell, Tennessee

Norris built travel trailers from 1966 until 1974. They had three different brands: the budget-priced Smokey, the medium-priced Volunteer and the luxurious Norris. The Norris line was available in standard or "Royal" editions. The company still manufactures homes today.

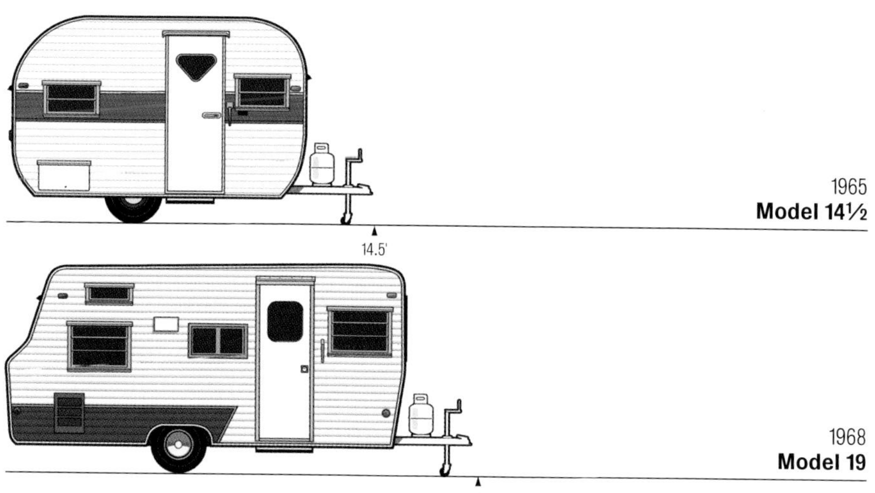

1965
Model 14½

1968
Model 19

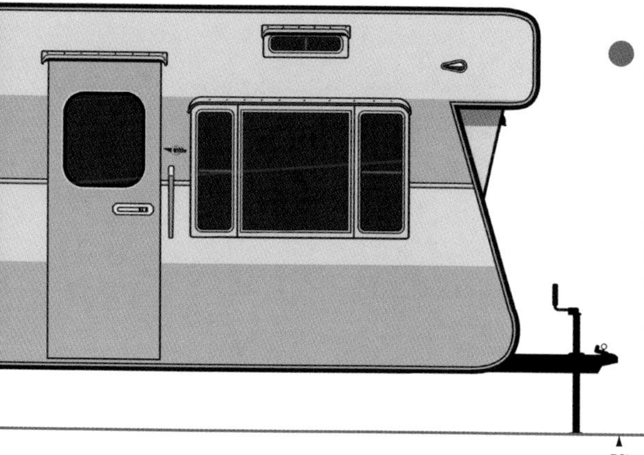

1953 New Moon 36': The Long, Long Trailer

The 1953 New Moon 36-foot model was featured in the 1954 film *The Long, Long Trailer* starring Lucille Ball and Desi Arnaz. The movie was based on the book of the same name by Clinton Twiss. A full-page color ad in the April 1954 *Trailer Dealer* magazine proclaimed the movie "the highlight of the greatest sales promotion in the industry."

Northwest Coach (1961–70)

Northwest Coach • El Monte, California

The Northwest Coach nameplate adorned a line of vacation trailers and pick-up campers. The trailers had a low profile, a winged graphic on their front, and a crest projecting from the back roof. Northwest offered fully self-contained models in 17-, 19-, 21-, and 22-foot lengths.

1965 Northwest Coach Little Dipper

Northwest Coach looked to the night sky when it named its models in the mid-1960s. The Little Dipper was a lightweight, fast looking, and low-slung model designed for vacation travel to remote areas of the western United States.

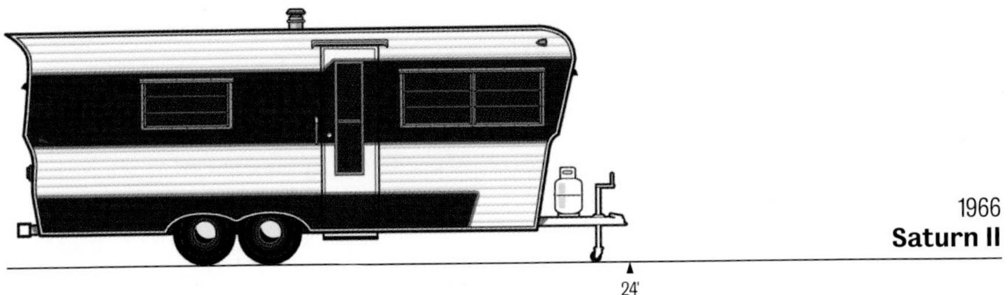

1966
Saturn II

Nu-Wa (1966–2013)

Nu-Wa Campers, Inc. / Nu-Wa Industries, Inc. • Chanute, Kansas

Travel trailers, fifth-wheel trailers, mini-motor homes, and park models were all designed and constructed by Nu-Wa over its long history. They had a reputation for making quality travel trailers that fit the needs of camping families and retired full-time trailerites.

1969
Model 15 Caravan

0

A bold graphic and notched front end marked models from 1957 to the mid-1960s

A cast metal badge was typically placed to the right of the entry door

Oasis (1957–69)

Donhal Inc. • Bellflower, California

Donald Herfter and Dwight Avery, coworkers in the aircraft industry during World War II, combined forces and founded Donhal Inc. in 1957. The two took pride in building trailers that had the seal of approval from the State of California Division of Housing.

By 1959 a complete line of vacation trailers and some park models flowed out of the Oasis plant. All models at the time had a heavy-duty welded frame, 2½-inch double floors, and glued construction joints.

After an extended road test in the early 1960s, *Mobile Home Journal* said, "The Oasis trailer tested is one lush, plush haven that for cost and accommodation beats any desert spa. The Oasis behaves wonderfully on the highway as if it is magnetized to the hitch. Even at high speed no wobble or sway could be detected."

In 1968, Oasis introduced a new "Air-O-Form" body design. The redesigned trailers had a one-piece fiberglass roof, front, and rear panels. A big trunk bumped out of their rear end.

The line disappeared from view in 1969.

1957 Oasis Fifteen

The first trailer made by Donhal Inc. was the 1957 Oasis 15-foot vacation trailer. Its body had a bold graphic painted on its sides. The interior featured ash paneling and cabinets with rounded corners. Customers could choose contemporary or provincial furnishings.

17.5'

1959
Seventeen Six

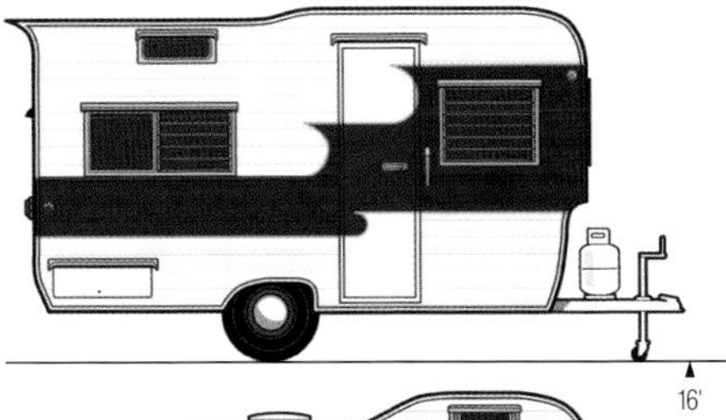

16'

1961
Sixteen

16.5'

1967
Sixteen Six Dual Level

18.5'

1968
Eighteen Six

Owosso (1939–early 1960s)

Millcraft Products Company / Owosso Coach Company • Owosso, Michigan

Owosso trailer coaches were sold coast to coast in the 1950s. In 1951 they introduced a low-cost line of canned ham–style trailers with smooth aluminum exteriors and plywood interiors. The company changed its name to the Owosso Mobile Home Company in 1959 and ceased making trailers.

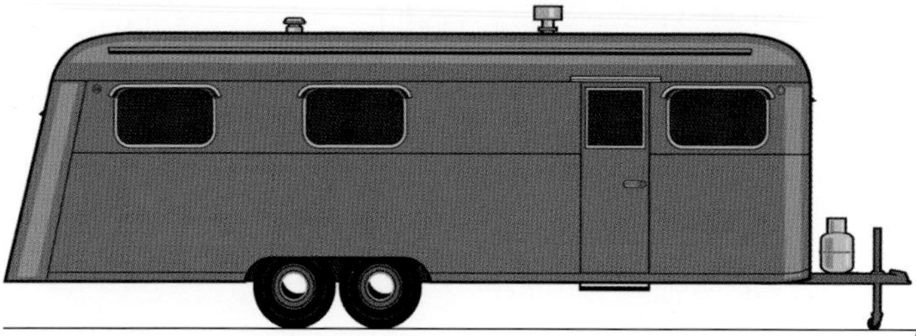

27'

1947
Model 27

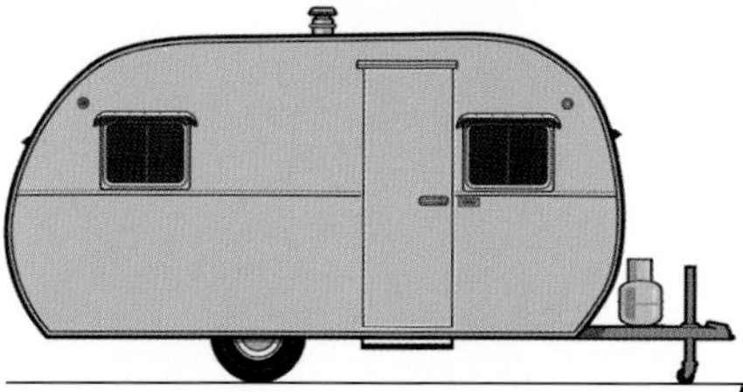

16.5'

1952
Model 16-6

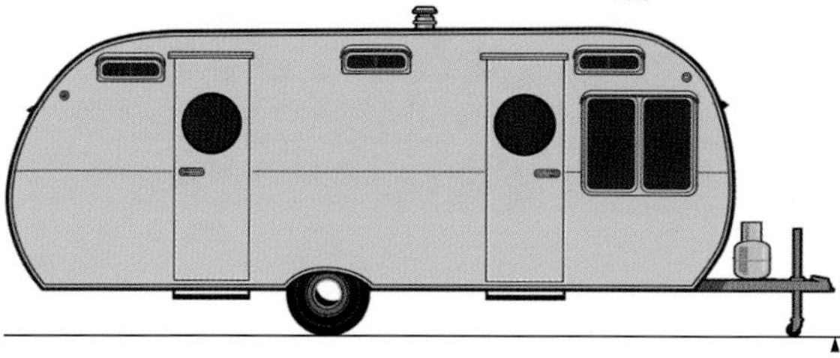

22'

1953
Model 22

P

Pathfinder

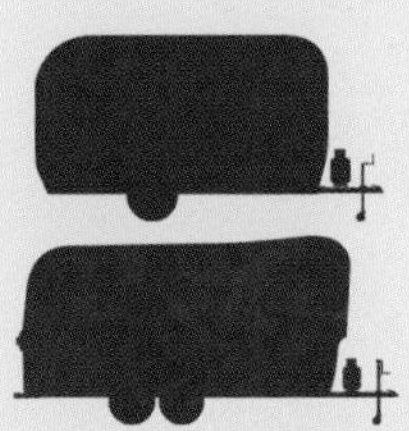

Two distinctive shapes on its sides give the trailer a sense of forward movement (1959–66)

An enlarged crown on the front of the trailer, with angled metallic panels set into its sides (1966–69)

Pathfinder (1953–73)

Pathfinder Mobilehome Inc. • Spencer, Wisconsin

The founders of Pathfinder Mobilehome named their company to honor Natty Bumppo (aka the Pathfinder), the courageous frontiersman from *The Last of the Mohicans*. Pathfinder ads from the 1960s show a coonskin-capped Bumppo leading the way forward.

The success of the Pathfinder line of luxurious mobile homes and trailers was attributed to careful planning. The marketplace was scouted for months before a new model was even mapped out by designers and engineers.

The finished plans were taken from paper to production by craftsmen in the metal and woodworking shops. All Pathfinder coaches were built using the finest materials available at the time. They had an all-aluminum roof and exterior walls, spun-glass insulation, and a vapor barrier seal.

By the mid-1960s mobile homes were dropped from the line. In 1966, Pathfinder introduced a fresh bread loaf–style model. It had a flatter front end, a bump-out tail, and a diamond-patterned stripe on their sides. Truck campers and motor homes were added in the late 1960s.

The Pathfinder name appeared on trailers through the 1973 model year.

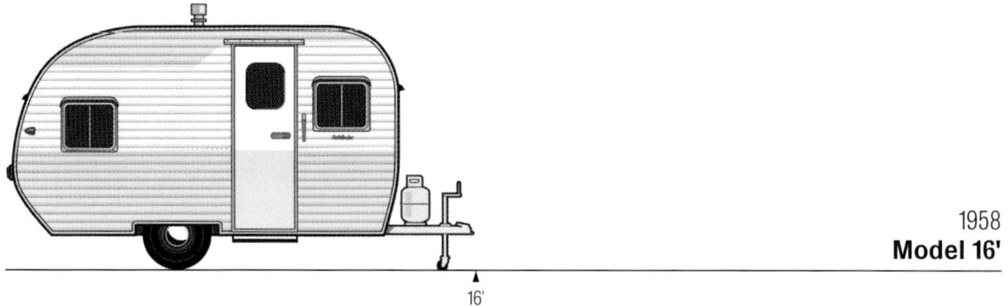

1958
Model 16'

1961 Pathfinder 16'

The Pathfinder 16', introduced in 1961, was made to be towed by compact cars like a Ford Falcon. It had electric brakes and "Torq-Less" axles that were said to give it a lower floorline, greater road stability, and better load distribution. Deluxe self-contained models had a marine toilet, a pressure water tank, septic tanks, and a gas light.

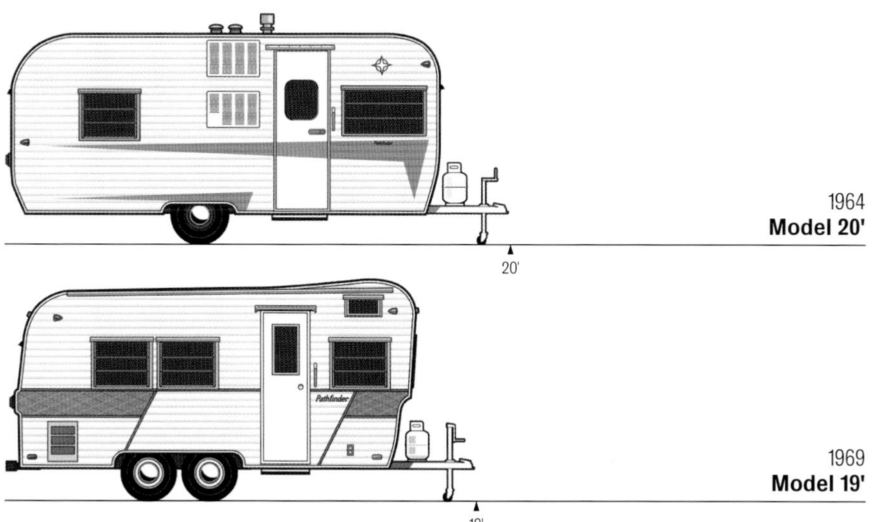

1964
Model 20'

1969
Model 19'

Palace

Palace (1935–early 1960s)

Palace Travel Coach Corporation / Palace Corporation • Flint, Michigan

Early Palace bread loaf–style models were offered with up to three bedrooms. During World War II, Palace made housing units for the army. After the war it constructed trailers with an aluminum "Panel-L-Frame" and body. The company phased out trailer production by the mid-1950s.

1939
18 Foot Standard Model

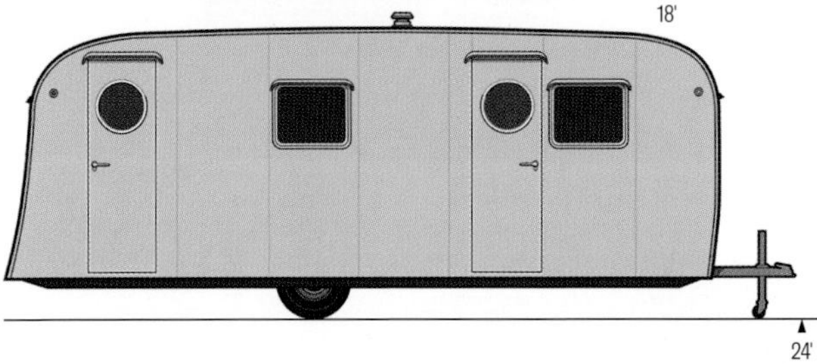

18'

1946
Wolverine

24'

24'

1948 Palace Royale

The body of the 1948 Royale, die formed like an automobile and made of aluminum, was lightweight and strong. It was painted with a two-tone enamel and had a three-piece chrome bumper. The Royale's other features included a full-height door, a handrail that became a night light, large windows, and a ventilation system designed into its raised roof.

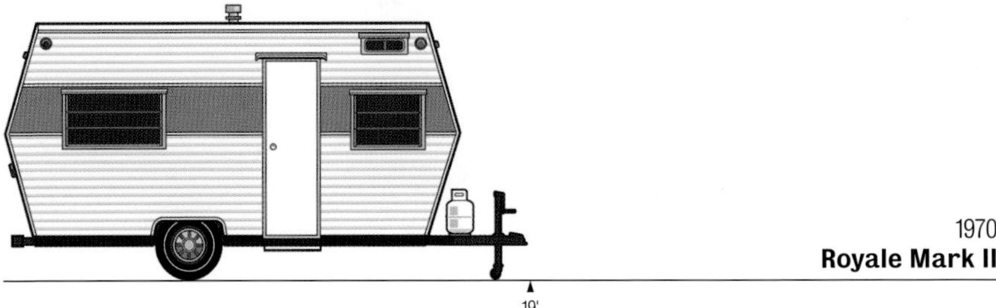

1970
Royale Mark II

19'

Phoenix (1959–73)

Heckaman Manufacturing, Inc. • Nappanee, Indiana

The "long grey line" of Phoenix-branded RVs included vacation, low-liner, pop-up, and fifth-wheel trailers. Early 1960s trailers had canned ham styling, a one-piece aluminum roof, and a gray and white body. Phoenix offered a wide variety of floor plans and colorful interior décor variations.

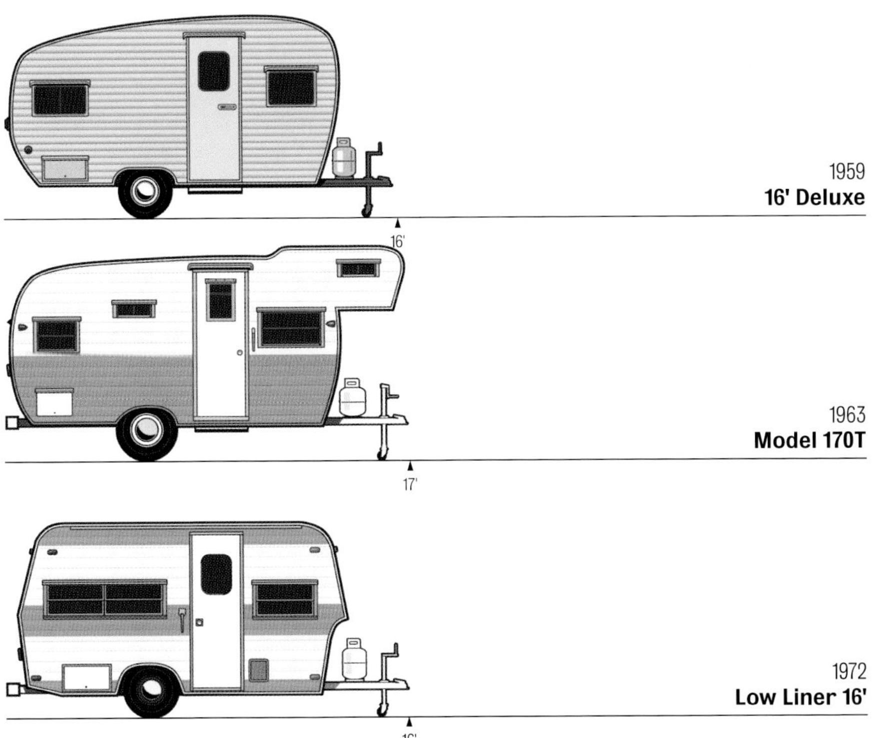

1959
16' Deluxe

1963
Model 170T

1972
Low Liner 16'

Pierce-Arrow (1936–37)

Pierce-Arrow Motor Car Company • Buffalo, New York

The Pierce-Arrow Motor Car Company went out of business in 1938, but not before putting their name on a travel trailer. The Travelodge had an aluminum skin riveted to an all-steel frame. Its exterior was coated with the same type of heat-refracting paint used on dirigibles.

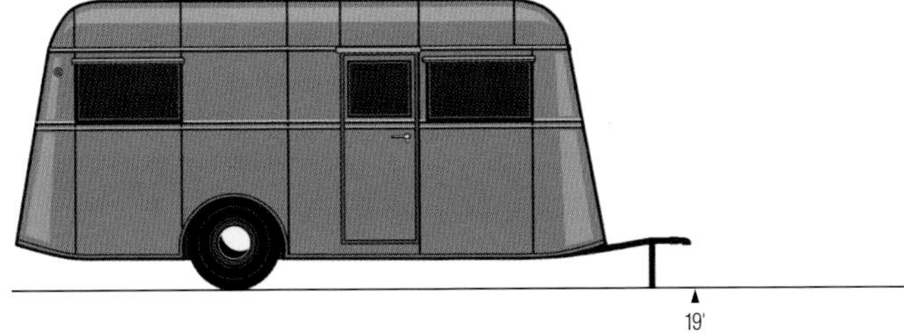

1937
Travelodge Model A

Play-Mor

Play-Mor (1964–present)

Play-Mor Trailers, Inc • Westphalia, Missouri

In the 1960s and '70s, Play-Mor specialized in building small trailers that were aerodynamically designed to cut wind drag and save gas. They were made to be superlightweight and easy to tow by compact cars and minitrucks.

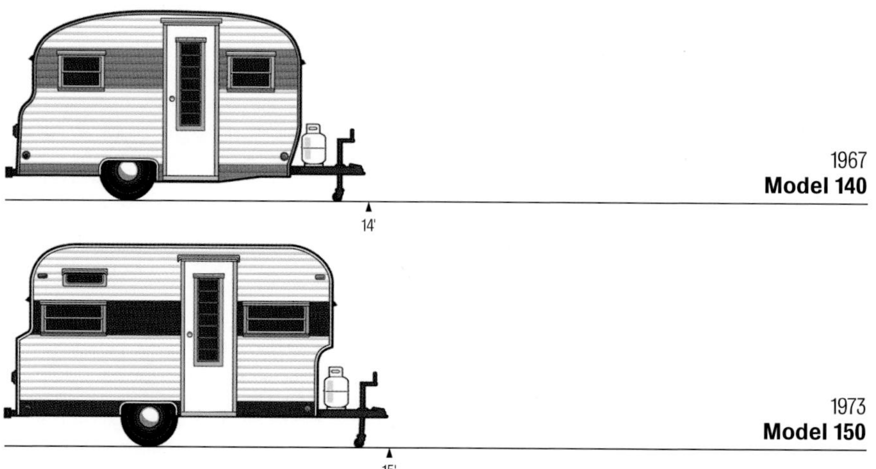

PleasureCraft

PleasureCraft (1955–58)

Ontario Trailer Works, Inc • Cucamonga, California

Early PleasureCraft ads claimed that their vacation trailers had the smooth, professional finish of a big mobile home. Their canned ham trailers had a three-color paint design on their all-aluminum body. In 1958, they introduced an all-fiberglass travel trailer with decorative fins that seem to have been inspired by the 1957 Chevy Bel Air coupe.

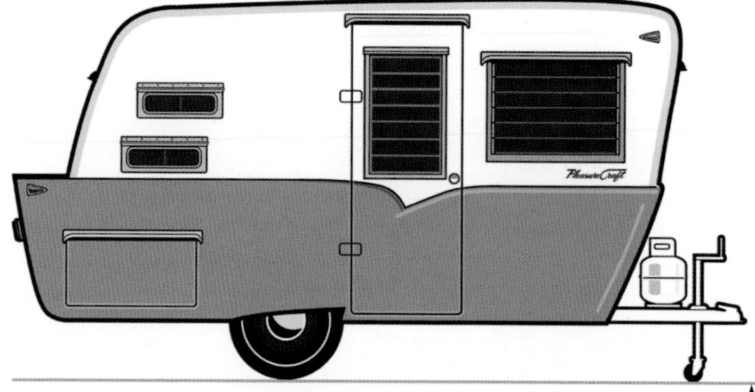

15'

1958 PleasureCraft Fibreglass

The 1958 PleasureCraft was an all-fiberglass travel trailer with decorative fins that seem to have been inspired by the 1957 Chevy Bel Air coupe. Because the trailer was made of lightweight fiberglass (including the cabinets, sink, water tank, walls, and ceiling), it required little maintenance, was easy to tow, and could support large louvered windows.

Prairie Schooner

Prairie Schooner (1936–1960s)

Prairie Schooner Trailer Company • Elkhart, Indiana

Prairie Schooner, a pioneer in the trailer industry, was one of America's most recognized brands. The company claimed that its trailers were rugged, built to last, and better every year. By the mid-1950s, they made mobile homes exclusively; however, the Prairie Schooner name did return on other manufacturers' travel trailers until the early 1990s.

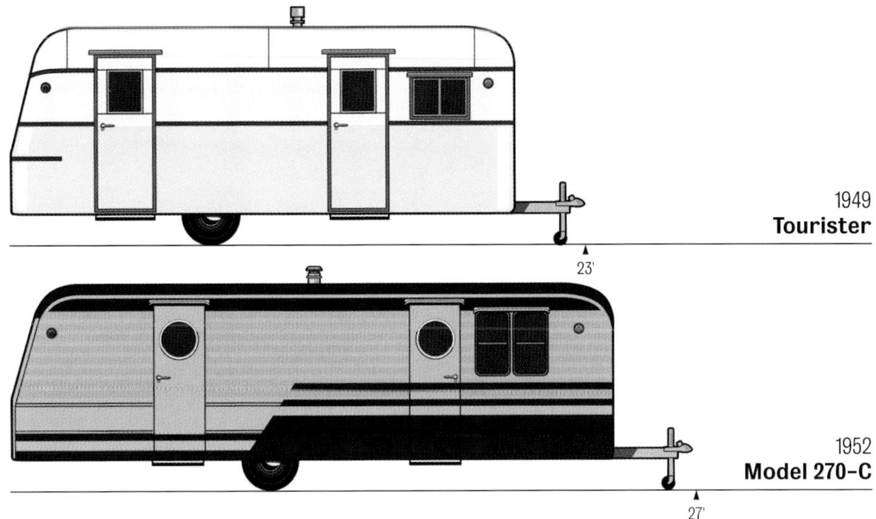

1949
Tourister

1952
Model 270-C

Prowler (1967–2009)

Fleetwood Enterprises, Inc. • Riverside, California

The 1967 Prowler line was a close relative to Wilderness and Terry travel trailer lines, and except for their different color palettes they looked nearly identical to the untrained eye. By the mid-1970s, Prowler had become the most popular trailer in the United States and was produced in several factories across the country. The trailers had long, low exterior lines and many interior layouts.

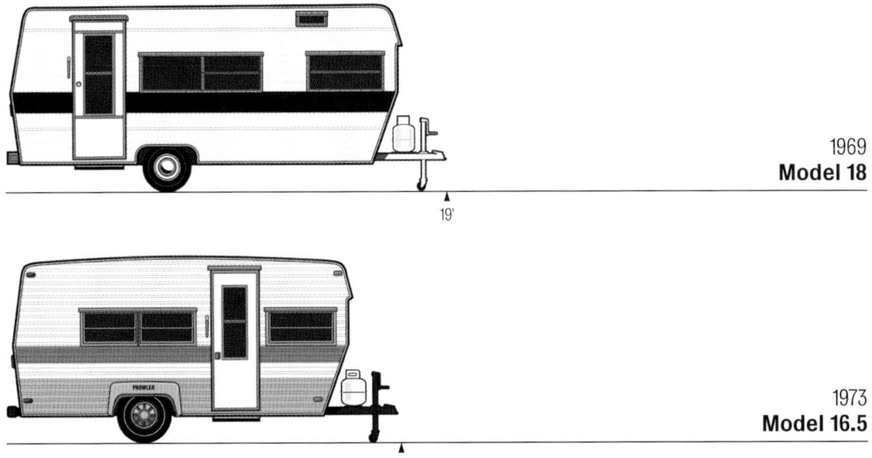

1969
Model 18

1973
Model 16.5

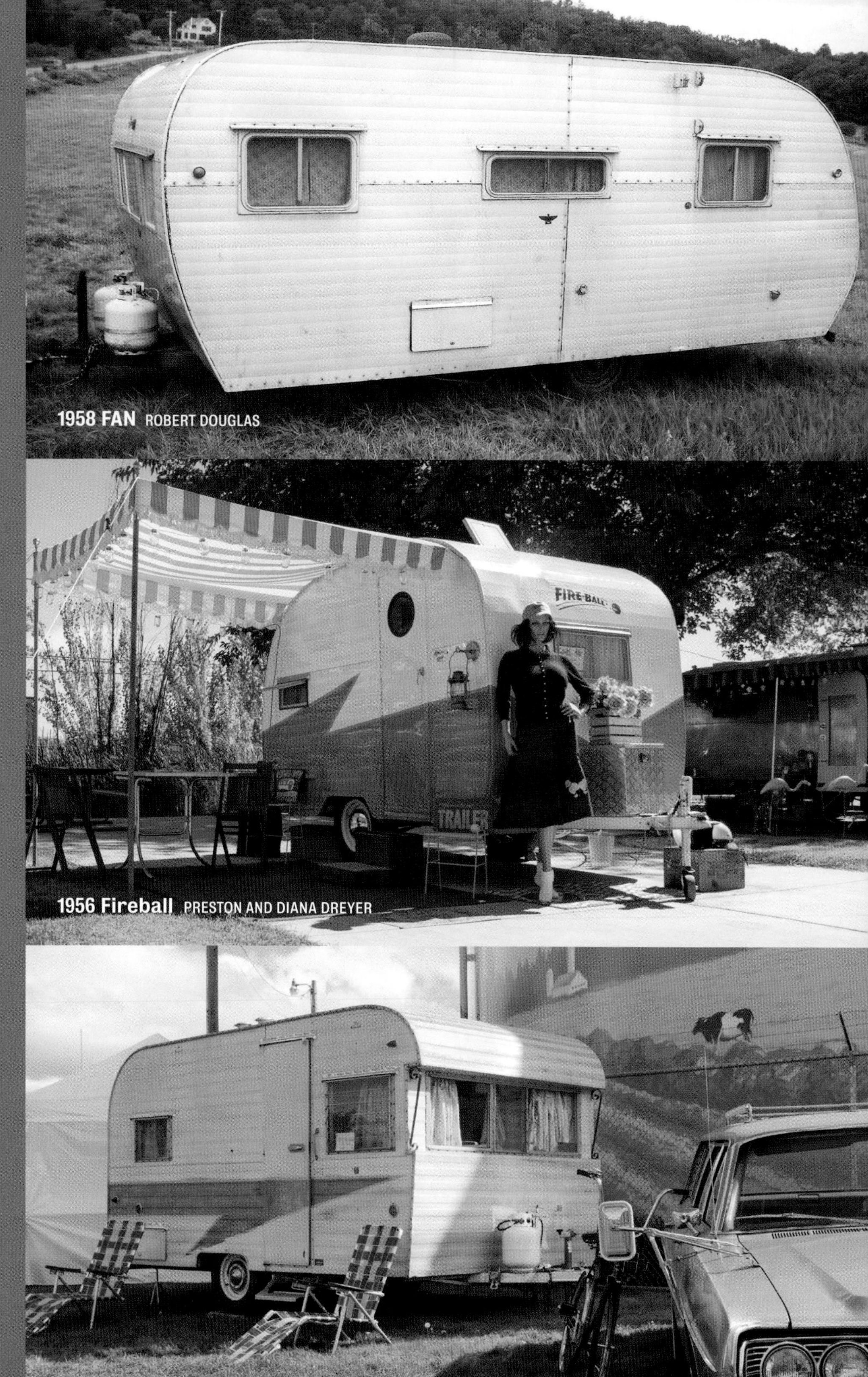

1958 FAN ROBERT DOUGLAS

1956 Fireball PRESTON AND DIANA DREYER

1961 Fireball RICK FARMER

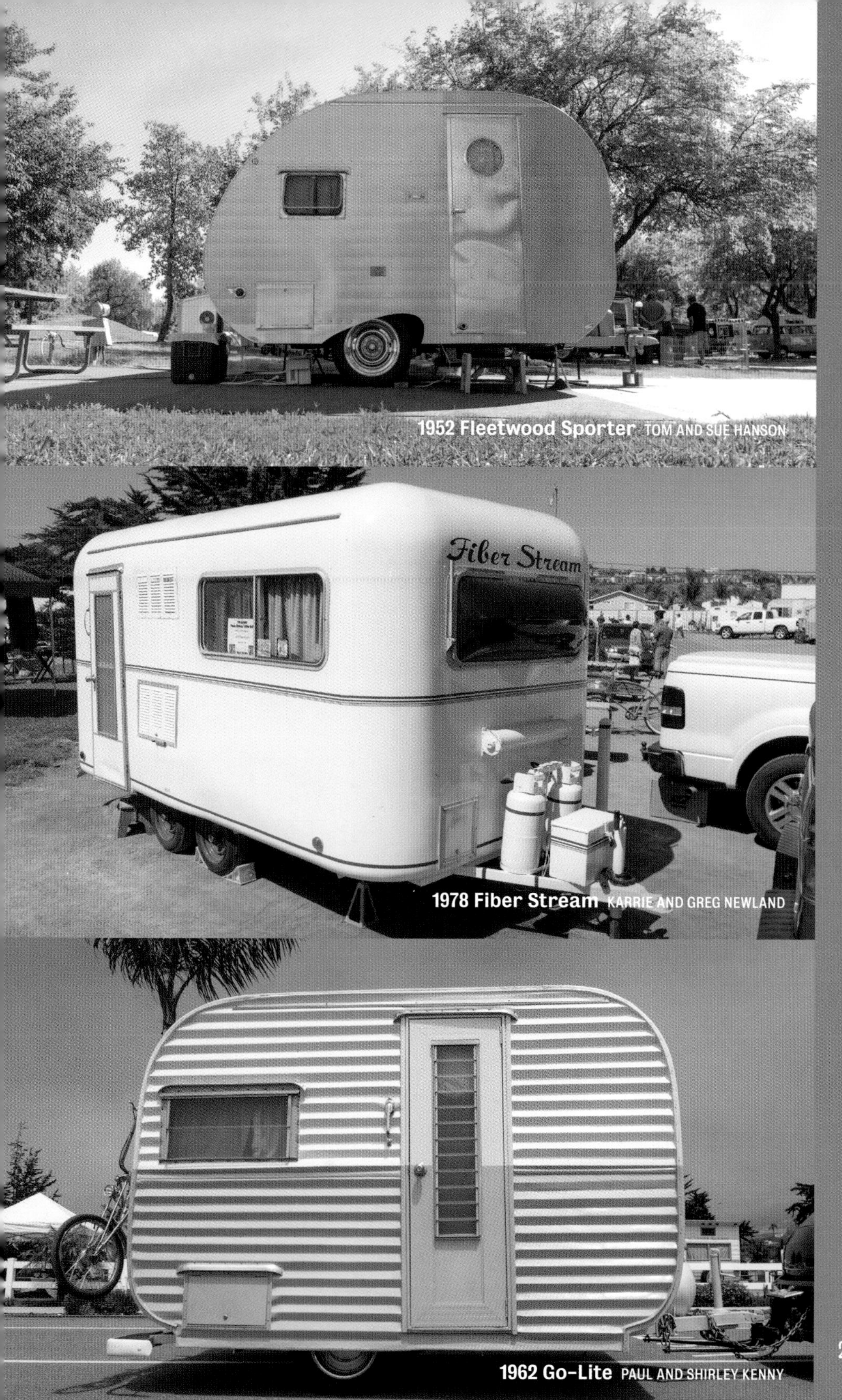

1952 Fleetwood Sporter TOM AND SUE HANSON

1978 Fiber Stream KARRIE AND GREG NEWLAND

1962 Go-Lite PAUL AND SHIRLEY KENNY

1962 Holiday House JIM STUEBE

1961 Holiday House Geographic FLYTE CAMP / JUSTIN AND ANNA SCRIBNER

HOLIDAY
HOUSE
MEDFORD, OREGON

1971 Go Tag-A-Long SASHA GLASS

1937 Hayes Cruiser MIKE PERINI

1952 Hanson Love Bug JUDY STAMM

1954 Hanson Love Bug JEFF AND ELAINE LEWIS

1954 Holiday Rambler RV/MH HALL OF FAME

1970 Holiday Rambler FIELD FIND

1941 Howard Hughes (one of a kind) TRAILER TRASH VINTAGE TRAILERS (LYNDEN, WASHINGTON)

1970 Ideal STACI BLOOMER AND TIMOTHY DUNKS

1962 Ideal DEB AND STEVE NOISEUX

1972 Ideal STEVE AND DEBRA LAMB

1954 Jewel CHRISTIANE HARRIS

1956 Jewel RENE PERRET

1955 Kenskill JIM AND DINA ELLIOTT

1947 Kenskill Kustom Kamper LARRY SHANK

1967 Kenskill GREGG AND CATHERINE LANDAKER

1955 Ken-Craft SHANNON AND ELLEN STEWART

1966 Ken-Craft TERRY M. LEWIS

1954 King Sport King TODD AND IRENE RILEY

1969 Kustom Koach Model 14 CHRISTOPHER WOODSUM

1955 Little Caesar DOUG AND ESTHER HALL

1965 Little Gem Bugg JENNIFER G.

1947 Kit Kamper TRACIE FORLER

1954 Kit Royal Chateau SCOTT PESCUMA

1969 Kit Companion BRAD AND SUE MEDLOCK

1947 Kit Sportsman FRANKIE AND JESSIE CORPENING

1962 Little Gem SASHA GLASS

1958 Mallard JERRY AND BEV STEMACH

1962 Mallard RV/MH HALL OF FAME

1958 Mercury LAURIE SISCO

1964 Mobile Scout KEITH AND CARRIE PARSONS

1965 Mobile Scout PAM GLASS

1949 Nashua Tour-It TRACY AND STEVE KENNEDY

1966 Nomad ROBERT AND LIZ SMITH

1966 Northwest Coach Little Dipper BRENDA LONGTON

1966 Oasis JANET LORENZ

1959 Pathfinder ALAN STEWART AND RHONDA WESTLUND

1966 Pathfinder JOY AND ED THURNER

1979 Perris Pacer MARK HENDRICKS AND BRENDA COOPER

1965 Play-Mor ROBERT DOUGLAS

1958 PleasureCraft MAURICE HOFF

R

1958–67 models had a sharp pointed nose on the front and a "shark fin" protruding from the back

Stamped logo badges with a desert theme were affixed above the front and back windows

Rancho El Rae (1958–89)

Rancho Trailers, Inc. • Salt Lake City / Nephi, Utah

Vern G. Miner started Rancho Trailers in Salt Lake City, Utah. The company offered custom trailer repair, parts, and rental Rancho truck campers and vacation trailers. In 1961 it moved south to Nephi, Utah, and added "El Rae" to its name. The town, with a population of 2,566 in 1960 and located on the banks of Salt Creek, had been a camping place on the Old Mormon Road to Southern California.

Rancho El Rae's unique style included models that had a sharp pointed nose, swept-back roofline, and an extended tail crown. For some reason models changed their body stripes yearly. They were distributed throughout the West and as far east as Nebraska.

The State of Utah's Economic Development Conference recognized Vern G. Miner for outstanding industrial achievement in 1969. Miner had built a $3,000 investment in a 1,000-square-foot plant into a firm that covered 50,000 square feet, employed 75–100 workers, and had yearly sales that exceeded $1.5 million.

In addition to travel trailers, Rancho El Rae built a line of truck campers and fifth-wheel trailers. The name continued until the late 1980s.

1957 Rancho 12' Deluxe (aka the Rancho El Ray Gun)

Before other manufacturers tried the bunk-over style to increase bed space in their small trailers, Rancho created the swept-back and gravity-defying design of the 1957 Rancho 12' Deluxe. It could have been a prototype, but it has the same wheel well shape and extreme rear extension of future models.

17'

1963
Model 17

17'

1966
Model 17

13'

1970
Model 13

Rainbow (1954–early 1960s)

Edwards Manufacturing Company • Sun Valley, California

Rainbow trailers came completely equipped and ready to roll for vacation, travel, fishing, and more. They had a two-tone paint scheme with a lateral band on their body. Tours of the Rainbow trailer factory and factory-direct pricing at their sales lot were offered seven days a week. Financing was available.

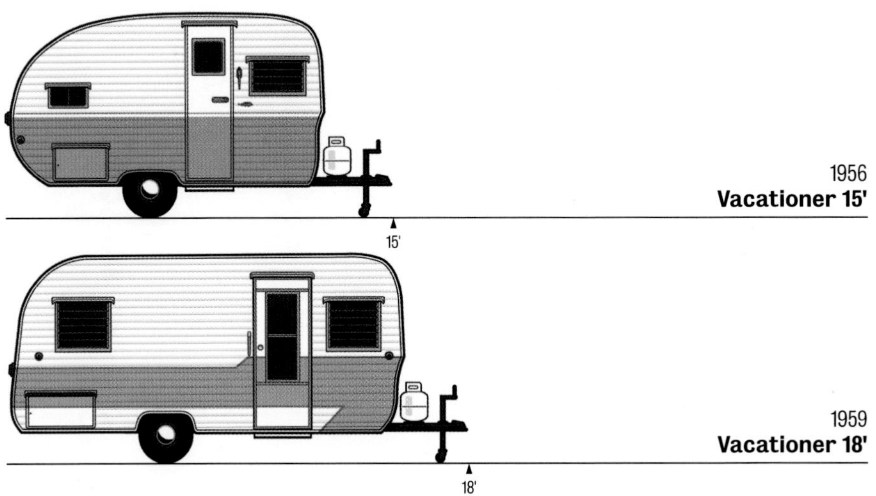

1956
Vacationer 15'

1959
Vacationer 18'

Red Dale (1961–79)

Red Dale Coach Company • Longmont, Colorado

Red Guthrie and Dale Martfeld joined forces and names to create the Red Dale Coach Company in 1961. Ads claimed that their trailers were "designed and built for people who demand the very finest." They were popular enough to have a national association of owners called the Red Dale Wagon Train Club. The group planned weekend campouts in the summer and potlucks in the winter.

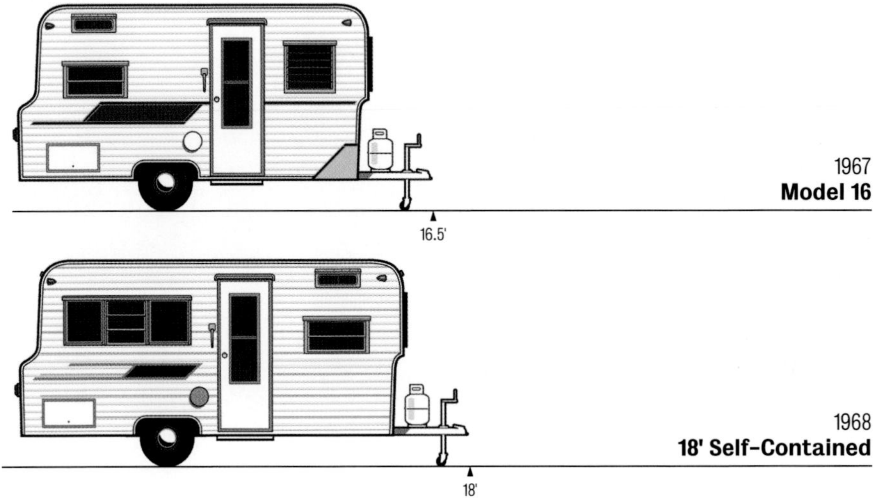

1967
Model 16

1968
18' Self-Contained

Ritz-Craft (1954–76)

Ritz-Craft Corporation • Argos, Indiana

Since its founding, Ritz-Craft was primarily a mobile home manufacturer. From 1966 to 1968 they added four different travel trailers to their line. They were built with double-wall construction, and had enclosed floors and 1-inch fiberglass insulation. The Ritz-Craft brand still appears on modular homes today.

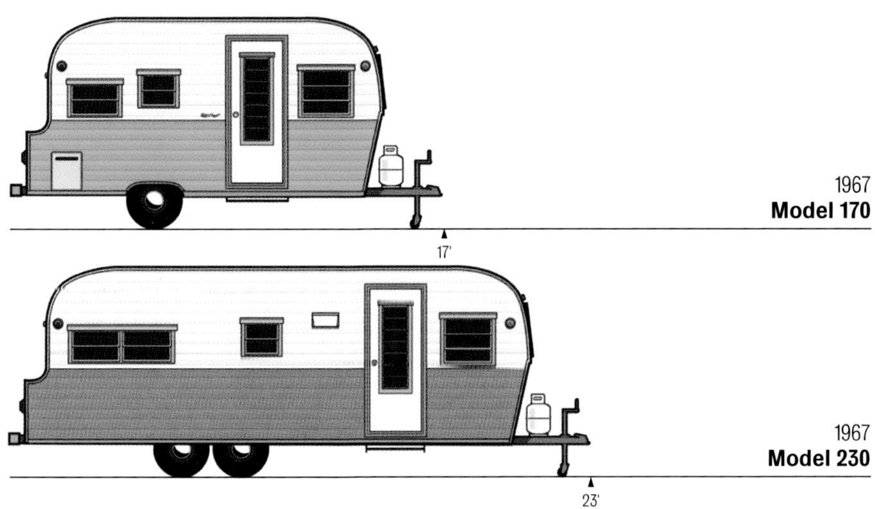

Roadmaster (1938–late 1950s)

Roadmaster Company / Roadmaster Coach Company • El Monte, California

Although built since 1938, the most popular Roadmaster towable trailers appear to be the early 1950s models. They came in four models, with lengths from 20 to 35 feet. All trailer models had metal exteriors, birch interiors, and a "skylite living room" with indirect lighting. Other Roadmaster models included 8-wide and 10-wide mobile homes.

1952 Roadmaster Custom 35'

A luxury trailer designed for long-term travel or as a park model, the Roadmaster Custom 35' was an 8-foot-wide model with room for a family of travelers. It had modern furnishings with a harmonizing color scheme, wall-to-wall carpeting, and a bathroom with a shower and large tub.

RoadRunner (1960–77)

L & M Trailer Manufacturing Company • Ephraim, Utah / Di Giorgio Leisure Products • Kalispell, Montana

Legend has it that a rancher named Harry Mosher made a hunting trailer and when Harry's friends and family saw it they swooned over his creation. So he started manufacturing RoadRunner trailers as fast as he could. Note that the roadrunner mascot's stylized tail feathers also sweep down the sides of Road-Runner trailers. Mosher sold out to Di Giorgio Leisure Products in the early 1970s.

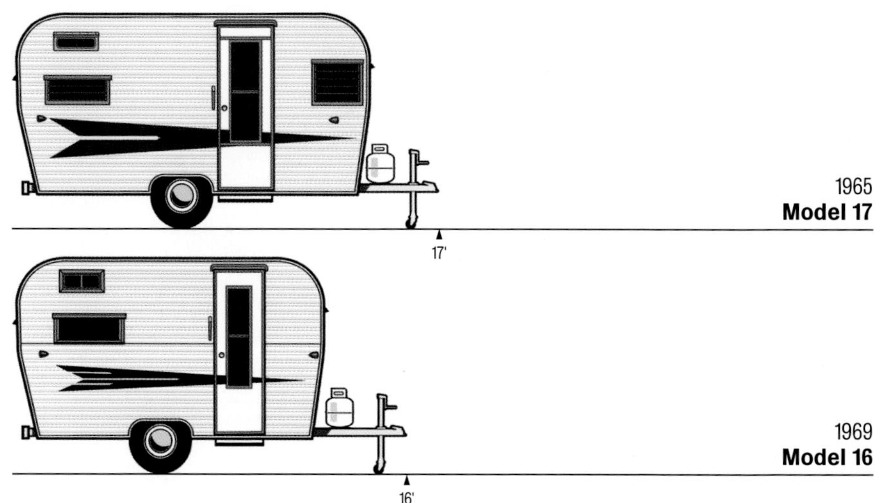

Robin Hood (1947–mid-1970s)

Cadet Coach Corporation • Seattle, Washington / Hammersley Inc. • Brighton, Michigan

The Robin Hood name has appeared on trailers since at least 1947. In 1958, Al Rose, the Trailer King, claimed to be the first to premiere "the Stupendous, Colossal and Low Priced Robin Hood 15 ft . . . trailer." The most well-known Robin Hoods today were built by Cadet Coach in the early 1960s. Hammersley Inc. of Brighton, Michigan, made them through the mid-1970s.

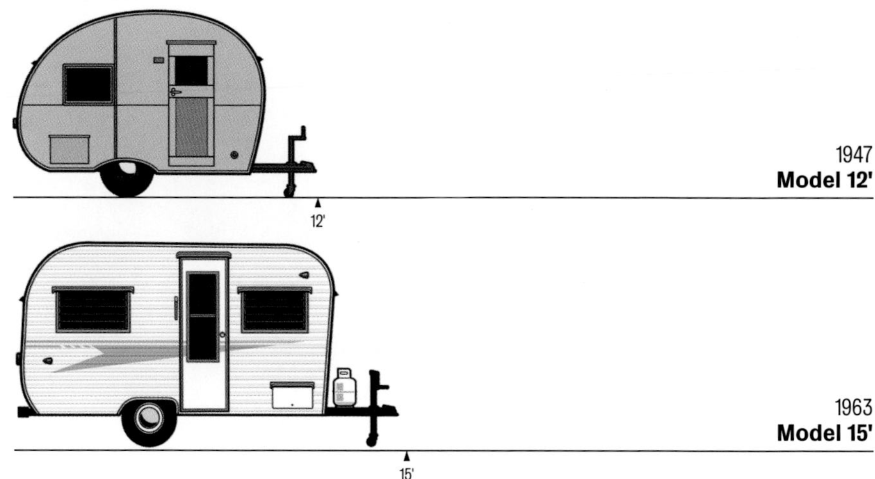

Rod and Reel (early–late 1950s)

Macoma Engineering, Inc. • Bellflower, California

An ad for the 1955 Sportsmen's Show in Los Angeles said that a Rod and Reel trailer was "just what you've been asking for—short enough, compact enough to track well at all speeds and road conditions yet carries all the features of larger bulkier trailers." The line debuted a 26-foot model at the show and soon after added 8- and 10-foot-wide mobile home models.

1952
Model 15

1955 Model 17

A true sportsman's trailer, 1950s Rod and Reel trailers finished their outdoors theme with a bold graphic that seems inspired by the pointed barb of a fishing hook. Two other characteristics to note are the aluminum trim that seals their lower sides and the fender skirts over the wheel wells.

Rollohome

Rollohome (1947–2009)

Rollohome Corporation • Marshfield, Wisconsin

The Rollohome brand of trailers grew up fast, wide, and long. Founded in 1947, by 1952 they had built 60,000 moderately priced trailer homes. They manufactured the first overwidth, or "10-wide" models, up to 40 feet long. By the late 1950s they made mobile homes exclusively. Elmer Frey, the founder of Rollohome, was inducted into the RV/MH Hall of Fame in 1972.

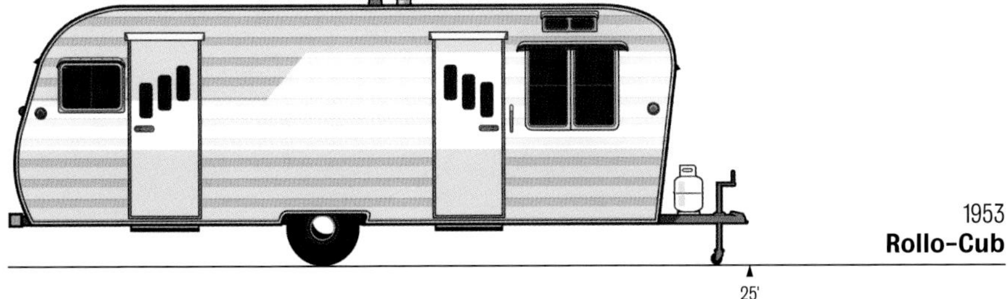

1953
Rollo-Cub

Roycraft (1929–late 1970s)

Roycraft Coach Company • Detroit / Chesaning, Michigan

Roycraft was first known as a furniture maker and boat builder. In 1929, Joseph Roy constructed a 10-foot-long trailer. By the late 1930s, his company offered the Cadillac of trailer coaches for sale. Over Roycraft's long life, it built trailers for the federal government and tracking stations for America's astronaut programs. In the 1960s it made mobile homes that were up to 60 feet long and 12 feet wide.

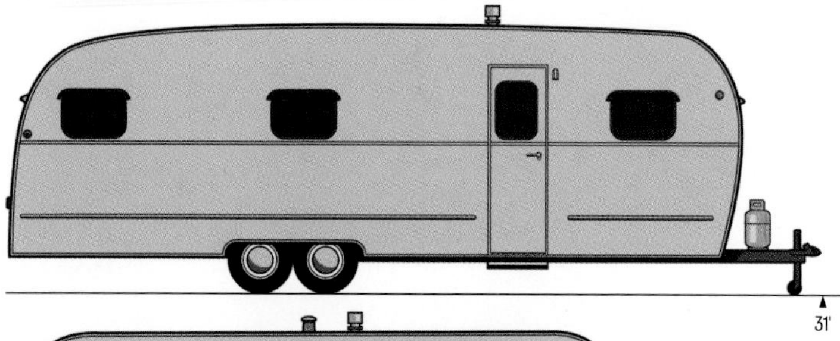

1944
Roycraft 31

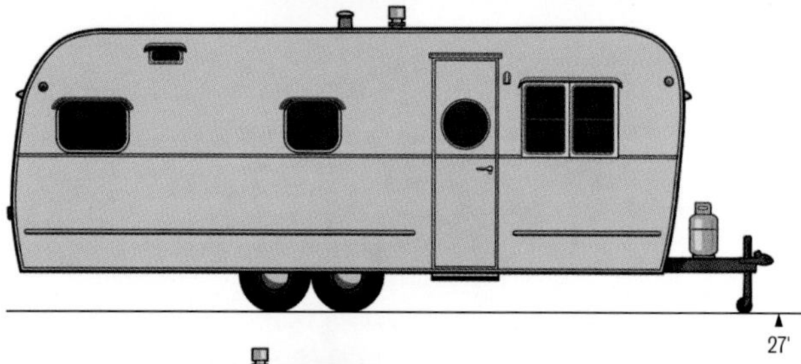

31'

1950
Roycraft 27

27'

1963
Breeze Model 19

19'

S

SERRO SCOTTY SPORTSMAN

Low-profile canned ham with teardrop wheel well cutouts

Aqua and white paint scheme (1964–78)

Serro Scotty (1957–97)

Serro Travel Trailer Company • Irwin, Pennsylvania / Ashburn, Georgia

John Serro must have had high hopes when he built the first Serro Scotty in his garage. It was a 16-foot canned ham with shiny aluminum skin. It should have been a hit with families ready for summer vacations. Unfortunately it didn't sell well, so Serro shifted gears and built a compact 10-foot teardrop, the 1957 Sportsman Jr., that was ideal for fishing and hunting.

The Sportsman Jr. sold well enough that in 1958 the company sent the 13-foot Sportsman Sr. out to the marketplace. Serro Scotty made their last teardrop trailer in 1960. By 1963 the line introduced their soon-to-be iconic aqua and white vacation trailers.

In 1963 the Scottyland Camping Resort, a 230-acre campground exclusively for Serro Scotty owners, welcomed its first visitors. Over the years John Serro and his family attended Scotty trailer rallies held there. The resort, open to all trailers, is still operating today.

By the mid-1970s the Scotty line ranged from 13- to 18-foot models that were simple in design, lightweight, and affordable. John Serro was inducted in the RV/MH Hall of Fame in 1987.

1957 Serro Scotty Sportsman Jr.

After failing in his first attempts to market a full-size trailer, John Serro introduced his 10-foot teardrop, the Sportsman Jr. It was the first in an enduring line of models that made Scottys some of the most beloved trailers on the road.

1959
Sportsman Sr. 13'

13'

1959
Sportsman Rear Door

12'

13'

1960 Serro Scotty Sportsman Sr. (w/winglets)

A Scotty rarity, the 1960 Sportsman Sr. featured winglets that were cleverly made using aluminum left over from the wheel cutouts. They were quickly discontinued after Shasta threatened a trademark lawsuit for infringing on their famed wings (see page 240).

1966
Hi-Lander 15'

1968 Serro Scotty Gaucho 13'

Serro Scotty's line of 13-foot trailers had model names based on their bed styles and kitchen configurations. Over the years model names included Gaucho, Mattress, and Front Kitchen. They had a dropped floor to give campers more headroom in the small trailers and to keep them at a garageable height.

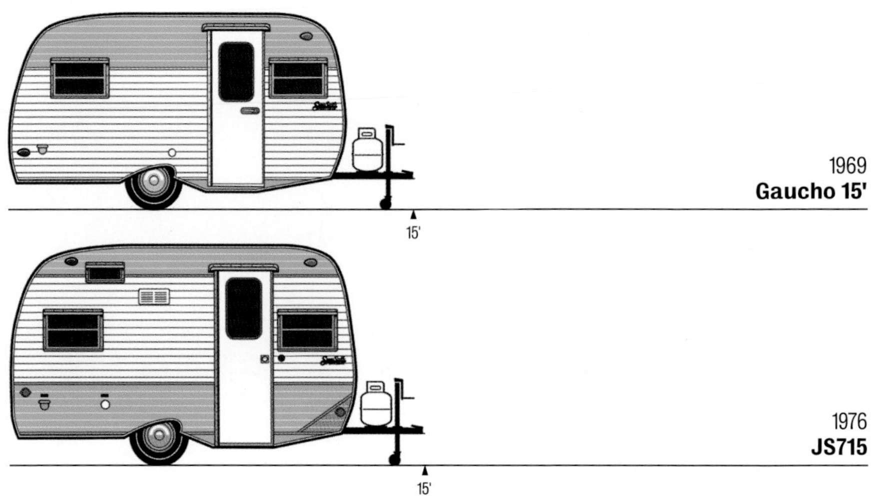

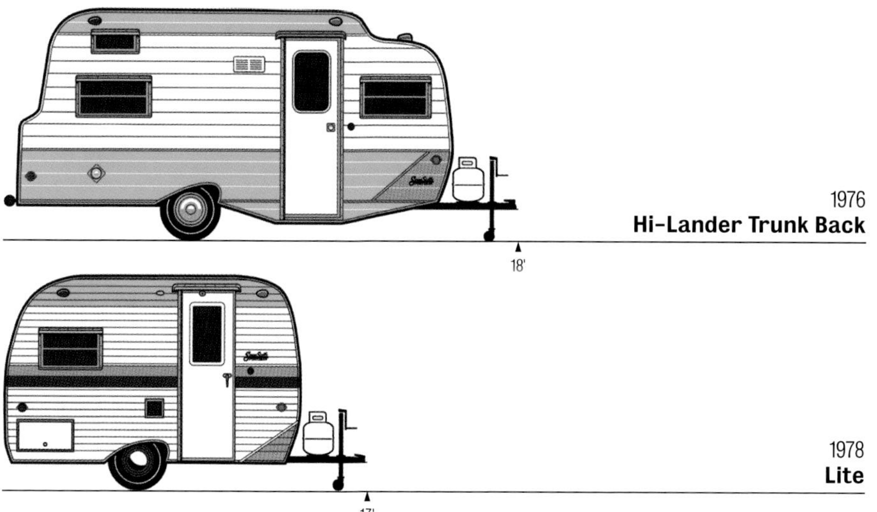

1976
Hi-Lander Trunk Back

1978
Lite

Serro Scotty Badge

All Serro Scotty teardrops and trailers displayed an iconic Scottish terrier mascot badge. The dog became a large part of the Scotty brand. An actual Scottish terrier puppy named Scotty greeted visitors from a miniature Sportsman Sr. at the Dallas Mobile Home and Travel Trailer Show in 1962.

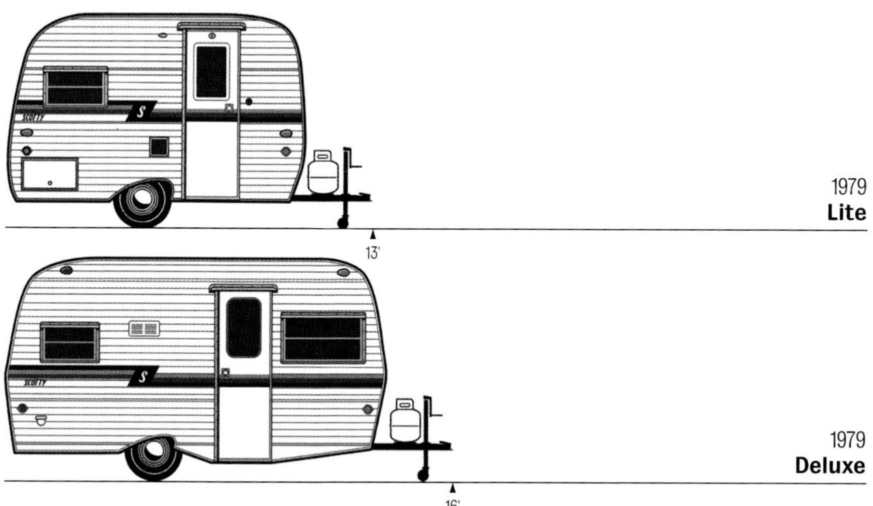

1979
Lite

1979
Deluxe

Shasta TRAILERS

Wings jutting off the back of trailer (post-1958)

Z-stripe graphic (1955–64)

Shasta (1941–mid-1980s)

Shasta Trailer Company / Shasta Industries • Los Angeles / Van Nuys, California

Shasta trailers were the best-selling trailer brand in the United States, and it's easy to understand why: everything about them speaks to mid-twentieth-century design, from the distinctive wings on their backs to the bold color design that featured either red, yellow, or aqua.

The Shasta Trailer Company was founded by Robert Gray in Los Angeles, California, in 1941 to build mobile military housing for the US armed forces. After World War II, the company sold Cozy Cruiser mobile homes until 1952.

The first Shasta trailers offered were aerodynamic canned hams sans their trademark wings. Their interiors featured birch or ash wood paneling and cabinets. The kitchen counter and dining table were color-coordinated with the exterior.

The wings, inspired by the jet age cars of the time, appeared with the introduction of the 1958 line. By 1965 their canned ham body and Z stripe graphic were replaced by a boxy style model with a contrail-like design on their sides.

In the 1960s, Shasta had manufacturing plants in California, Indiana, Texas, Washington State, and Pennsylvania. They continued to soar down America's highways until the mid-1980s.

14'

1954
Model 1400

15'

1956
Model 1500

13'

1961
Compact

17'

1958 Shasta Airflyte

The 1958 Airflyte is iconic of the Shasta brand and one of the most recognizable of all vintage trailers. In 2015 it was reissued by Shasta as a replica, updated with modern systems.

16'

1962
16 SCS

1964 Shasta Astroflyte and Astrodome

From 1961 to 1964, Shasta made the cabover Astroflyte and Astrodome. The bump-out created a bunk space, and the Astrodome model also included a toilet in its floor plan.

1964
Model 20

Slashes and Squares

By 1965 the iconic canned ham body and Z-stripe graphic had been phased out and replaced by a more boxy style and a slanted slash.

1966
Compact

1966
Starflyte

17'

1966
16 SC

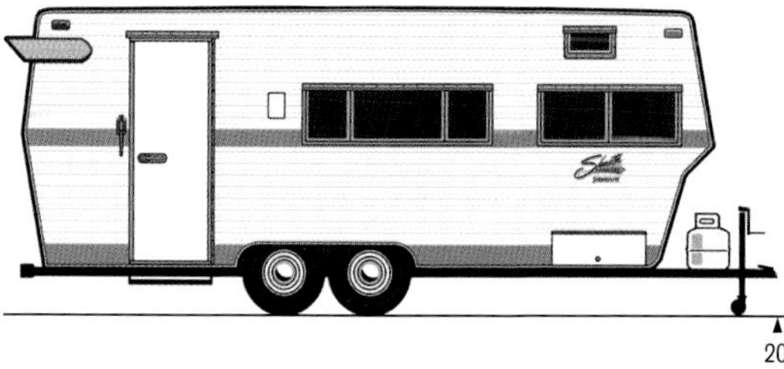

17'

1969
Stratoflyte

20'

16'

1971 Shasta Loflyte

Introduced in 1966, the Loflyte could be easily confused with an Aristocrat Lo-Liner, were it not for its Shasta wings. Like the Lo-Liner, its low profile allowed it to fit in most home garages.

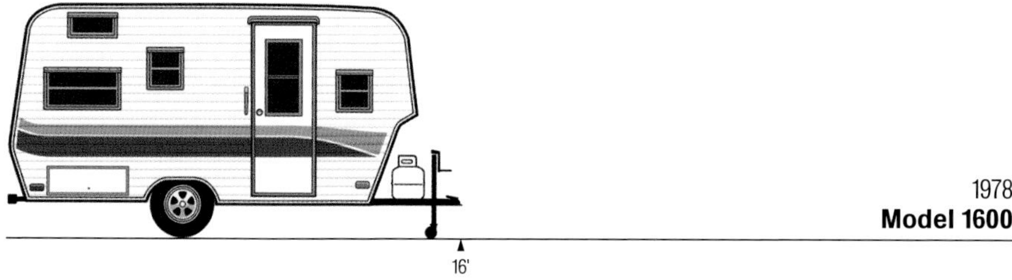

1978
Model 1600

16'

Silver Streak

1949–54 models have the classic clipper style, with a rounded profile and eye-shaped front windows

Post-1955, the aircraft-style body is more squared off, with anodized gold-colored panels added in 1964

Silver Streak (1949–97)

Silver Streak Trailer Company • El Monte, California

The founders of the Silver Streak Trailer Company, Kenny Neptune, James "Pat" Patterson, and Frank Polito, bought the plans for the Clipper model trailer built by Curtis Wright Industries when it shed its trailer division in 1949.

The progenitors of their first model, the streamlined Silver Streak Clipper, can be traced all the way back to the 1934 Bowlus Teller Road Chief and up through Wally Byam's design of the 1936 Airstream Clipper and the 1946 Curtis Wright Clipper. The 1947 Airstream Clipper is a close relative.

Silvers Streaks were all-aluminum, lightweight, high-speed, luxury travel trailers. They were built using aircraft construction techniques with a sturdy frame, thick walls, and insulated floors to make them comfortable year-round. Although advertised "For Those Who Love to Travel," longer models were more than likely to land in a trailer park as their final destination.

Over the years Silver Streak became a venerable brand and was made until 1997. In 2016, a new Silver Streak Trailer Company started to build early-era-style Clippers, but with updated building techniques and materials.

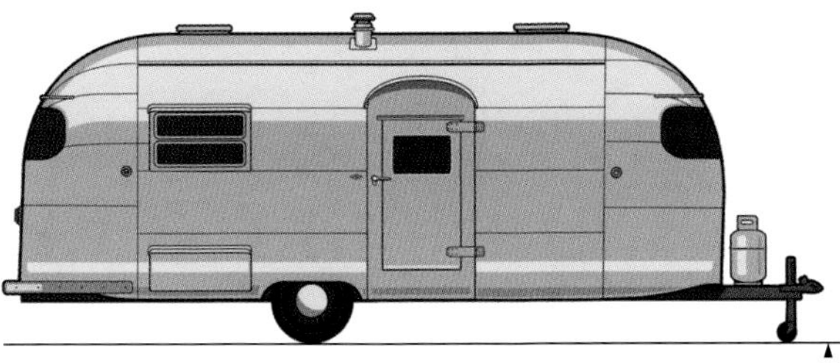

1949
Clipper 22'

22'

Silver Streak and Curtis Wright

The 1949 Silver Streak Clipper is a direct descendant of the Curtis Wright Clipper. The Silver Streak Trailer Company bought the plans from Curtis Wright Industries when they went out of business that same year. Judging by these two ads, they were identical except for their name badges. Clippers, no matter the manufacturer, all share a classic streamlined look. They were aerodynamic, built with lightweight aluminum, and easy to tow.

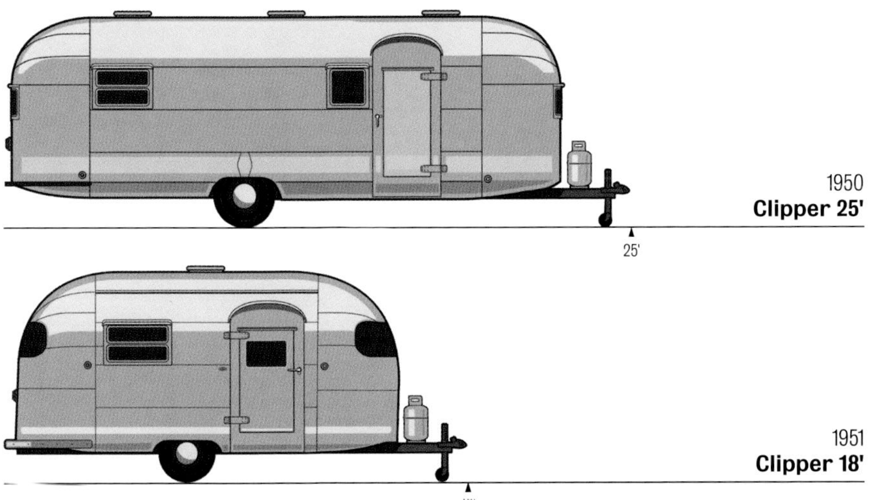

1950
Clipper 25'

25'

1951
Clipper 18'

18'

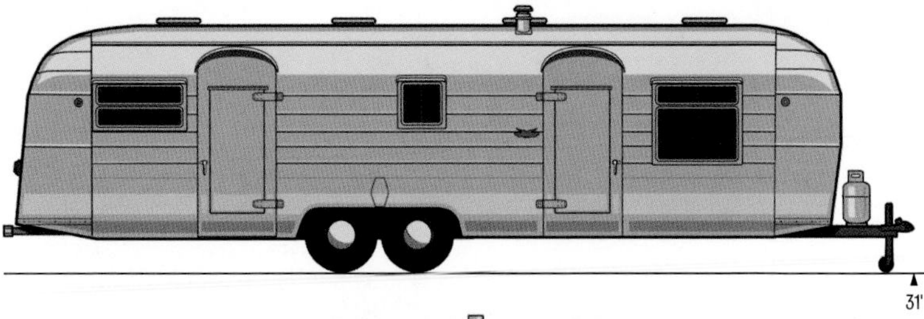

1954
Luxury Liner 31'

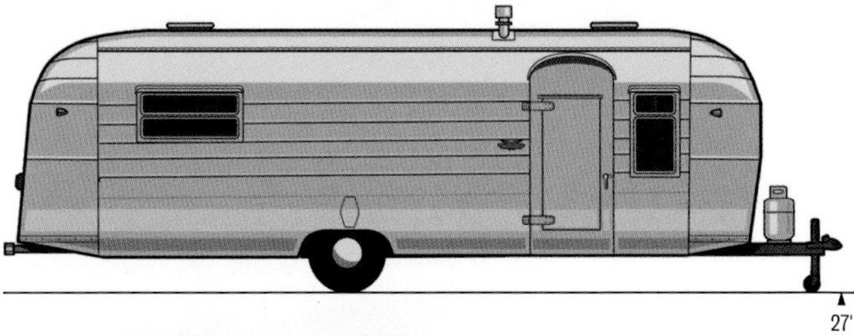

31'

1956
Rocket 27'

27'

1956
Jet 19'

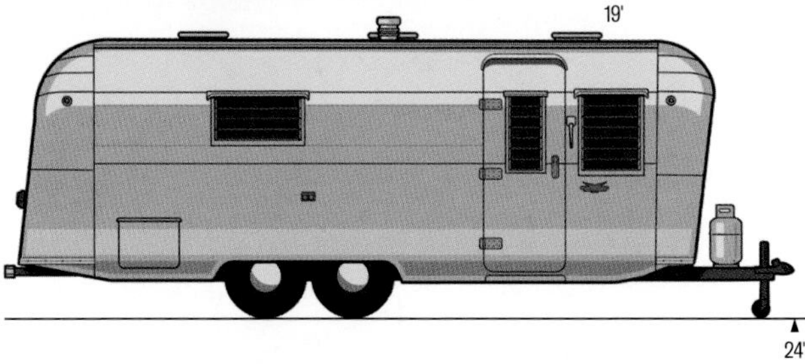

19'

1959
Clipper 24'

24'

The Raven

Silver Streak was well known for their all-aluminum aircraft-type models, but in 1959 they introduced the Raven economy line of wood-framed vacation trailers. The company seems to have designed the line to attract first-time buyers and compact car owners. The Raven line existed through 1961.

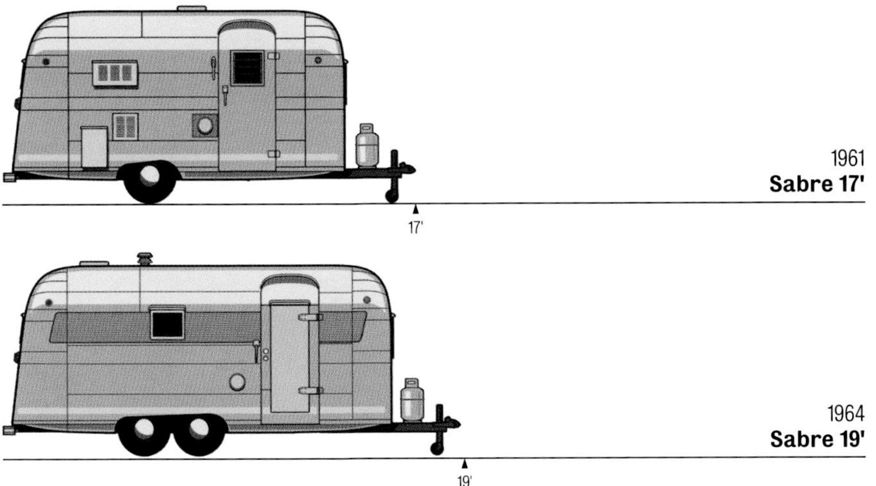

Twin Taillights

In the mid-1960s some models added twin taillights. The lights protruded from the rear of the trailer in gold anodized fixtures. The extra lights gave the line a distinctive rear profile that emphasized its luxurious appeal, and at the same time made Silver Streaks more visible to other motorists and increased highway safety.

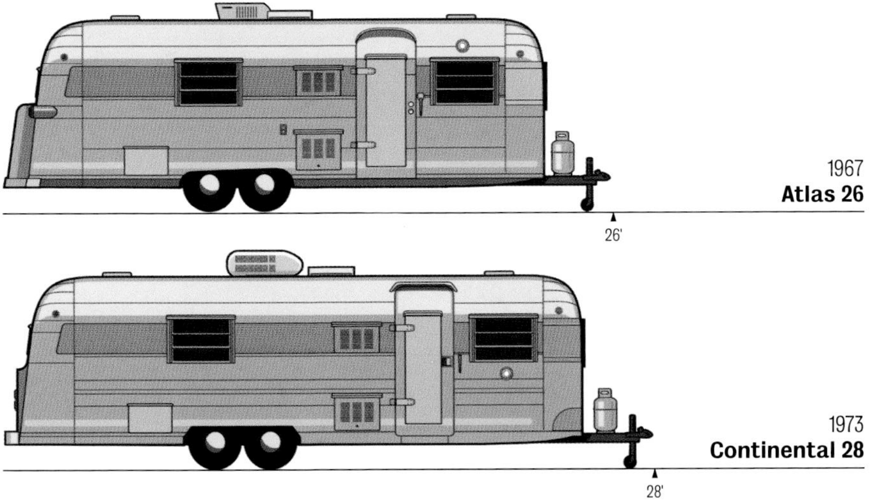

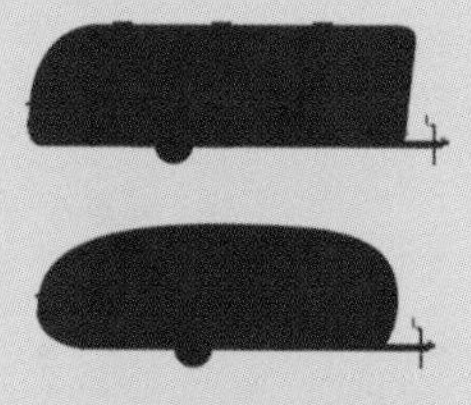

The Manor and Mansion feature a bread loaf body covered with a bare aluminum skin with rounded tail

The Spartanette is an elongated canned ham trailer with a bare aluminum body (note the straight underbody)

Spartan (1945–61)

Spartan Aircraft Company • Tulsa, Oklahoma

When J. Paul Getty transformed his aircraft business into a trailer company, the result was the Spartan trailer line. Introduced in 1945, Spartans offered all the comforts wealthy executives from the Tulsa area had grown accustomed to since the discovery of oil in the Panhandle.

Spartan had produced lightweight and robust planes like the aptly named Executive, and in its new incarnation made travel trailers with deluxe monikers like Manor, Mansion, and Royal Mansion. By the mid-1950s, the trailers were genuinely mobile homes. They featured all-riveted, all-aluminum construction borrowed from aircraft manufacturing, and high-quality interiors.

The only thing that kept Spartan trailers from flying out of the showroom was their price. The 1948 Royal Spartanette started at $3,670. A bathroom, electric fridge, and other extras were optional. At the time a new suburban home with a backyard cost $7,700, so the math didn't add up for most growing families.

Spartan offered to finance buyers and introduced lower-cost models, but all of their efforts to increase their market share were for naught, and they went out of the trailer business in 1961.

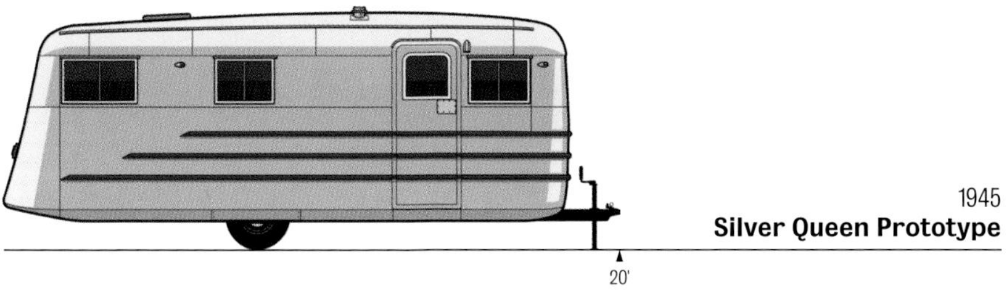

1945
Silver Queen Prototype

20'

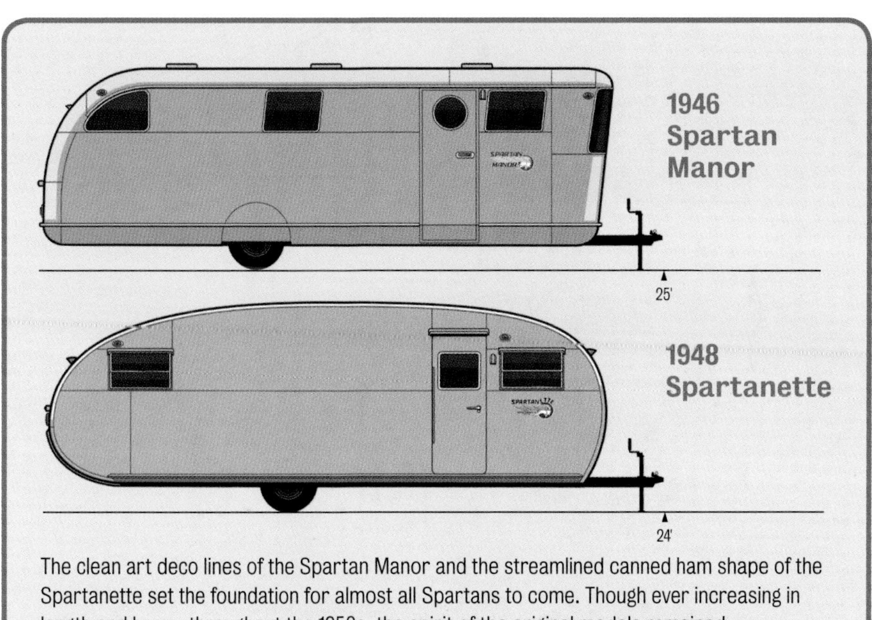

1946 Spartan Manor

25'

1948 Spartanette

24'

The clean art deco lines of the Spartan Manor and the streamlined canned ham shape of the Spartanette set the foundation for almost all Spartans to come. Though ever increasing in length and luxury throughout the 1950s, the spirit of the original models remained.

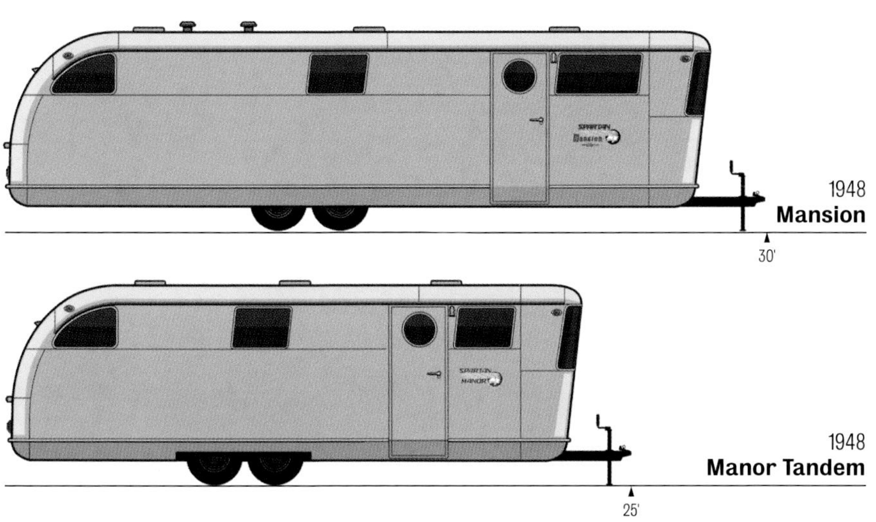

1948
Mansion

30'

1948
Manor Tandem

25'

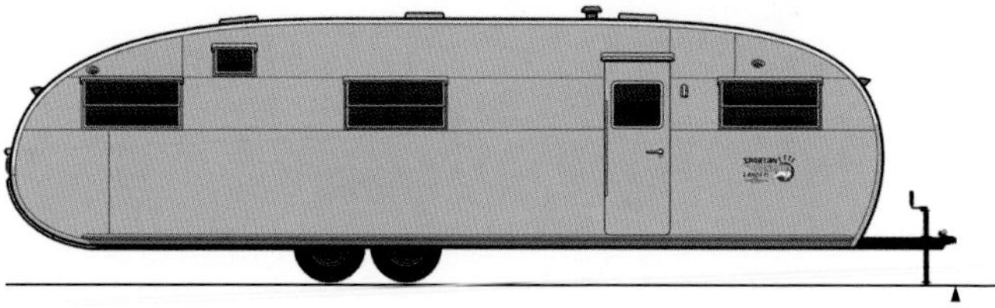

1950
Spartanette Tandem

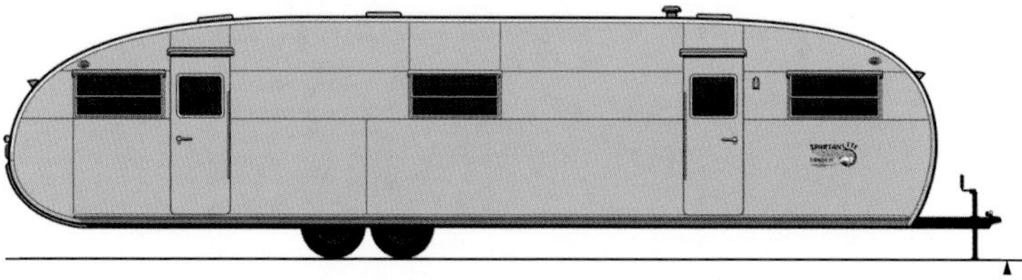

30'

1951
Royal Spartanette

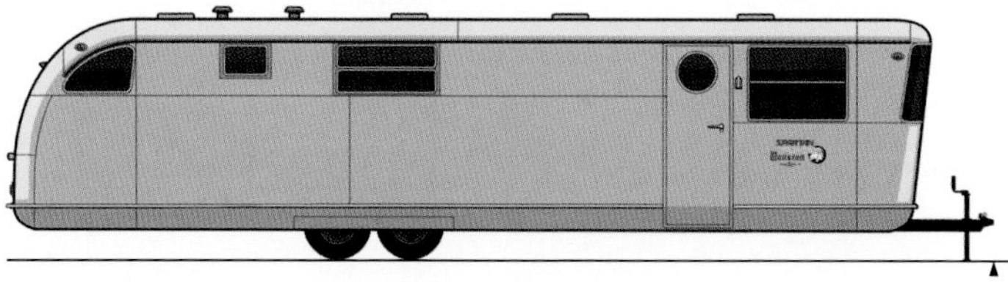

35'

1951
Royal Mansion

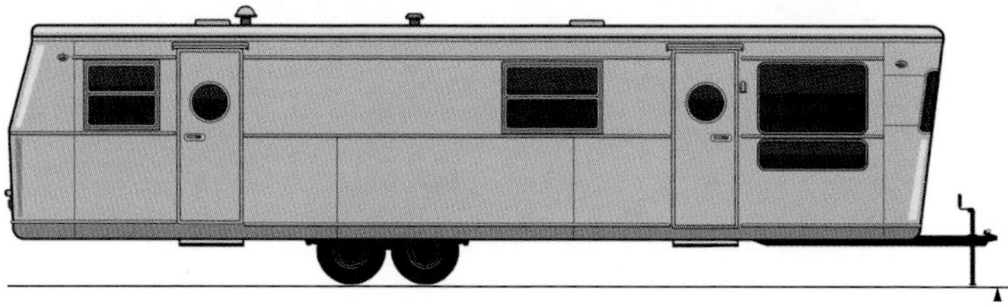

33'

1954
Royal Manor

35'

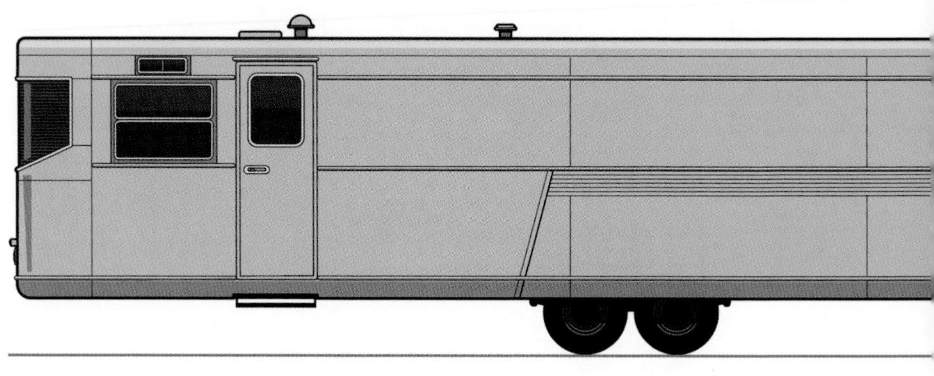

S

Spartan Naming Conventions

For the most part, Spartans fall within the Spartan Manor, Spartanette, or Spartan Mansion styles. Within those lines are variations such as the Royal, Tandem, Imperial, and Executive models. To compete in the late 1950s, Spartan began introducing the economy Sparcraft and Sparlane lines, along with mobile home models Crescendo and Carousel.

1956 Imperial Mansion

Always as much at home in a trailer park as they were in a campground, Spartans continued to grow in length over time. While stylistically resembling the smaller Mansion models, the 45-foot Imperial Mansion is decidedly a mobile home.

45'

STREAMLINE

Streamline (1957–74)

Streamline Trailer Company • El Monte, California / Thorntown, Indiana

The Streamline Trailer Company began in 1957 when Pat Patterson, a founder of the Silver Streak Trailer Company, was bought out, and along with Harry Lovett, began to manufacture their own aircraft-style trailers.

Streamlines were constructed and looked similar to other all-aluminum trailers of the day, but in addition to their aerodynamic design, they had heavy-duty shocks and a low center of gravity that made for easy towing. In 1960, Streamline began to market their trailers as "The Aristocrat of the Highway!" The royal family, from smallest to largest, included the Prince, Princess, Duchess, Duke, Countess, Empress, Count, and Emperor.

All models were road- and travel-tested by factory personnel, who lived and worked in the units in all weather and travel conditions. Members of the Streamline owners association, the Streamline Royal Rovers, crisscrossed the country led by wagon masters confident because their trailers came with a guarantee for the lifetime of the original owner. Streamline trailers ended their 17-year reign on the American highway in 1974, when the company went out of business.

Embossed aluminum ribs in a streamline design stand out in an aircraft-style body

A stamped Streamline logo is found above the front and rear windows, often accompanied by the model name

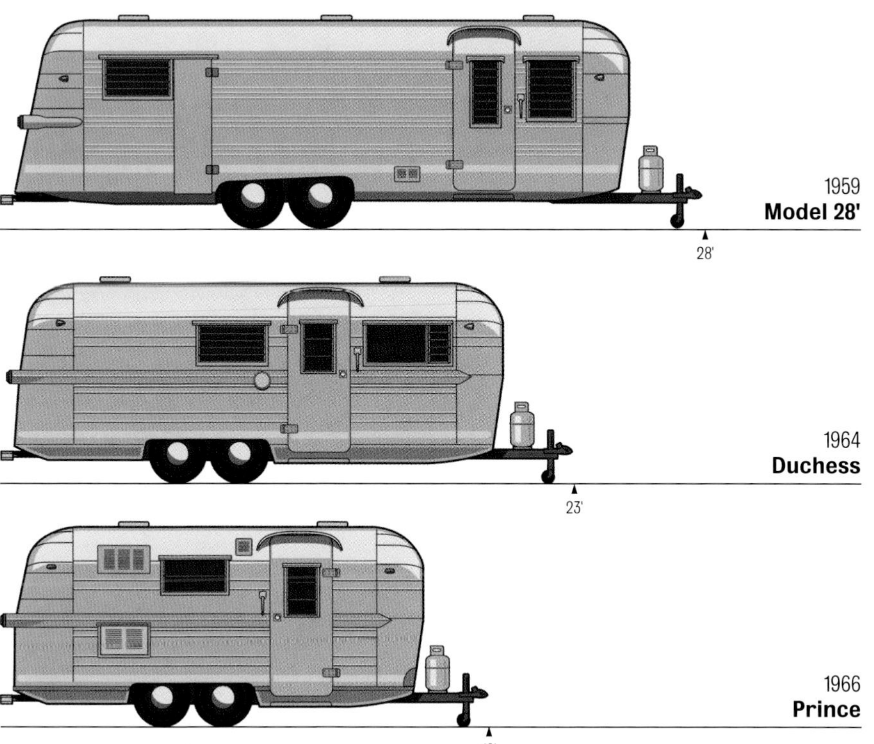

Streamline Ribs

Their aircraft-style body is differentiated from similar trailers by the streamline design–style ribs on their sides, instead of smooth aluminum panels. A gold-colored strip was added to their sides in 1963. It ran just below the windows, from the taillights to a pointed tip near the front.

Safari (1961–late 1960s)

Safari Trailer Manufacturing • Portland, Oregon

It took an expedition to find Safari Trailer Manufacturing on the outskirts of Portland, Oregon. They were made in limited quantities, only sold from a lot in front of the factory, and their badge didn't have the company name on it. Safari advertised in the classified section of the local newspaper, but there is little other documentation available.

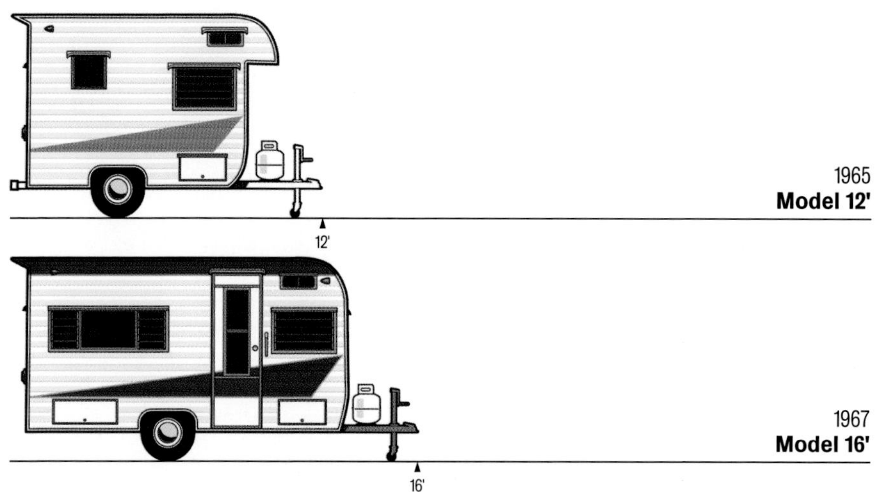

Santa Fe (1956–mid-1970s)

Santa Fe Travel Trailers • Sun Valley, California

Santa Fe trailers were distributed throughout the western United States. A review of the trailer line from the late 1950s said, "The extras, totally unexpected in a trailer priced so low, make [Santa Fe] a good buy and excellent all-around vacation trailer." In 1967 a plant was added in Kansas to extend their reach east across the Rocky Mountains.

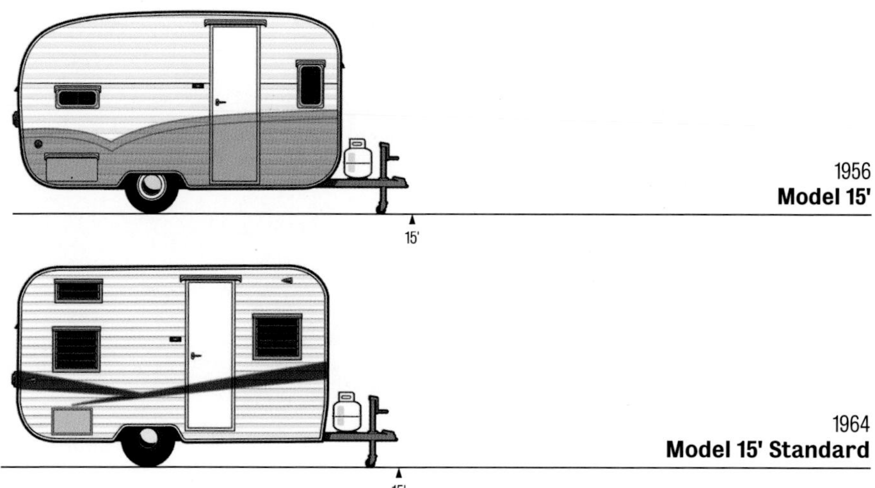

1968 Santa Fe 12' Cub Convertible

The Santa Fe Cub Convertible was a small but fully equipped trailer. It had space for either a queen bed or double beds and could sleep five with a retractable double bunk. The kitchen included a breadboard and utensil drawer. Its dinette table could be used inside or attached to the trailer outside.

Scamp (1972–present)

Eveland's, Inc. • Backus, Minnesota

Scamp trailers were a direct descendant of the Boler fiberglass trailer. They were lightweight and easy to tow for small vehicles. Corrosion free and watertight, the Scamp's molded exterior shell, interior cupboard bodies, and walls were all constructed of fiberglass. Models are currently available in 13-, 16-, and 19-foot lengths and sold factory direct.

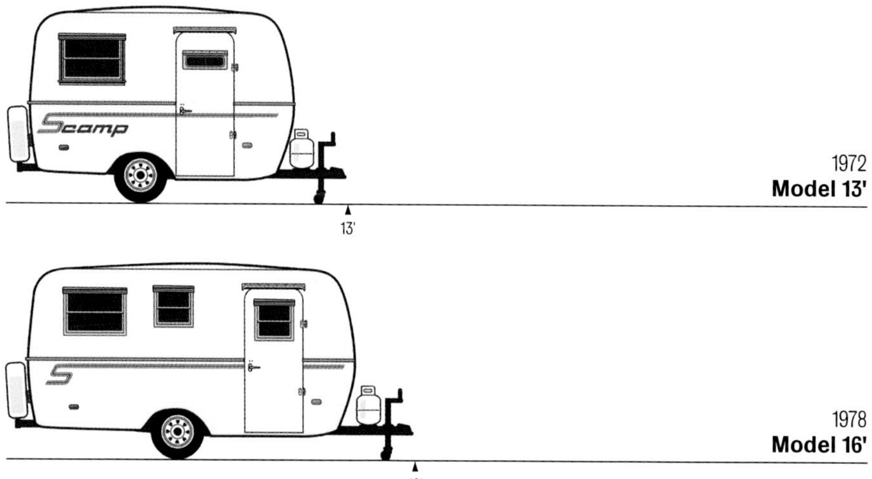

1972
Model 13'

1978
Model 16'

Schult (1936–present)

Schult Trailers, Inc. / Schult Corporation • Elkhart, Indiana

A 1938 ad said that Schult took a lesson from shipbuilders on how to engineer trailers with solid construction and good balance. They must have learned how to build models too as they offered to send prospects a scale model of a trailer for a $10.00 deposit. They made bread loaf–style trailers until 1957. They are known today as Schult Homes.

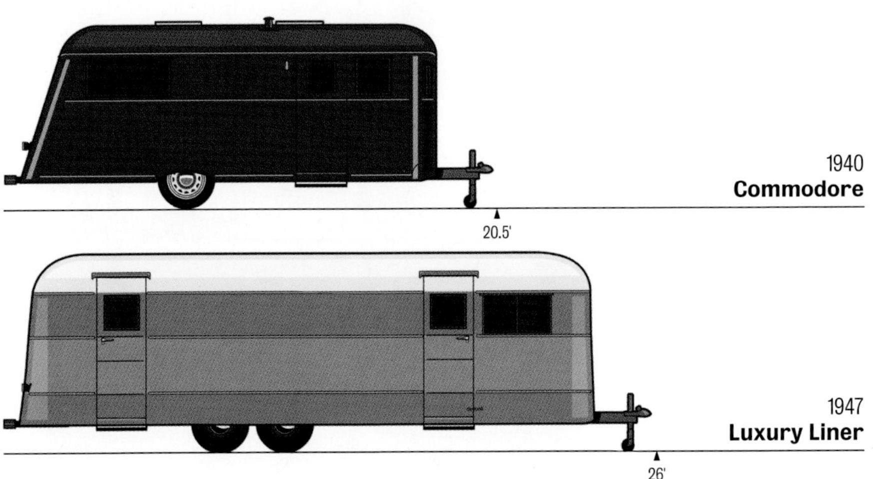

Scotsman (1947–early 1970s)

Scotsman Industries • Gardena, California

Jack's Trailer Service (before the company was known as Scotsman Industries) introduced a line of low-priced trailers designed for the rental trailer market in 1957. Ads claimed that renters would be comfortable towing a Scotsman trailer after only a few minutes on the road. Scotsmans had an extended rolled front roofline, solid plywood walls, and a low drop axle.

1957 Scotsman 14

The Scotsman's distinctive front end makes it easy to spot among vintage trailer brands. Its rounded brow gave it considerable cabinet space for a trailer of its size. The closest cousin to the Scotsman 14 is the Aladdin Genie, also from the West Coast (see page 45).

Siesta (1940s–1981)

Siesta Trailer Manufacturing Company, Inc. • Santa Clara, California

The most recognized vintage Siesta models today date from the late 1950s through the early 1960s. The Models 15', 16', and 17' had painted aluminum bodies with an intersecting arrow design. They featured a full wraparound front window and rear picture window. The Siesta brand was affixed to truck campers in the late 1960s and motor homes in the early 1970s.

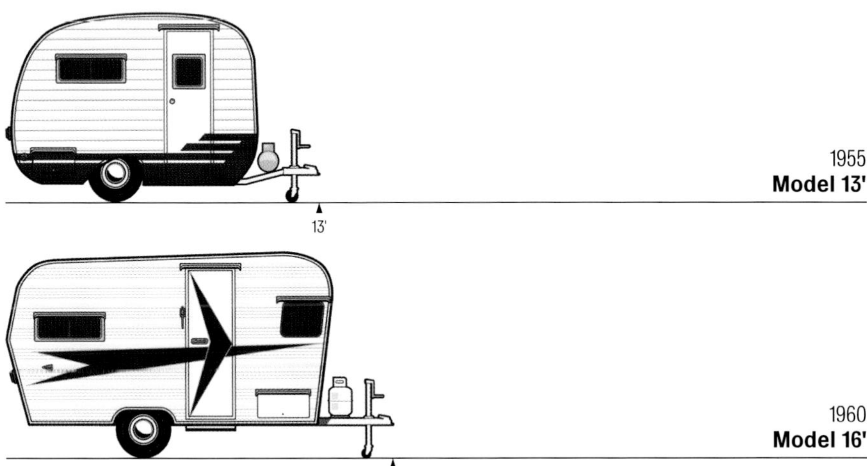

Skyline (1951–present)

Skyline Coach Company, Inc. • Elkhart, Indiana

In the 1950s, before Skyline was an industry giant and parent company to brands like Layton, Nomad, Golden Falcon, Aljo, and others, it made travel trailers and mobile homes that carried the Skyline name. Its early trailers had all-aluminum bodies and came in 21- to 35-foot models. Art Decio, the founder of Skyline Coach Company, was inducted into the RV/MH Hall of Fame in 1975.

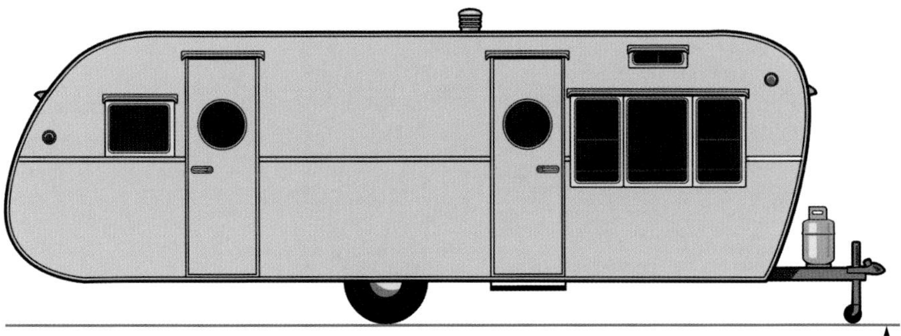

1953 Skyline Invader

The modestly priced Invader had an all-aluminum exterior, two doors with portholes, and a single axle. A 6-inch Jr. "I" beam frame provided a strong base of support for its body. The inside featured birch paneling and tile floor throughout. Its kitchen had white pine cabinets, twin sinks, and a snack bar.

Southland (1946–mid-1950s)

Mathison Aircraft & Trailer Manufacturing Company • Long Beach, California

E. O. Mathison built, sold, and repaired trailers at Southland Trailer Sales. In 1946 he announced the new Southland Runabout, a 14-foot Masonite-clad model with plexiglass windows. By the early 1950s the line was offered in up to 32-foot lengths with an aluminum exterior and glass windows.

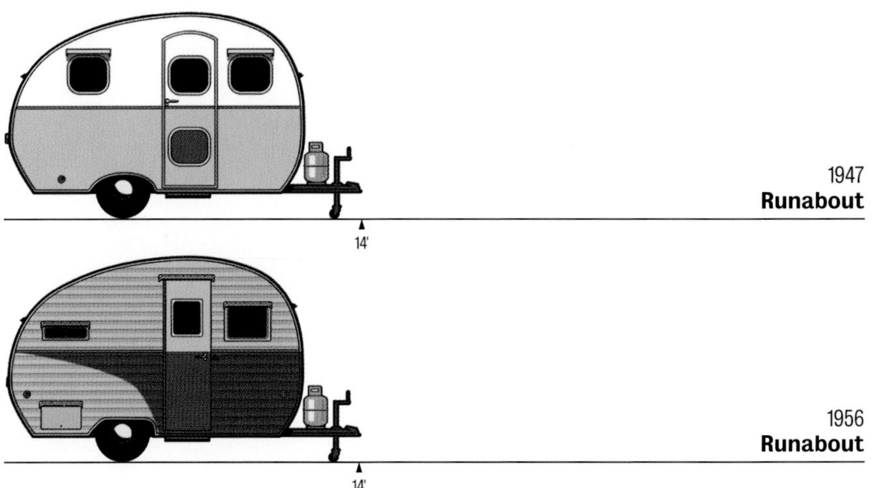

Sportcraft

Sportcraft (1955–late 1960s)

Sportcraft Trailer Manufacturing Company • Cortland, Ohio

In 1955, Ray Allen introduced the Sportcraft line to the eastern United States. They were advertised as being "lightweight, economical, and built for fast, safe traveling." Sportcraft built travel trailers into the early 1960s. The Sportcraft brand name appeared on mobile homes until the late 1960s.

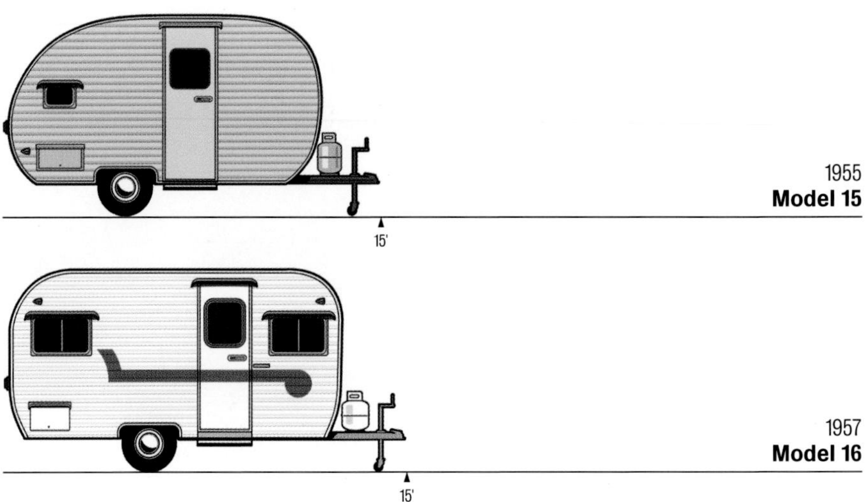

STARCRAFT

Starcraft (1968–present)

Starcraft Corporation • Goshen, Indiana

In 1963, Starcraft employee Lloyd Bontrager invented the first lifter mechanism for tent campers. One year later, Starmaster, Starliner, and Star Rambler tent campers hit the road. Bontrager went on to found Jayco, Inc. in 1968, the same year the Starcraft Corporation built its first travel trailers. Truck campers and fifth-wheel trailers soon followed.

1972
Model 161

SUN CRUISER

SunCruiser (1957–60)

United States Mobilehome Industries • Osceola, Indiana

There is little information to be found about the SunCruiser line of trailers. They didn't leave much of a trace beyond some brochures and classified ads from midwestern newspapers. SunCruisers featured brilliant graphics and wings but were otherwise a typical canned ham–style vacation trailer.

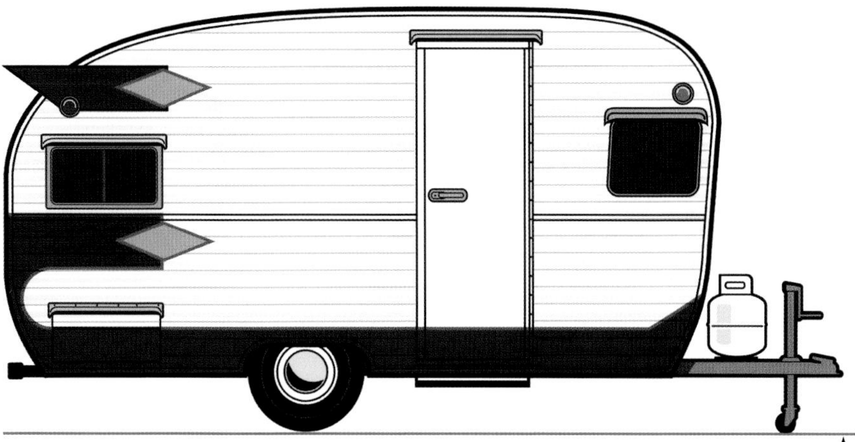

1959 SunCruiser 16

While the SunCruiser's wings and body shape were similar to a Shasta Airflyte, its graphics were decidedly bolder. It featured a diamond pattern on its sides and painted wings that thrust out from the rear of the trailer. Shastas had an angled graphic painted on their bottom half and aluminum wings bolted to their sides. There are differences in the running lights too. The rear running light on the SunCruiser is on its wing, while the Shasta's rear running light is *under* its wing.

1961 Shasta Airflyte

Superior

Superior (1941–mid-1950s)

Superior Coach Corporation / Superior Industries Inc. • Goshen, Indiana

The clerestory roof, or trolley top, originated on trailers by Superior Coach. The raised roof provided ample headroom, cross ventilation, and light. Hidden under their aluminum skin was a patented bow strut frame. Inside they featured mahogany or birch paneling, a complete kitchen, and a private bedroom.

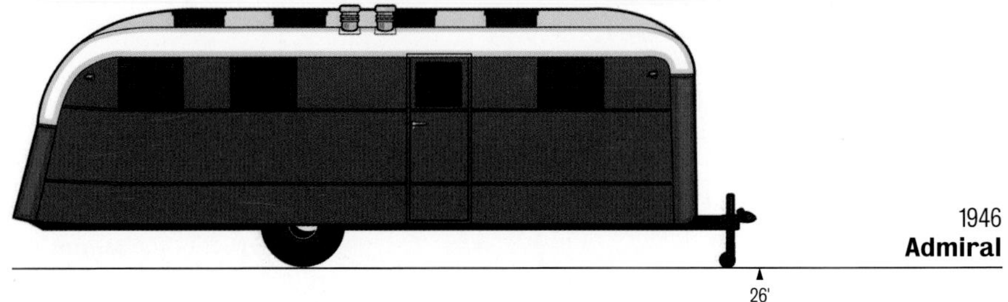

1946
Admiral

Swiss Colony (1963–80)

Swiss Colony Travelers, Inc. • Elkhart, Indiana

A 1963 ad said that Swiss Colony trailers were “designed by the same engineers and built by the same craftsmen who have built the finest in 10 wides for years.” In the mid-1960s all models were self-contained and came in vacation-sized lengths up to 21 feet. By the late 1960s, larger trailers and truck campers carried the Swiss Chalet name. Fifth-wheel trailers models followed.

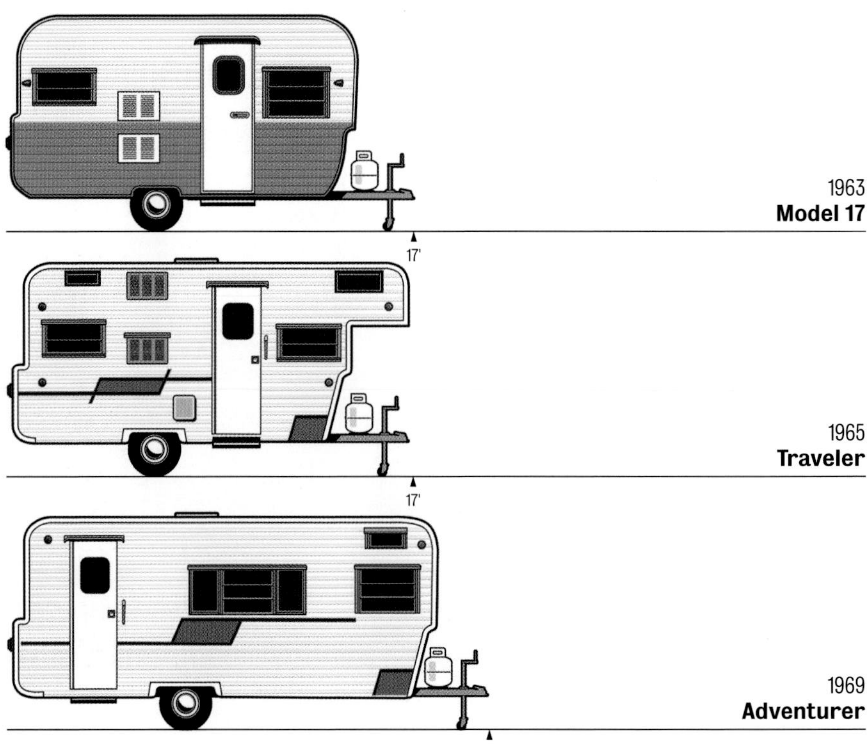

1963
Model 17

1965
Traveler

1969
Adventurer

T

Terry

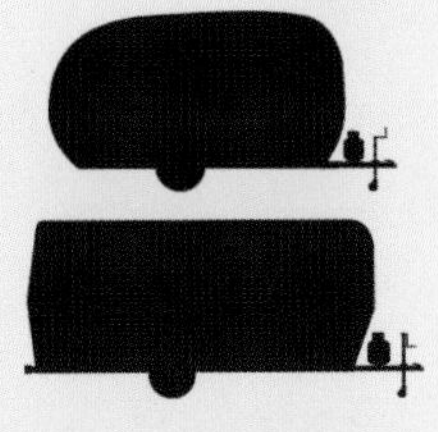

Three white stripes in a V pattern adorn the front of the trailers until the 1966 models

The 1958 models were the first to feature a compass in the Terry logo

Terry (1948–2009)

Western Trailer Service / Terry Coach Industries, Inc. • Huntington Park, California / Fleetwood Enterprises, Inc. • Riverside, California

The first in a long line of Terry-branded trailers, a 12-foot canned ham called the Terry Rambler, originated in 1948 from Western Trailer Service in Huntington Park, California. By 1953 the company had changed its name to Terry Coach Industries, Inc. and sold a complete family of vacation, travel, and park models.

Terry's slogan for most of the 1950s, "You can take it with you," underscored its dedication to building a low-priced but high-quality trailer. The trailers had steel truss sidewalls and baked-enamel aluminum skin, while the interiors featured a custom midcentury "Charm Design." National advertising on TV programs like *Queen for a Day* and their use of recognizable brand-name materials, paints, tires, and appliances made them a very popular choice.

That's probably why Fleetwood Enterprises, Inc. bought Terry Coach Industries, Inc. in 1964. Their iconic compass logo decorated Terry-brand trailers through the 2009 model year, when Fleetwood ceased manufacturing all travel trailers.

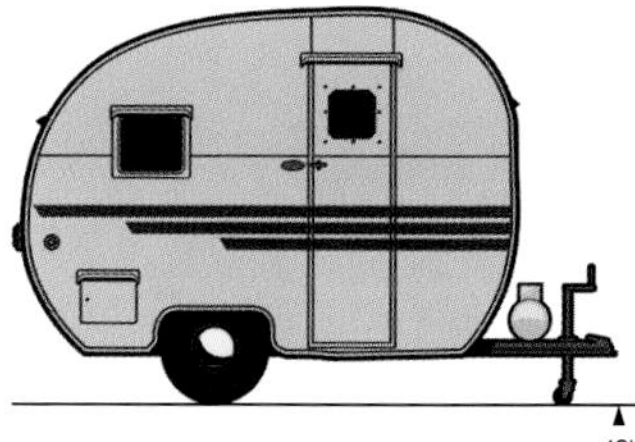

1948
Rambler 12

12'

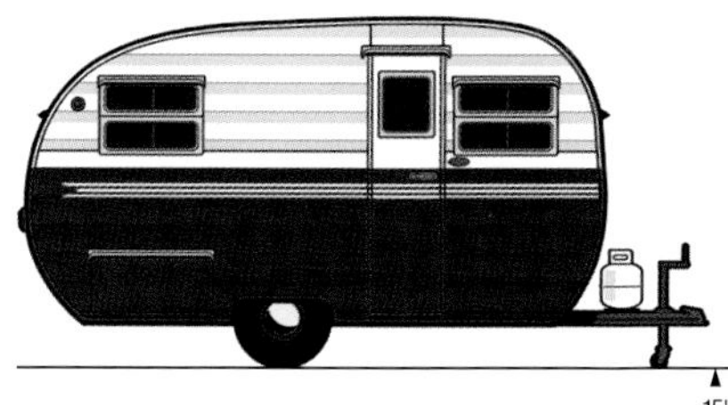

1952
Rambler 15

15'

TERRY

Charm Design For '59

1959 Terry 17

A "Charm Design for '59" teaser advertisement announced what would be "the greatest advancement of any year and will set the pace for travel trailers for years to come," but didn't show it. Terry ads later revealed two new interior design options: Driftwood Moderne, with a black and white theme, pink appliances, and turquoise accents; and an Early American style that had bronze and beige tones, cherrywood, and color-matched name-brand appliances.

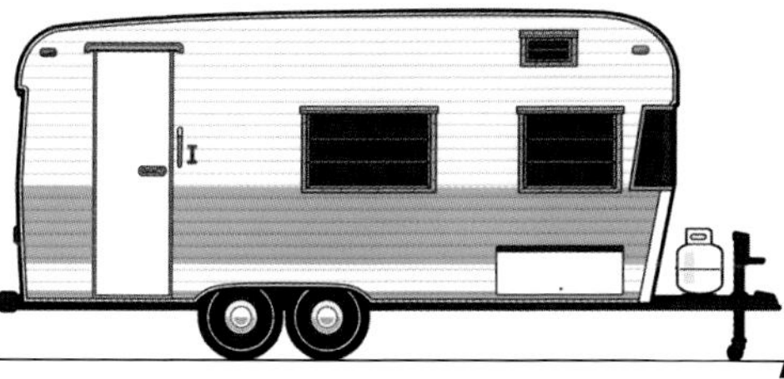

1965
Travel-Pak 19

19'

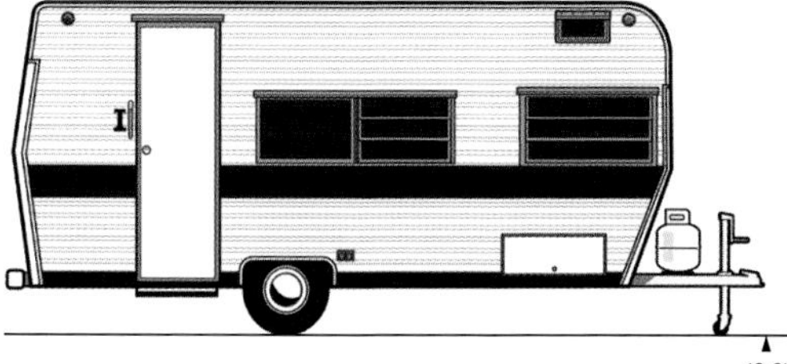

1969
Travel-Pak 18

18.9'

TRAVELEZE

SUN VALLEY Calif

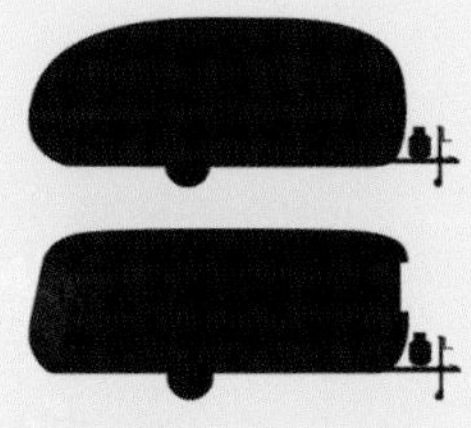

Early models were bare aluminum canned hams with three feather-shaped stripes

Bold offset stripes and an inset front window became a standard feature in the mid-1950s

Traveleze (1931–89)

Traveleze Trailer Company, Inc. • Sun Valley, California

In the early 1930s, Kenneth Dixon taught high school woodshop, mechanical drafting, and electricity classes, and built trailers in his spare time. He sold them through classified ads until 1936, when he entered a canned ham–style model into a weekend auto show. By that Sunday night he had all-cash deposits on seven trailers.

The following Monday morning he resigned as a high school teacher, and over the next 58 years Dixon and his family built one of the longest-lived lines of travel trailers. Part of the company's success was its willingness to innovate. Traveleze was the first to make a motorcycle trailer and the first to construct a chassis-mount truck camper.

In 1950 their trailers were the first to have a butane refrigerator, which allowed fishermen to freeze their catch quickly. Soon, all-butane models offered complete independence for those camping in remote areas. By the late 1950s, Traveleze was making longer and more luxurious models.

The company went on to build fifth-wheel trailers, park models, and motor homes. In 1983, Kenneth Dixon was inducted into the RV/MH Hall of Fame.

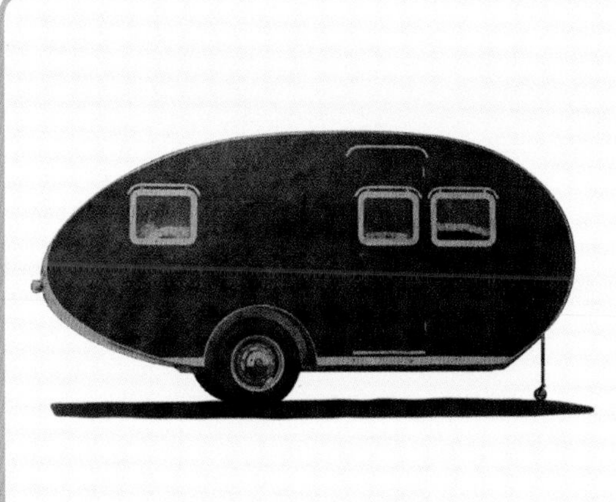

1936 Model

The streamlined 1936 model had plywood walls covered with leatherette and muslin, a sunken floor, and hand-crafted window frames. After Traveleze had built 86 of them in six months, founder Kenny Dixon had second thoughts about the future of the trailer industry and quit the business to build a house in Hollywood. He returned to making trailers after a brief hiatus.

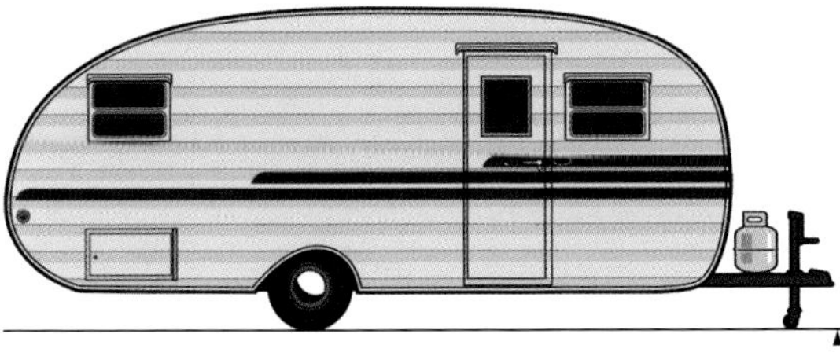

21'

1950
Model 21

19'

1955
Model 19 ES

21'

1958
Model 21

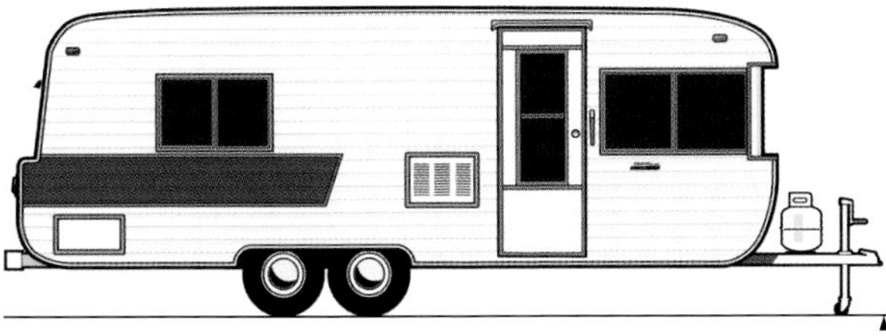

23'

1968
Model 23T

Talisman (1958–61)

La Verne Industries, Inc. • La Verne, California

A 1958 Talisman ad quoted the philosopher Baruch Spinoza: "Love is a sensation of pleasure coupled with the thought of an external object." The external object in this case being a Talisman trailer. The short-lived line of midpriced vacation trailers came in lengths from 12 to 30 feet. They had aluminum exteriors, were designed for easy towing, and were expected to last.

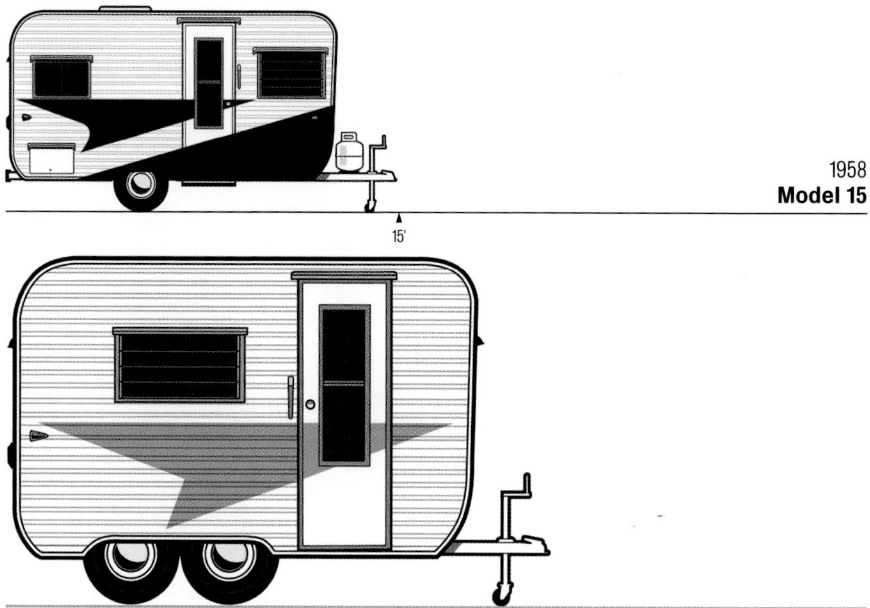

1958
Model 15

1961 Talisman Tandem Twelve

The Tandem Twelve was possibly the shortest travel trailer with a tandem axle. Compact and sports cars could tow a 1,330-pound, fully equipped Tandem Twelve with little drag because the axles shifted its weight toward the rear of the trailer and shaved off about 80 pounds of its tongue weight.

Thunderbird Castles (mid-late 1960s)

Thunderbird Products Corporation • Alliance, Ohio / Miami, Florida / Paso Robles, California / Sebring, Ohio

The Thunderbird Products Corporation named their travel trailer models after famous castles. There were the Ferrara 1700, Belvedere 170 Cab-Over, Windsor 1900, and Glamorgan 2300. Glamorgan Castle, located in Alliance, Ohio, was their corporate headquarters in the mid-1960s.

1967
Ferrara 1700

Tour-A-Home

Tour-A-Home (1957–1970s)

Tour-A-Home Manufacturing Corporation • Flint, Michigan

The Tour-A-Home Manufacturing Corporation built trailers and mobile homes. The standard features of 1958 Tour-A-Home trailers included a tricolored aluminum exterior, a one-piece welded roof, and two doors. The doors on the Models 15, 17, and 19 were on the opposite sides of the trailer. The doors on the Model 23 were on the same side of the trailer.

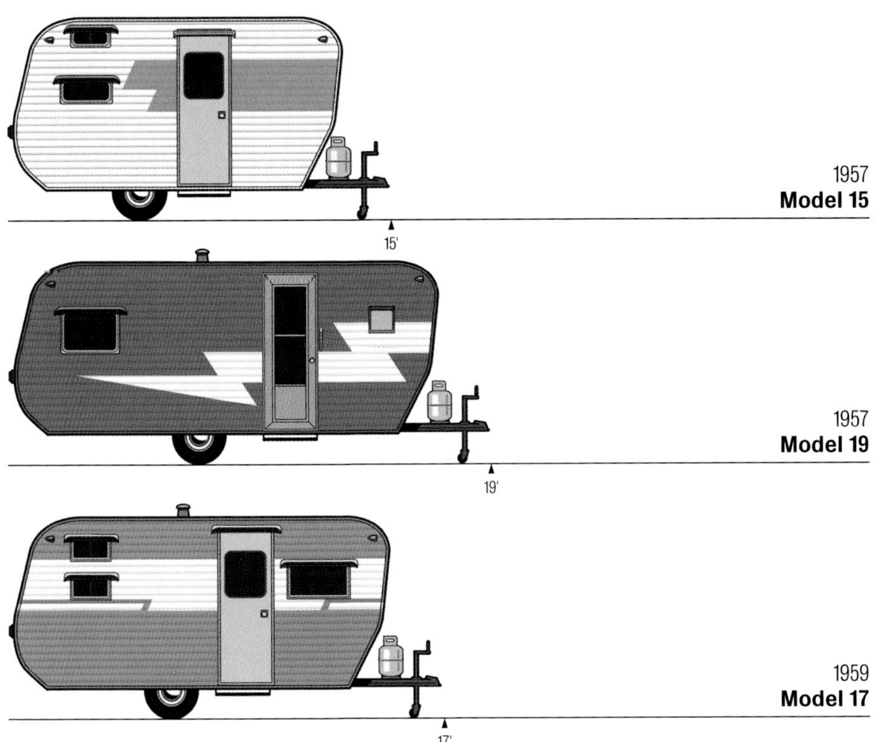

TOUR-ETTE

Tourette (1947–48)

Universal Trailer & Manufacturing Corporation • Kansas City, Missouri

The Tourette teardrop trailer was marketed as a home on wheels "for tourists, businessmen, traveling salesman, sportsman, field workers, show people and construction crewmen." The all-aluminum trailer was 10 feet long and weighed less than 720 pounds. It came fully equipped for $495. Options included a tent that extended the kitchenette by 8 feet.

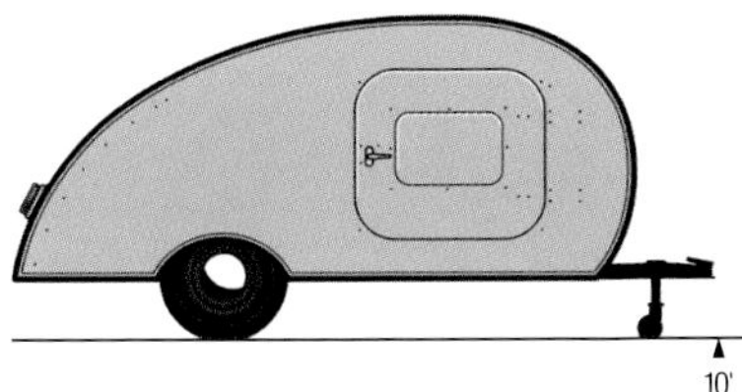

10'

1947
Teardrop

Trailblazer (1961–74)

Spencer Sports Products, Inc. • Spencer, Wisconsin

The first Trailblazer vacation trailers had prefinished aluminum exteriors and colored shutters. By 1964, Trailblazer offered cabover versions of the 15-, 17-, and 20-foot models. In 1972 the company organized its models into three new lines based on quality and price. They branded them as the Tenderfoot, Explorer, and Eagle lines.

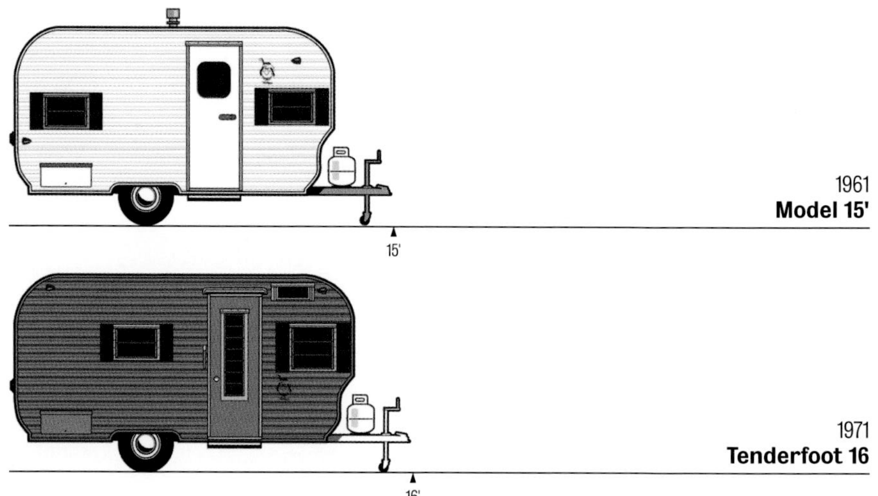

Travelo (1930–86)

Raymond Products Company, Inc. • Saginaw, Michigan

The long-lived Travelo name first appeared on trailer coaches. Over the next two decades, Travelo trailers had Masonite, steel, aluminum, and even cedar siding. During World War II all of their coaches were sold to the US government. After the war they made models for "travel, camping or permanent living." By 1953, Travelo built mobile homes exclusively.

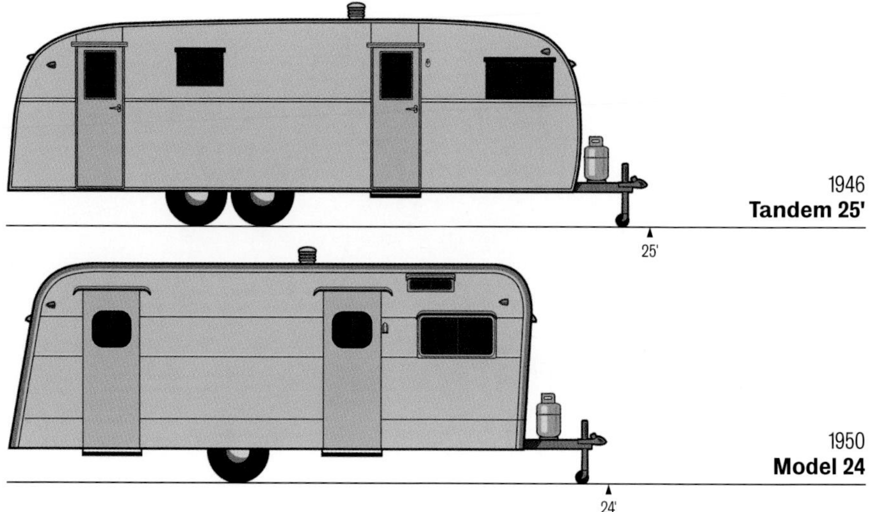

Trillium (1974–late 1970s)

Trillium Recreational Vehicles, Ltd. • Markham, Ontario

Trillium Industries trailers were a direct descendant of the Boler molded fiberglass trailer. They were lightweight and easily towed by small vehicles. Their molded fiberglass shell was designed to be corrosion free and watertight. Its interior cupboards and walls were made of fiberglass too. The Trillium name currently appears on Outback trailers based on an original Boler mold.

1975
Model 1300

Trailorboat (1961–63)

Trailorboat Engineering Company • San Rafael, California

With its easily removable boat, kitchen galley, and cozy sleeping cabin, the fiberglass Trailorboat was an all-in-one solution for the outdoorsman on the go. The interior had a storage shelf, fishing rod racks, and flip-up windows. The American Dream Trailer Company, in Portland, Oregon, bought the original fiberglass molds for the Trailerboat and currently offers its own version.

1961
Trailorboat

A Fisherman's Dream

Trailorboats carried a small fiberglass boat on their roof. The boat, once unclipped and lifted from the trailer, was ready for a day on the water. An integrated bracket held an outboard motor on the trailer's tongue. There was storage space for rods, reels, lures, line, and assorted tackle inside the cabin.

Trotwood (1920–mid-1980s)

Trotwood Trailers, Inc. • Trotwood, Ohio

The venerable line of Trotwood trailers lasted for over 60 years. In 1932, Trotwood was the first manufacturer in the United States to make a canned ham style–trailer. Its later models led and kept up with decades of material, technical, and design innovations within the industry.

1940
17' Economy

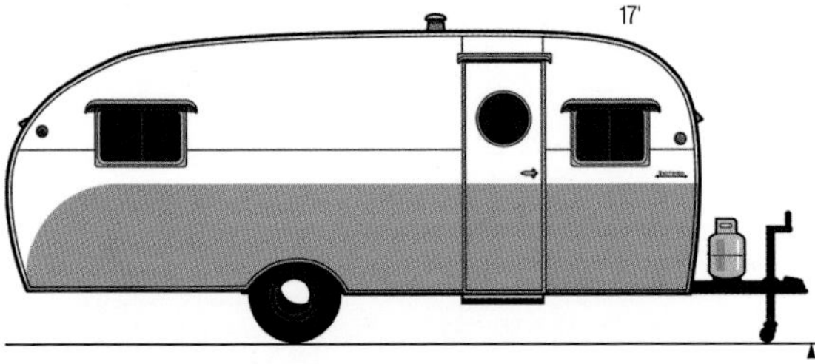

17'

1950
19–A

22.5'

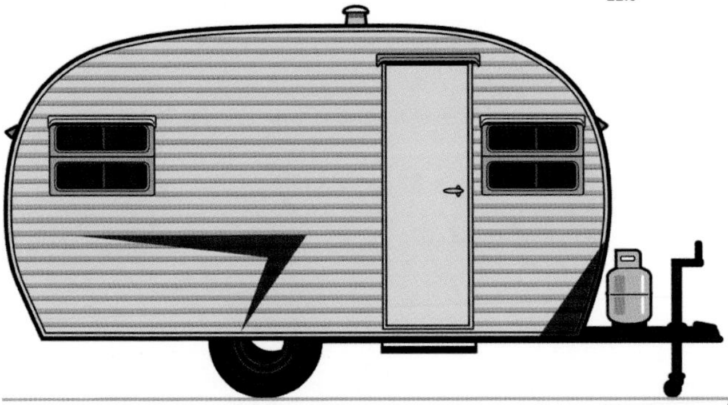

16'

1957 Trotwood Cub Deluxe

The elegant canned ham–shaped 1956 Cub Deluxe had an unpainted aluminum body decorated with two slashes of color on its sides. It was self-contained, and some floor plans had a dinette and all-in-one stove, sink, and oven unit. There was a second exit door on the port-side rear of the trailer.

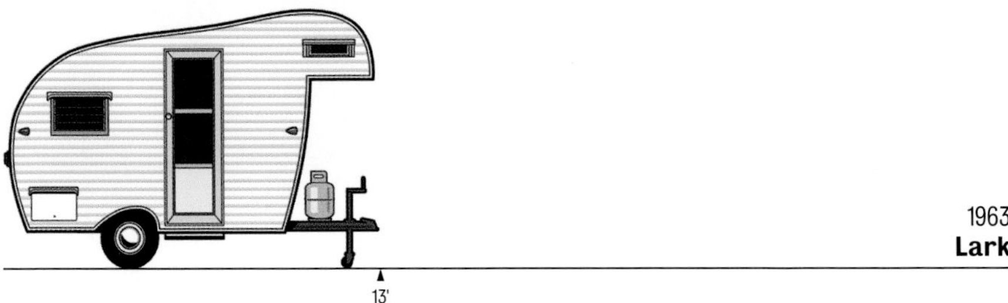

U *thru* Z

UTOPIA

Front wraparound jalousie windows gave Pan-O-Ramic models a wide view

All models have a trunk back with a bold angled graphic trimmed in aluminum

Utopia (1963–72)

Utopia Coach Corporation • Elkhart, Indiana

The Utopia Coach Corporation started production of their trailers in a small workshop in June 1963. By November of that same year they had moved to a 5,500-square-foot plant. In 1966 they constructed a 15,000-square-foot plant in Elkhart, Indiana, where they attempted to develop the perfect trailer.

Utopia initially built two trailer lines. The Economy line of canned ham–style models had a rounded roofline and came in 15- and 17-foot models. They had an all-aluminum exterior with a two-tone baked-enamel paint design and a trunk.

The Pan-O-Ramic line's models, made in 15½- to 28-foot lengths, were all self-contained, had a large trunk, and notably panoramic windows. Their other noteworthy traits included a door with large jalousie windows, polished aluminum trim, and automobile taillights.

While Utopia trailers were distributed mainly in the Midwest, in the mid-1960s several shipments of the trailers headed out to the western United States via railroad. Truck campers and the Executive trailer line name appeared fleetingly in ads in the late 1960s. The brand discontinued production with the 1972 model year.

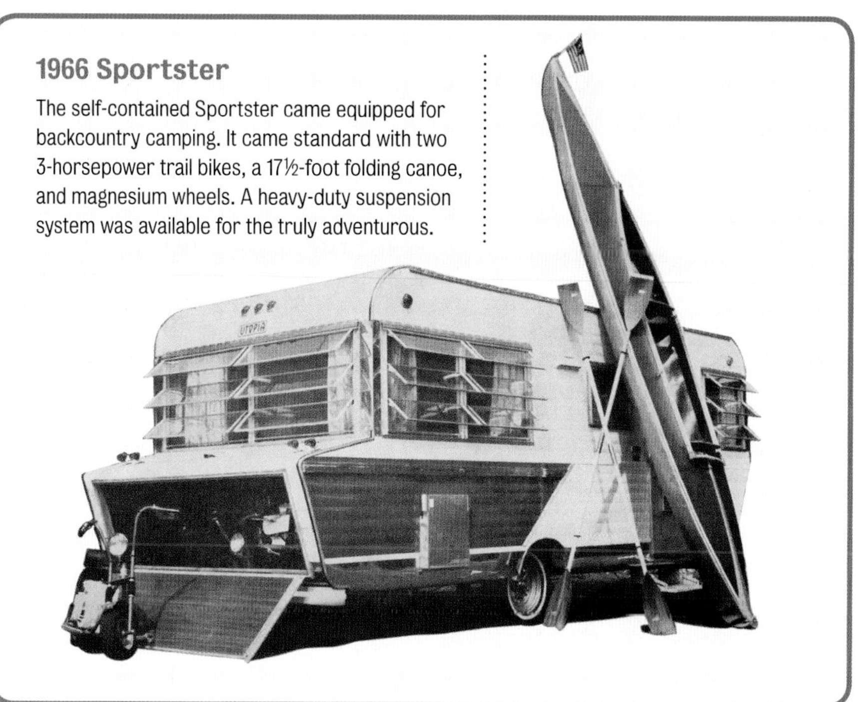

1966 Sportster

The self-contained Sportster came equipped for backcountry camping. It came standard with two 3-horsepower trail bikes, a 17½-foot folding canoe, and magnesium wheels. A heavy-duty suspension system was available for the truly adventurous.

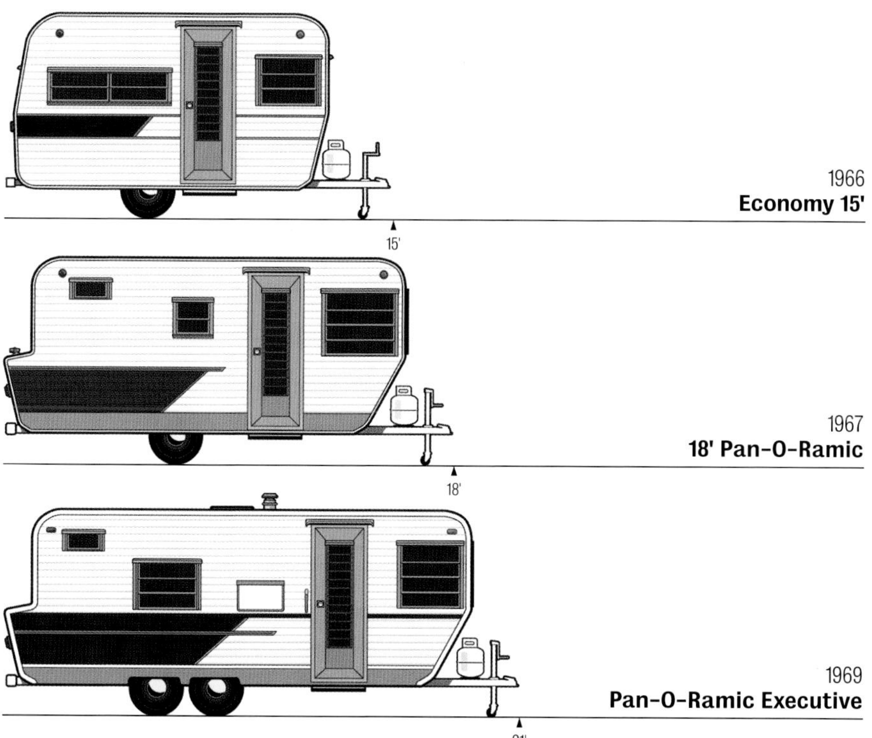

Vagabond

Bread loaf–style models with sheet aluminum sides (1931–46)

A die formed aluminum body with a rounded roof and rear end (1946–mid-1950s)

Vagabond (1931–late 1960s)

Vagabond Coach Manufacturing Company • New Hudson, Michigan

Vagabond coaches from the early 1930s, like other trailers of the time, had a Masonite skin that while strong in the short term couldn't endure cold, hot, and wet weather conditions for very long. The durability of the trailers increased dramatically in 1936, when Vagabond began skinning their models with sheet aluminum.

In the late 1930s, a Vagabond ad said, "People expect more in a Vagabond, and get it. All have truss-type steel frames. All have hydraulic jacks. All have trunks in the rear. All have turret tops. All have optional permanent beds. All have full insulation."

The 1940 models had a forced-air heating system that sent warm air through a vented double floor. In 1942 the company issued the 22-foot Victory model to dealers nationwide. The trailers were made by the thousands to house itinerant military and civilian workers.

The 1946 Vagabonds introduced a new die-formed all-aluminum exterior, a lighter frame, and a more spacious interior. The company turned to mobile home construction in the mid-1950s. In 1978, George Miles, a long-time Vagabond executive, was inducted into the RV/MH Hall of Fame.

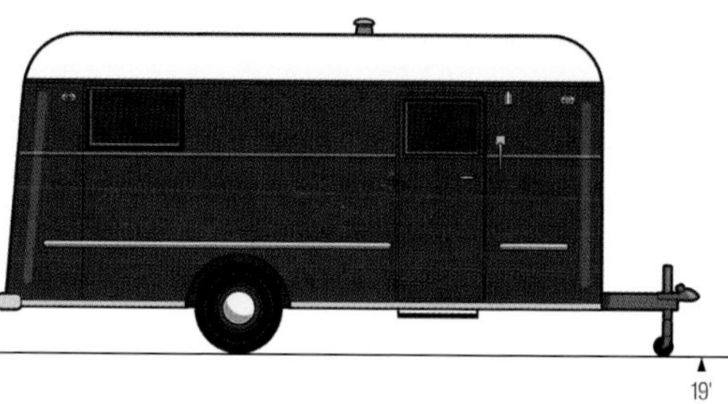

19'

1941
Model 16

Hobo Emblem

A cartoon rendering of a stereotypical hobo wandered across Vagabond badges and emblems. His hunched figure branded Vagabond as an essential part of a carefree, nomadic trailering life.

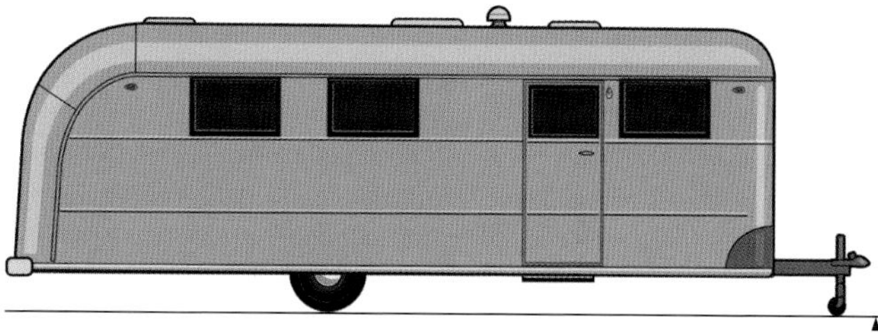

26'

1946
Model 23

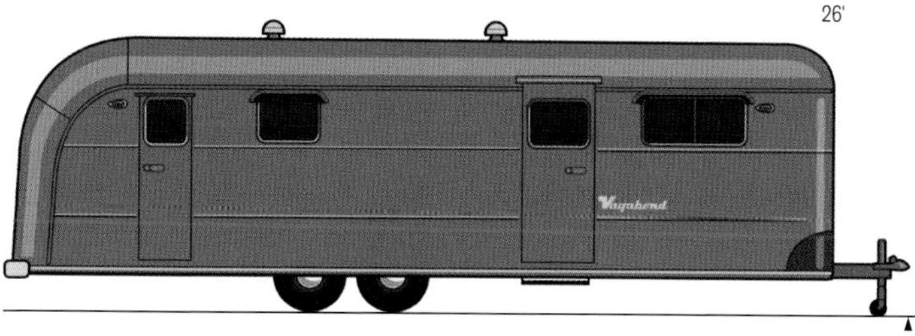

29'

1949
Model 262

22'

1950
Model 19

WESTCRAFT

Westcraft (1932–55)

George T. Hall Company • Los Angeles, California

The George T. Hall Company, a pioneer in trailer manufacturing and distribution, introduced the Westcraft trailer brand in the early 1930s. Models carried names of California towns, mountains, and trees that rolled off the tongue: Coronado, Montecito, Shasta, Sequoia, and Yosemite.

The Westcraft line of smooth-skinned bread loaf models featured a clerestory roof called a Pullman top. The roof's design gave it 6 feet 4 inches of headroom and improved cross-ventilation throughout its luxurious interior.

The company took part in defense programs during World War II. The postwar Westcraft line returned to civilian life with all-metal frames and aluminum bodies. The trailers would prove to be long lived, lighter, and stronger.

In 1946, Westcraft debuted the less expensive Westwood trailer line. According to its ads, the new models featured the "exacting craftsmanship of aircraft design and construction." They had a typical bread loaf–shaped body and roof. Westwoods only lasted through 1948.

The George T. Hall Company stopped making Westcraft trailers in 1955. Today the company sells automation and control systems, equipment, and services.

Westwoods have a plain bread loaf body

Westcrafts feature a Pullman-style roof

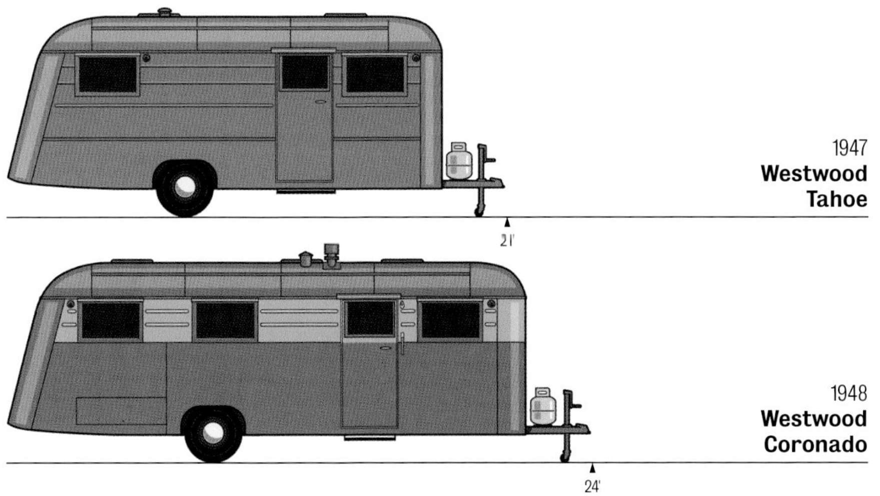

1947
Westwood
Tahoe

1948
Westwood
Coronado

How to Tell a Westcraft from a Westwood

Westcraft and Westwood trailers shared body types, similar window placement, and some model names. The easiest way to distinguish between the two lines is to look at the roof. If it has a Pullman-style top at the center of its roof it's a Westcraft.

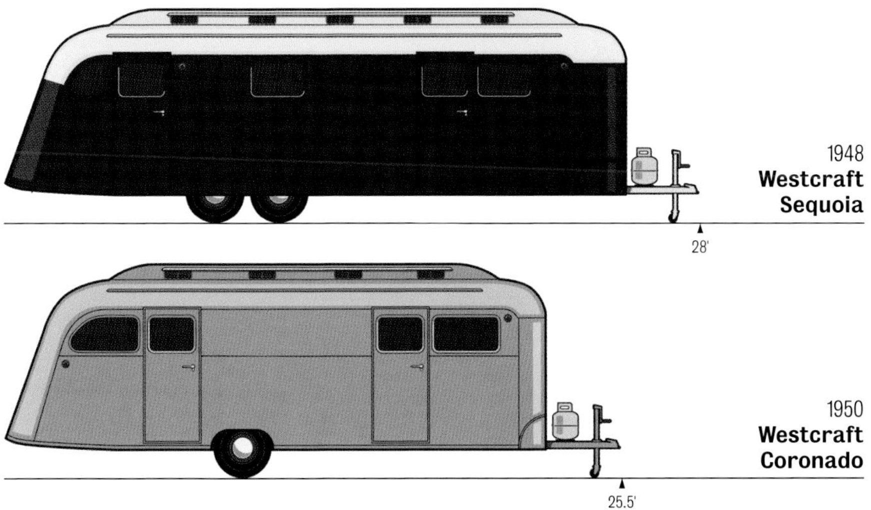

1948
Westcraft
Sequoia

1950
Westcraft
Coronado

Winnebago (1958–present)

Winnebago Industries, Inc. • Forest City, Iowa

John K. Hanson wanted Forest City, the county seat of Winnebago County, Iowa, to thrive. Since the end of World War II, the area had been losing farm workers to factory jobs in distant cities. The city wanted to build a foundation for future economic and population growth.

So a group of local businessmen led by Hanson made a deal to build Aljo-brand trailers for the Midwest market. They built their first trailers in 1958. The firm floundered when a dissenting group left the organization and formed Forest City Industries, Inc. (see page 139).

By 1960, Winnebago offered free delivery to all points in the lower 48 states, and through 1964 had a "W" painted across their front end. Winnebago trailers had wood frames through 1965. Later models used Thermo-Panel construction methods. The panels required no frame and made the trailers up to 30 percent lighter.

Winnebago announced a new series of motor homes in 1966. They continued to make trailers until the early 1980s. John K. Hanson was inducted into the RV/MH Hall of Fame in 1983. In 2010, Winnebago reintroduced travel trailers to its line.

A bold "W" on the front, flowing into stripes on the sides (1958–64)

Angular styles were introduced in the mid-1960s, with the "W" graphic moving to the sides

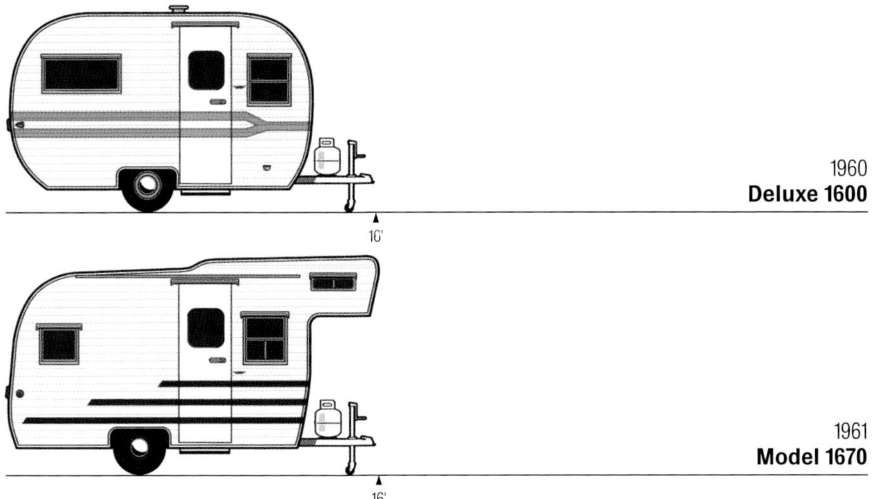

1960
Deluxe 1600

1961
Model 1670

1966 Winnebago Model 217

Built using new Thermo-Panel construction materials, the 1966 Model 217 was lighter and stronger than previous Winnebagos, but still proudly displayed a bold "W" on its sides—arguably the most recognized symbol in the history of recreational vehicles.

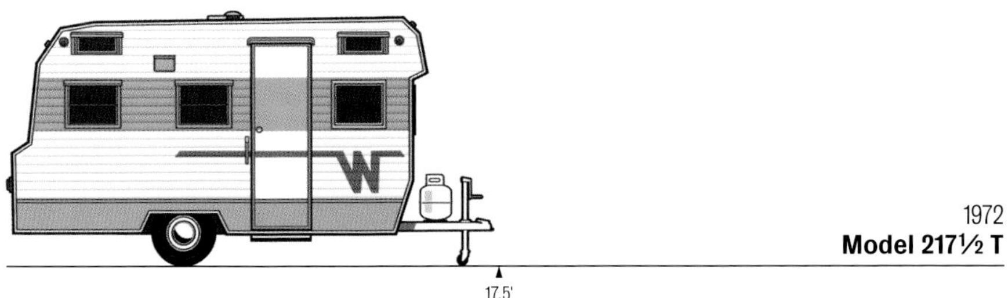

1972
Model 217½ T

YELLOWSTONE
COACH CO. ELKHART, IND.

Caravan shaped with a round or rounded door window, Yellowstones featured bare aluminum skins up to the early 1960s

The distinct stamped badge mounted forward of the door

Yellowstone (1945–90)

Yellowstone Coach Company • Wakarusa / Elkhart, Indiana

Elmer Weaver, the founder of the Yellowstone Coach Company, probably took a lot of time naming his new company in 1945. After all, choosing a name can set the tone of an organization for years to come. He chose wisely by naming his trailers after Yellowstone National Park. The park was the first national park in the United States and a well-known tourist destination.

Yellowstone built trailers for both vacationers and long-term travelers. Models in the mid-1950s came in 19- and 23-foot lengths with two doors. They had a bare aluminum body, an all-birch interior, and apartment-sized appliances.

In 1960 it added a 16-foot model and a 27-foot model. All of Yellowstone's trailers were available on a made-to-order basis. Most customers ordered their trailers wholly self-contained and ready to travel to any location.

The new 1963 line erupted in color and models. Yellowstone trailers for the first time came painted with a two-tone enamel exterior, and the new 13-, 16-, and 19-foot models had a cabover option. Truck campers, park models, fifth-wheel trailers, and motor homes carried the Yellowstone name until 1990.

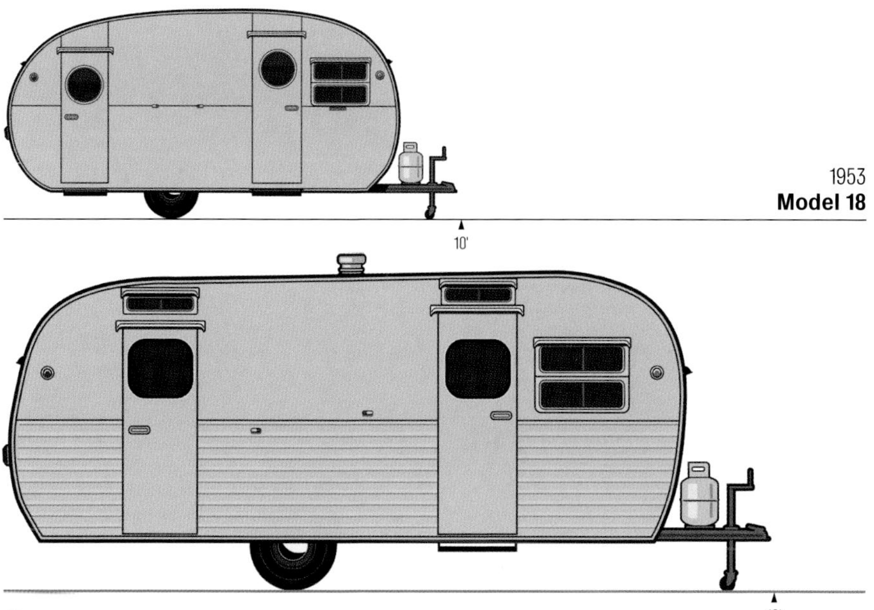

1953
Model 18

1957 Yellowstone Model 19B

Yellowstone ads claimed “the most liveability in a trailer designed for travel.” The Model 19B had a private dressing room, a full-sized bath, and an apartment-sized gas range. Campfire storytellers swear that Yellowstones were the trailer brand of choice for carnival barkers, clowns, and magicians.

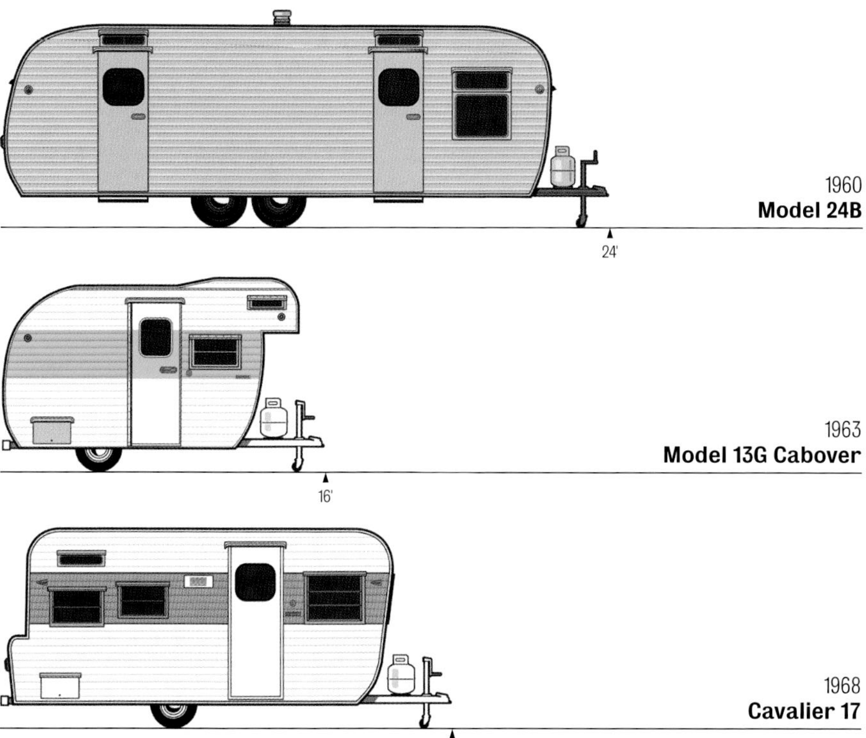

1960
Model 24B

1963
Model 13G Cabover

1968
Cavalier 17

A caravan shaped body similar to Boles-Aero models

Beveled ribs run horizontally on their aluminum sides and front

Zenith (1956–early 1960s)

Boles-Aero, Inc. • Burbank, California

Throughout their history, Boles-Aero made riveted aircraft-style models and sold them as high-end, high-quality, and high-priced trailers. In 1956, Boles-Aero sought to increase the depth of their trailer line with the introduction of the new Zenith trailer brand.

Zenith trailers were lower-priced versions of the Boles-Aero line. They looked similar on the outside, but their construction, materials, and furnishings were more like those of a vacation trailer than a trailer that could serve for long-term travel or living.

The caravan-shaped Zeniths came in lengths from 16 to 35 feet and appeared to have wood frames. They had all-aluminum skin and louvered windows in their door. A 1957 Boles-Aero advertisement claimed that "every Zenith is tow-tested to track straight and true. With freedom from side-sway and sure stopping power, you'll arrive at your destination rested and ready for fun."

By 1960, the two Boles-Aero lines seemed to compete with each other. They came in many overlapping sizes and the quality of the Zenith line neared that of the more expensive Boles-Aero trailers. The Zenith model name was folded back into the Boles-Aero line in the early '60s.

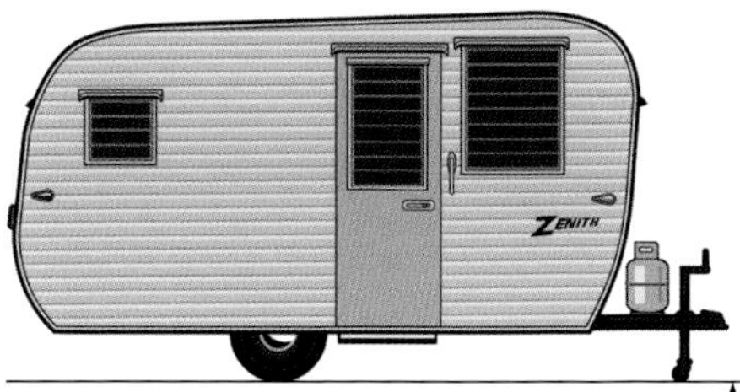

1956
Model 16

16'

Zenith/Boles-Aero

This 1957 ad shows how Boles-Aero marketed Zenith trailers to dealers as a lower-priced companion line to the Boles-Aero models that they were already selling on their lot.

It was a win-win situation for the manufacturer and the dealer. Boles-Aero kept competing brands *off* the lot and dealers kept potential customers *on* the lot.

Offering the new Zenith line would result in more sales and more satisfied customers because the dealer could be sure of the quality of Boles-Aero products. And the differences between the two trailer lines were only in the details.

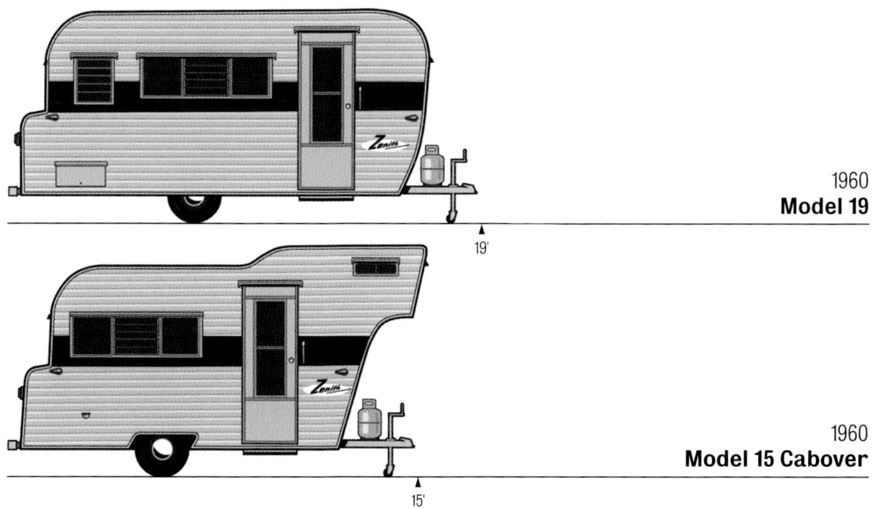

1960
Model 19

19'

1960
Model 15 Cabover

15'

United

United (1946–late 1950s)

United Manufacturers, Inc. • Williamston, Michigan

The founders of United Manufacturers, Inc. got their start building war housing during World War II. In 1946 they began making aluminum-sided mobile homes. They came in 15- and 16-foot vacation-sized versions and longer year-round-living lengths. In 1950, United introduced a 35-foot-long, 8-foot-wide "house trailer" to the market. Today it would be called a manufactured home.

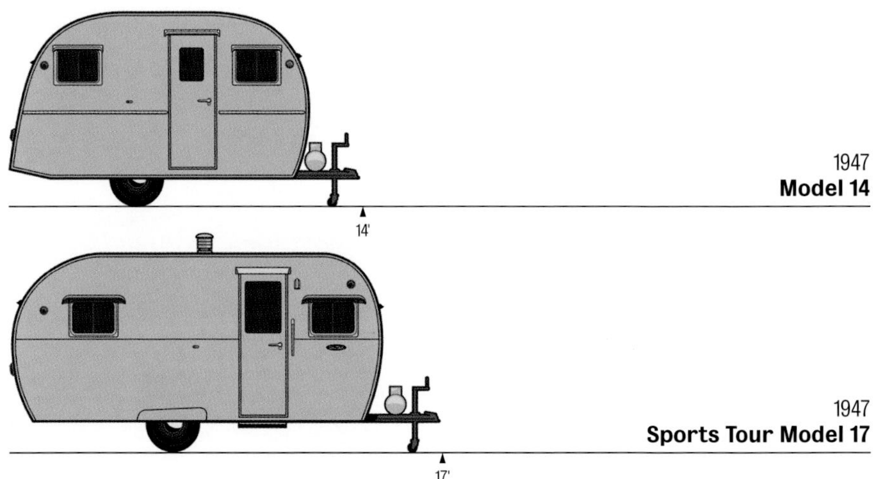

VA-KA-SHUN-ETTE

Va-ka-shun-ette (1947–65)

Zollinger Trailer Company • Elkhart, Indiana

Adolph and Bernice Zollinger founded the Zollinger Trailer Company as a trailer repair company. The first trailer Zollinger sold was a rugged all-aluminum canned ham. The company focused on making small vacation trailers until the mid-1950s. In 1957 luxurious models began to be added to the line.

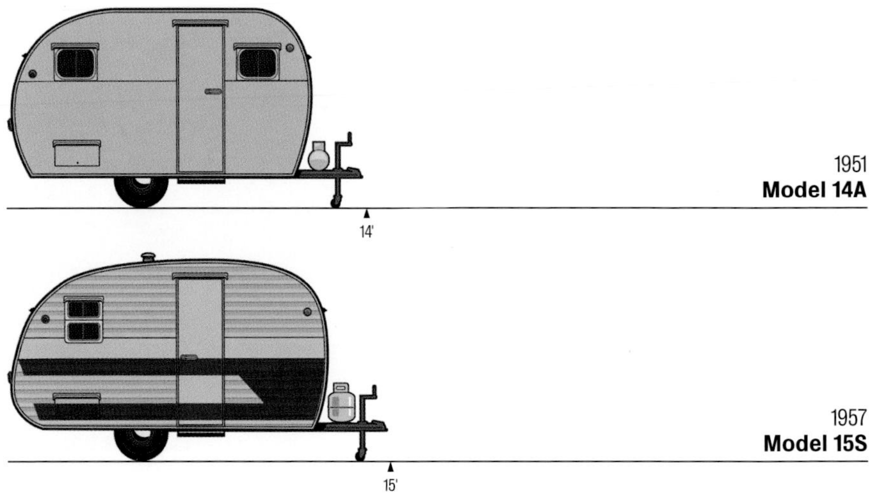

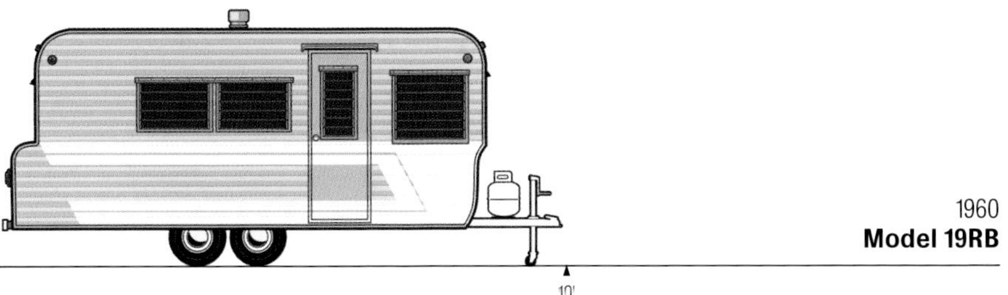

1960
Model 19RB

Wally Byam's Holiday (1954–55)

Airstream, Inc. • Jackson Center, Ohio

Wally Byam designed the Holiday to be similar to trailers he had seen while traveling in Europe. He had it built as a test for the American market. Instead of having a streamlined body like an Airstream trailer, the Holiday was a flat-sided canned ham–style model. It carried Byam's name so as not to dilute the Airstream brand.

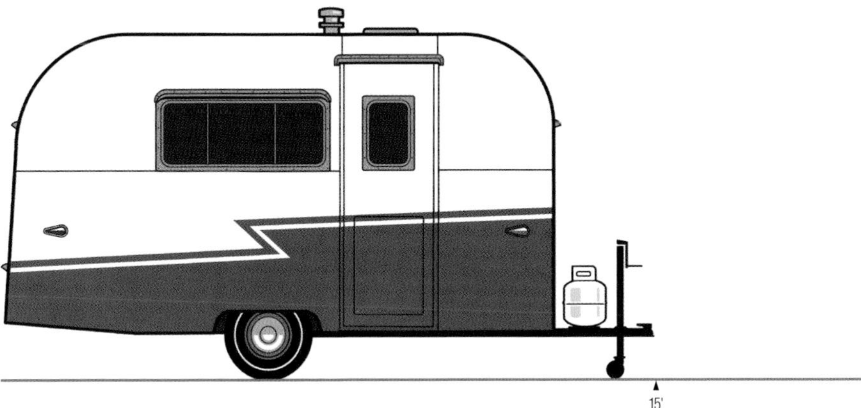

1955 Holiday

The 15-foot Holiday had a two-tone painted aluminum body riveted to a mostly aluminum frame. Standard equipment included a butane stove, oil or propane heater, and chemical toilet. Holidays could sleep five close friends in a convertible dinette, a rear bed, and a bunk.

Westerner (1952–late 1950s)

Westfield, Inc. • Azusa, California

The Westerner brand is best known for making 15-foot canned ham vacation trailers. They could be bought at the factory or from trailer dealerships in Southern California. Although Westerner trailers were lightweight, they were said to be "strongly built and able to withstand fast travel."

1957
15' Deluxe

WILDERNESS

Wilderness (1972–present)

Fleetwood Enterprises, Inc. • Riverside, California

The Wilderness line advertised itself as being comfortable and convenient family vacation trailers. They came in a wide variety of models and floor plans. In the 1970s, the Wilderness brand emphasized sleek styling designed to complement the look of their tow vehicles.

1973 Wilderness Model 18

The Wilderness, Prowler, and Terry trailer lines were close relatives, and except for their different color palettes, they looked nearly the same to the untrained eye. In addition to logos on the front and back of a Wilderness trailer, its wheel well guard displayed a “W.”

Williams Craft (1964–late 1970s)

Williams Manufacturing Company, Inc. • Arlington, Texas

The most recognizable trailers built by Williams Craft are their mid-1960s boxy-style models. They had a “baked enamel lifetime aluminum exterior” with a band of color on their sides and a door that featured a large triangle-shaped window. The company also made truck canopies, truck campers, chassis-mounted campers, and watercraft.

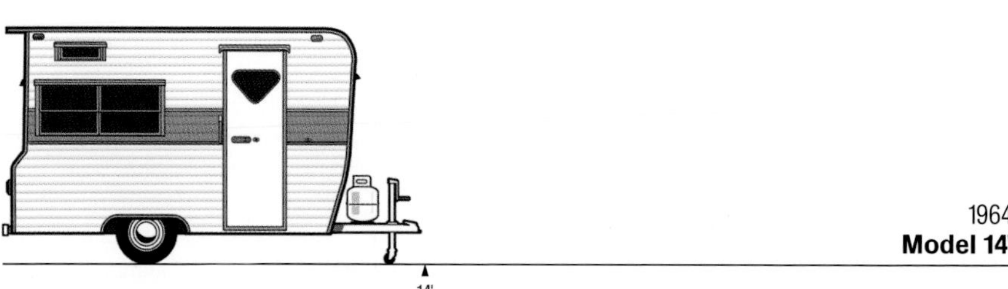

1964
Model 14'

1968
Model 16' Low-Profile

Zimmer (1938–late 1980s)

Zimmer Boat and Trailer Company • Detroit, Michigan

The Zimmer brand of trailers first appeared in the late 1930s. The line disappeared during World War II, then reappeared in 1945. Zimmer bread loaf–style trailers had an all-aluminum body, a reinforced top, and a balanced chassis. By the late 1950s, Zimmer stopped making trailers and evolved into a manufactured-housing company.

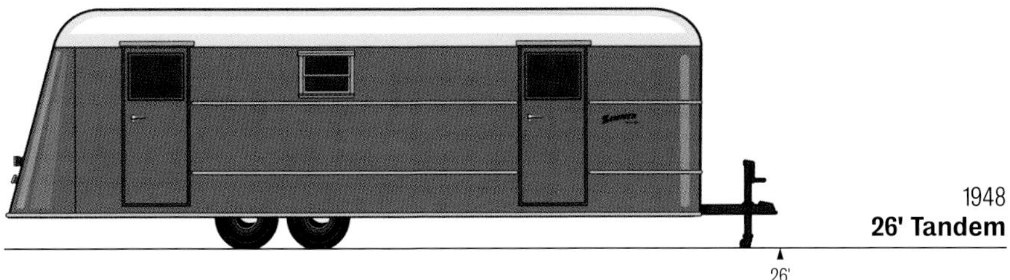

1948
26' Tandem

Zipper (1957–69)

Zipper Inc. • Clinton, South Carolina

The story goes that the founders of Zipper Inc. were former Shasta employees. Whether true or not, some Zipper models did have the shape and wing-like stylings of the Shasta line. The inside of a Zipper had birch paneling and a letter "Z" routed into a closet cabinet. In 1957 a Zipper travel trailer could be bought for $795 with $99 down or rented for $7 per day.

1964 Zipper Model 12

An advertisement for the 1964 Zipper Model 12 claimed that it had up-to-the-minute appliances, jalousie and awning windows, and a unique appearance. The Model 12's shape and triangle wings make the case that it's descended from a Shasta Compact (see page 241).

1961 Shasta Compact

1956 Rainbow CHRIS HART

1960 Relic Reissue JAYNE BAROCELA

1951 Roadmaster RON AND NANCY ROBERTS

1962 Robin Hood STEVE AND BEA WELZBACKER

1956 Rod and Reel JIM AND MICHELLE PROCTOR

1937 Royal Wilhelm SKOT AND JUDY RANDALL

1967 Safari KATHY AND MIKE JONES

1958 Santa Fe FRANK AND CAROL POWELL

1946 Schult PAUL LACITINOLA

1959 Scotsman JIM AND LINDA TUTTLE

1962 Serro Scotty Sportsman Sr. DAN AND MINDY ZEN

1957 Serro Scotty Sportsman Jr. RV/MH HALL OF FAME

1961 Shasta Compact JOHN AND ALICE O'HARE

1956 Shasta 1500 LESLEY AND LEW PULS

1965 Shasta SLS JEFF AND MICHELLE NALL

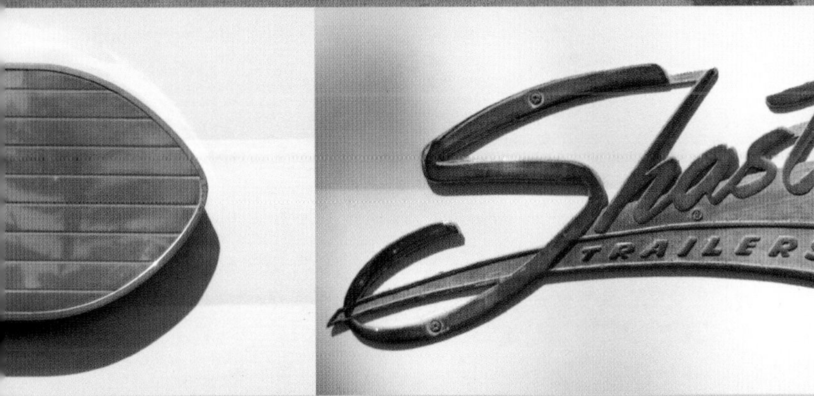

1969 Shasta Starflyte JESSICA PIERCE AND SEAN PAYNE

1960 Siesta MIKE AND DEBI BROCKETT

1949 Spartan Spartanette CRAIG AND PATTI HOLROYD

1949 Spartan Manor STAN JAMESON

1955 Starfire DAVID GONGORA

1963 Streamline Duke JOHN AND TAMIE BOERSEMA

1966 Streamline Prince CINDY BUSER

1959 Silver Streak Clipper CHRIS AND TRINA CHAPMAN

1952 Silver Streak Clipper TRAILER TRASH VINTAGE TRAILERS (LYNDEN, WASHINGTON)

1967 Silver Streak Atlas CATHY AND RAY SCOTT

1957 **Sportcraft** ROBERT DOUGLAS

1954 **Terry** DANIEL AND DEBORAH NESSIM

1972 **Terry** JULIA HIGGINS

1966 Thunderbird ROBERT DOUGLAS

1947 Tourette CARLOS AND SHERRY VIVAS

1954 Traveleze JEREMY CHINN AND KATY STONE

1959 Traveleze JOHN AND KRISTEN DAMAZIO

1947 Travelite BRIAN AND CATHY GEARY

1961 Trailorboat DAN MORLEY

1978 Trillium 4500 JEFF AND DONNA JOHANNSEN

1953 United PATRICIA CLARKE

1966 Utopia Pan-O-Ramic MATTHEW BRANDES

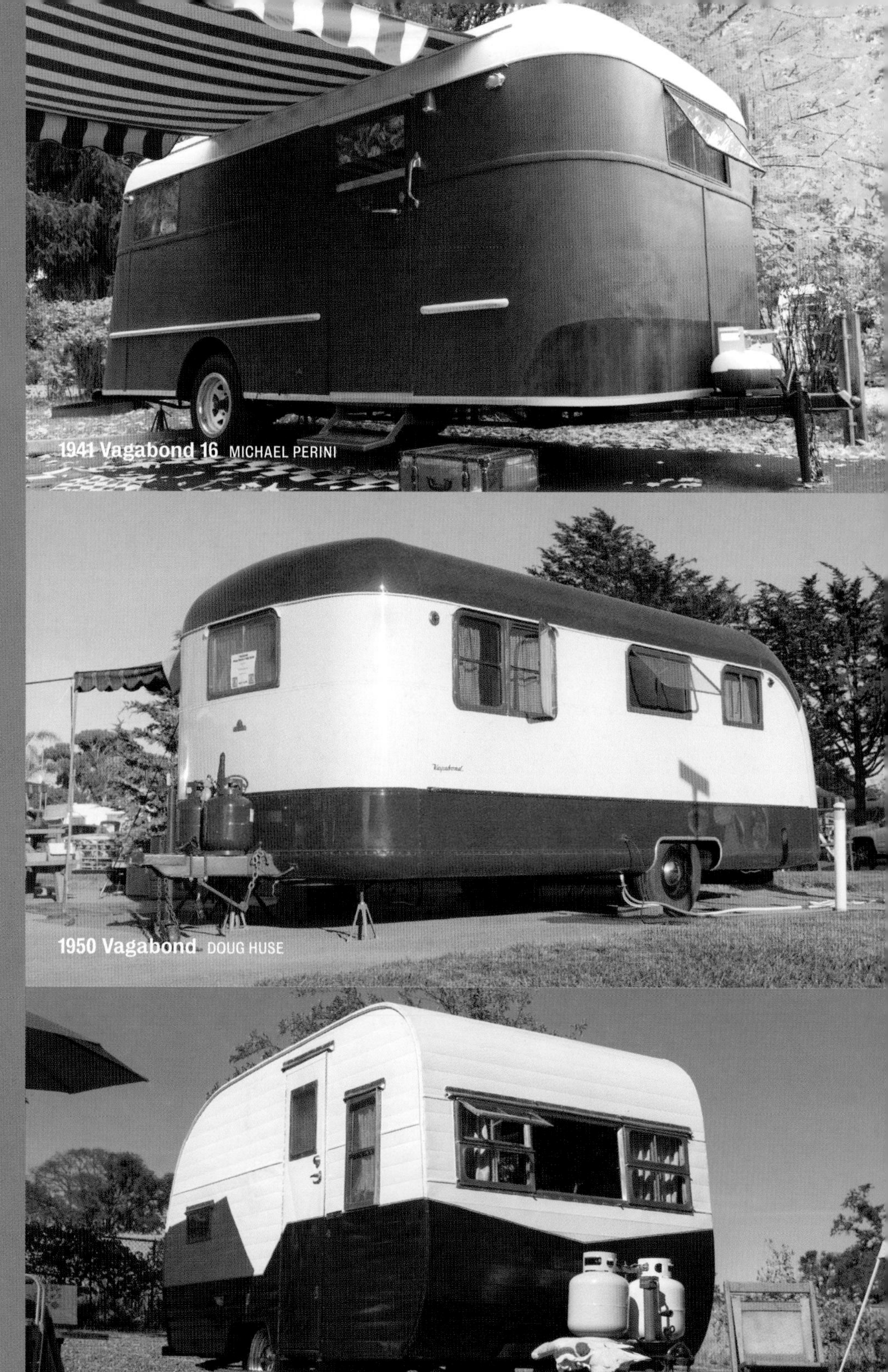

1941 Vagabond 16 MICHAEL PERINI

1950 Vagabond DOUG HUSE

1958 Westerner JOE AND CAROLE POLAND

1959 Winnebago KEN AND HAZIE STOLLMEYER

1956 Yellowstone STEVE AND RITA BABCOCK

1958 Zenith MOSELY MANOR (OAK GROVE, OREGON)

1950 Westcraft Coronado Pullman CHUCK AND TONI MILTENBERGER

1946 Westwood Coronado JASON AND ROCHELLE PALL

1950 Westcraft Tahoe JAY LEVIN

1947 Westwood Coronado GARY AND SALLY LODHOLM (BADGE AND INTERIOR)

STORIES FROM *the* FIELD

Have you ever wanted to run away from home? Vintage trailers allow you to do that and to take your home with you on your travels. But a vintage trailer can be much more than a house on wheels; it can be anything you imagine it to be.

When we rebuilt our first trailer we just wanted to go camping in style. What we found along the way was a lifestyle that honors the past and brings it into the present via a lot of sweat. And we got to meet a lot of different trailerites with different interests.

There are the old-school types who rebuilt their trailers to original specifications. Restoration experts who take the ruins of a trailer and turn it into a piece of camping heaven. Glampers who make their trailers shine with decorations. And those who clean up their trailers, give them a new paint job, and head down the road to the nearest rally.

True nostalgia lovers make their trailers into altars to the mid-twentieth century, and many vintage trailers become an integral part of a small business's brand. There are food trailers serving a full menu of the world's cuisine, trailers that during the day are strewn with vintage clothing, and some that are rented out as backyard getaways for tourists. You can spot these reimagined trailers just about anywhere across the country. They pop up on street corners, and at rallies, events, and fairs.

Throughout the field guide we've shown and written about how to spot standard models, but in the next few pages we highlight a handful of vintage trailers and their owners. There is a traveling museum, a rugged teardrop, a trailer event company, and a seaside resort. We can't wait to discover the many other stories about vintage trailers.

Mid Century Mobile Museum

Paul Lacitinola of *Vintage Camper Trailers* magazine and his family often tour the western United States with a 1955 Spartan Manor in tow. The rebuilt trailer is fully functional and equipped with a bathtub, toilet, bedroom, desk, and hundreds of pieces of vintage camping gear on display inside and out. Visitors are welcome to walk through the 28-foot, two-door, midcentury trailer while they reminisce about the gear they remember camping with growing up.

midcenturymobile.com

Sou'wester Historic Lodge and Vintage Travel Trailer Resort

Seaview, Washington

The Sou'wester Resort in historic Seaview, Washington, on the Long Beach Peninsula, includes a generous mix of accommodation types: suites, cabins, vintage travel trailers, RV spaces, and campsites. Vintage trailers include everything from a one-person rustic Shasta to a two-story mobile home called the African Queen. There's plenty of things to do too. Pacific Ocean beaches are only a block away, and there is live music, workshops, and an artist residency program.

souwesterlodge.com

Silvercloud Trailer Events®

Austin, Texas

Silvercloud Trailer Events® offers beer-tap trailer, photo booth, and mobile bar rentals in vintage Airstreams. The founders, Chris and Yvonne Johnson, are professional wedding photographers. In 2011 they converted a 1962 Airstream Bambi into a photo booth trailer and began a "party on wheels" journey to over 1,000 events since. Their growing fleet of trailers are popular attractions for events, weddings, and marketing tours around the country.

silvercloudtrailerevents.com

The Shank Family's Kenskill Kustom Kamper

Glendale, California

Owning a vintage trailer can give deep meaning to your life. For Larry Shank, who inherited his Jeep CJ-3B and Kenskill Kustom Kamper, it means carrying on his love for his parents. From a young age, Larry remembers his family exploring the rugged back-country of the southwestern United States. His father modified his Kustom Kamper with racks and mounts for carrying boats, extra fuel, and other sundries. Larry's parents passed in the early 2000s, but thanks to some rejuvenation, the Jeep and trailer are still going strong.

WHERE *the* TRAILERS WERE MADE

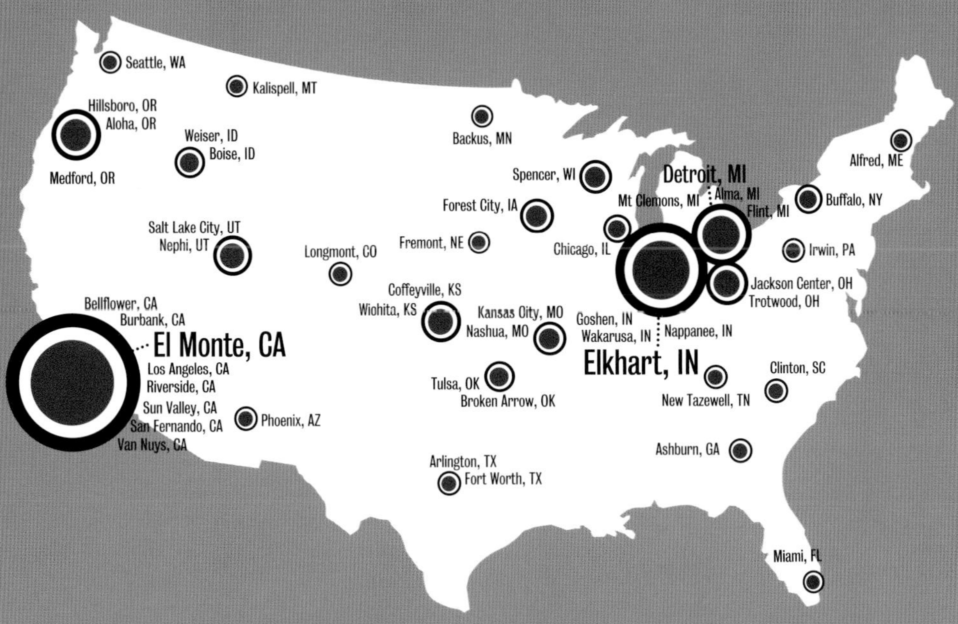

This map of the United States is a visual representation of where vintage trailer manufacturers that have entries in *The Illustrated Field Guide to Vintage Trailers* clustered during the mid-twentieth century. While not all company locations are shown on the map, two significant manufacturing centers are easy to see.

The Southern California area, centered in and around Los Angeles, was home to most of the all-aluminum streamlined models. Many of them grew out of the area's aircraft industry and practically fill up the "A" section in the field guide.

The northern Indiana area, with Elkhart at its heart, was influenced by Detroit and the automobile industry in the early 1930s. Many trailers, types, and brands flocked to the area in the past and today.

The Pacific Northwest was another hot spot of trailer manufacturing. The area produced some well-known travel trailer brands, like Aloha and Aladdin, and unique trailers, including the Holiday House and Kom-Pak.

GLOSSARY

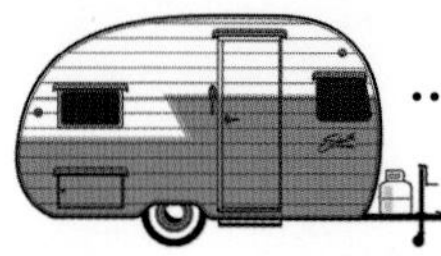

Aircraft / Streamlined: A trailer style that borrows aircraft design and construction techniques.

Art Moderne / Streamline Moderne: A design style known for its curving and long horizontal lines.

Atomic Age / Jet Age / Space Age: Cold war design styles that celebrated a technological future.

Badge: A metal plate engraved with the trailer's brand name and other information.

Barn Find: A vintage trailer that was found stored in a barn or building. Considered lucky.

Boondocking / Off Grid: Camping at a site without available water, electrical, or bathroom facilities.

Brand: A trailer line that had a different name than that of the manufacturing company.

Bread Loaf: Long, flat-sided trailers rounded off at the top like a loaf of bread.

Bump-Out / Trunk Back: A trunk or storage area that protrudes from the back of a trailer.

Bunk-Over / Cabover: A trailer with a sleeping area that extends out of the front of the trailer and over the hitch.

Canned Ham: Flat, aluminum-sided trailers with a round profile like a canned ham.

Canopy / Topper: A hard, protective, lightweight shell mounted on the bed of a pickup truck.

Caravan: 1. A style of trailer with the shape of an extended canned ham. 2. Name given to trailers in some countries outside of the United States. 3. Trailerists traveling together in an organized group.

Clerestory / Pullman-Style Roof / Trolley Top: A raised roof with windows in the center of a trailer.

Coach: A long, streamlined trailer with a rounded body and roofline.

Crimped Seam / Pittsburgh Seam: A seam that clamps metal sheets together and hides their exposed metal edges.

Daveno: A sofa or couch.

Dinette: A dining table area that can be converted into a sleeping area.

Dolly Wheel / Slimp Wheel: A wheel and suspension system that sits beneath the trailer's tongue and coupler, thereby decreasing a trailer's tongue weight.

Double-Wall Construction: A wall frame with panels on its inside and outside surfaces.

Dropped Floor: A lowered floor designed to decrease a trailer's overall height and make it garageable.

Fiberglass Egg: An egg-shaped trailer made of molded fiberglass.

Field Camping: Camping in an open field with no designated spots.

Fifth Wheel: A type of trailer that connects to a coupling installed in the bed of a pickup truck.

Garageable: A trailer designed to fit in a single-car garage.

Gas Light: A fixture or lantern that burns fuel, such as butane or propane gas, to produce light.

Gaucho: A couch that converts into a bed.

Glamper: A person that owns a vintage trailer decorated in a glamorous style.

Glue-and-Screw Construction: Trailer walls built using glue and screws, rather than nails.

Googie: A design style influenced by car culture, jets, the atomic age, and the jet age.

Jalousie / Louver Windows: A row of angled glass slats set in a single window frame.

Masonite: A low-cost and flexible pressboard often used to side trailers in the 1930s and '40s.

Midcentury: Referring to a design, style, or artifact from approximately the 1940s through the 1960s.

Mobile Home / Park Model: A trailer that still has wheels, but used for long-term living in one location.

Model: A specific trailer with distinguishing characteristics in a trailer line.

Motor Home: A motor vehicle with living accommodations.

Pop-Up Camper: A trailer with a hard top that is lifted into position via cranks to a full-height trailer.

Recreational Vehicle (RV): Any motor home, trailer, fifth-wheel, pop-up camper, or truck camper meant for travel and temporary living.

Rolled Front Roofline: An aluminum roof extension that rounds over the top front of the trailer.

Self-Contained / Utility-Independent: A trailer that can go off grid with its own water supply tank and bathroom facilities, DC electrical system and lights, and propane-powered appliances and lights.

Shore Power: AC electrical power provided to a trailer from a camping or parking site.

Skin / Shell: The material, often aluminum, that covers a trailer's frame.

Teardrop: A small trailer with a shape like a teardrop, with a sleeping area in its main body and a kitchen in the rear.

Tent Camper: A trailer that has a tent-like top.

Three-way refrigerator: A refrigerator that can operate using AC or DC current, or propane.

Tongue Weight: The weight of the trailer when connected to a tow vehicle's hitch.

Trailerite / Trailerist: A person who vacations or lives in a trailer.

Travel Trailer: A trailer used for vacations or longer-term living.

Truck Camper: A type of RV tall enough to stand in that includes living accommodations and is designed to slide into the bed of a pickup truck.

Unique Style: A trailer style that pushed the boundaries of design and construction techniques of the era.

Vacation Trailer: A trailer, generally lighter and under 30 feet long, meant for periodic travel.

Vehicle Identification Number (VIN): A number that identifies the manufacturer, length, model, and date of a vehicle's manufacture.

Vintage Trailer: A trailer built from the early 1930s through 1980.

Whale Tail: The nine-panel end cap on the back of mid-1950s Airstream models made in California.

Wheel Well: The area that covers the tires under the trailer.

ACKNOWLEDGMENTS

Here's to the people we've met on the road who inspired us, shared their knowledge, or otherwise pointed us in the right direction as we wrote *The Illustrated Field Guide to Vintage Trailers*:

First and foremost we are thankful to everyone that let us photograph their trailer. The pictures provide an invaluable compass for trailer identification. It took us several years to gather all the photos, but we soon learned that buying a vintage trailer is often just the beginning of a life-changing journey for many of us. Thank you for sharing your stories too.

And special thanks to our proofreaders and expert fact-checkers at every rally. You lead us to rare trailers—often parked only a few feet away—that we were able to share in the field guide.

We made several trips to the RV/MH Hall of Fame in Elkhart, Indiana, where we were welcomed by president Darryl Searer and his staff into their library for days at a time. We appreciate both their hospitality and access to their invaluable collection of books and magazines.

Thank you to these other important contributors:

Jill Angle
Jayne Barocela, Relic Custom Trailers
Bob Cooper, Gibbs Smith
Al Hesselbart
Sharon Jameson
Chris and Yvonne Johnson, Silvercloud Trailer Events®
Paul and Caroline Lacitinola, *Vintage Camper Trailers* magazine
Kyle LeMire, Elle Poindexter, and their daughter, Paloma
Marie Murphy and David Hackney
René Perret and Jeremy Ralston, Down River Vintage Trailer Restoration
Larry Shank
Sou'wester Historic Lodge and Vintage Travel Trailer Resort
Gordy Seeley and Kate Dyer-Seeley
Meg Storey
Deirdre Thompson
Tin Can Tourists
Dave and Lori White

Special thanks to Douglas Keister for writing *Teardrops and Tiny Trailers.*

PHOTO CREDITS

All photos by Carl Jameson except:

Matthew Brandes: Pages 272 (top), 301 (Utopia)

Morgan Casner: Page 192 (bottom)

Robert Douglas: Pages 114 (Arrow Little Chief), 115 (Banner), 128 (DeCamp), 130, 142 (top), 208 (FAN), 272 (bottom), 298 (Sportcraft)

Jennifer G.: Pages 178 (bottom), 219 (Little Gem Bugg)

Pam Glass: Page 223 (1965 Mobile Scout)

Sasha Glass: Pages 142 (bottom), 178 (top), 212 (Go Tag-A-Long), 222 (Little Gem)

Chuck High: Page 282 (top)

Rob and Mechelle Merrill: Page 228 (top, bottom), 288 (Rancho El Rae)

Toni Miltenberger: Page 39 (Airstream Silver Cloud)

Paul Lacitinola: Pages 14 (bottom left), 53 (Aloha World's Fair Model, courtesy of Northcraft Vintage Trailer Restoration), 290 (Schult)

Gary Olguin: Page 104 (top, bottom)

Carrie Parsons: Pages 186 (top), 223 (1964 Mobile Scout)

Larry Shank: Page 310

Silvercloud Trailer Events®: Page 309

Sou'Wester Historic Lodge and Vintage Travel Trailer Resort: Page 308

Leonardo and Christy Taylor: Page 186 (bottom)

Bob Thompson: Pages 5, 11, 12 (top left, top right), 14 (top right, middle), 20, 111 (Aladdin Sultan's Castle)

Deirdre Thompson: Pages 175 (top), 221 (Kit Companion)

CHECKLIST *of* TRAILERS

Check off the vintage trailers you've seen on the road, at rallies, or in the field. Don't forget to note the date and the number found. You'll likely see some manufacturer's names more than others, but that only makes spotting the rare trailer more memorable. Happy hunting!

- ❑ Ace
- ❑ Aero Flite
- ❑ Airfloat
- ❑ Airlight
- ❑ Airstream
- ❑ Aladdin
- ❑ Aljoa/Aljo
- ❑ Alma
- ❑ Aloha
- ❑ Alumacoach
- ❑ Anderson
- ❑ Argosy
- ❑ Aristocrat
- ❑ Arrow
- ❑ Arrowhead
- ❑ Avalair
- ❑ Avalon
- ❑ Avion
- ❑ Banner
- ❑ Barth
- ❑ Bee Line
- ❑ Beemer
- ❑ Bell
- ❑ Bellwood
- ❑ Benroy
- ❑ Blazon
- ❑ Boler
- ❑ Boles-Aero
- ❑ Bonanza
- ❑ Bowlus
- ❑ Broken Arrow
- ❑ CabinCar
- ❑ Cal-Craft

- ❏ Cardinal
- ❏ Caveman
- ❏ Century
- ❏ Clipper
- ❏ Coachmen
- ❏ Comanche
- ❏ Comet
- ❏ Compact Jr.
- ❏ Corvette
- ❏ Covered Wagon
- ❏ Cozy Cruiser
- ❏ Cree
- ❏ Crown
- ❏ Curtis Wright
- ❏ Dalton
- ❏ Davron
- ❏ DeCamp
- ❏ Detroiter
- ❏ DeVille
- ❏ Driftwood
- ❏ Easy Travler
- ❏ El Rey
- ❏ Elcar
- ❏ Empire
- ❏ Excel
- ❏ FAN
- ❏ Fiber Stream
- ❏ Field and Stream
- ❏ Fireball
- ❏ Fleetwing
- ❏ Fleetwood
- ❏ Forester
- ❏ Franklin
- ❏ Frolic
- ❏ Garway/Garwood
- ❏ Glider
- ❏ Go Tag-A-Long
- ❏ Go-Lite
- ❏ Great Western
- ❏ Hanson
- ❏ Hayes
- ❏ Hi-Lo
- ❏ Hiawatha
- ❏ Holiday House
- ❏ Holiday Rambler
- ❏ Holly
- ❏ Honorbuilt
- ❏ Hummingbird
- ❏ Ideal
- ❏ Jayco
- ❏ Jet

- ❑ Jewel
- ❑ Ken-Craft
- ❑ Kenskill
- ❑ King
- ❑ Kit
- ❑ Kom-Pak
- ❑ Kozy Coach
- ❑ Lakewood
- ❑ Layton
- ❑ Liberty
- ❑ Lighthouse
- ❑ LintzCraft
- ❑ Little Caesar
- ❑ Little Gem/Gem
- ❑ "M" System
- ❑ Main-Line
- ❑ Mallard
- ❑ Masterbilt
- ❑ Mercury
- ❑ Metzendorf
- ❑ Mobil-Glide
- ❑ Mobile Scout
- ❑ Monitor
- ❑ Mustang
- ❑ Nashua
- ❑ New Moon
- ❑ Nomad
- ❑ Norris
- ❑ Northwest Coach
- ❑ Nu-Wa
- ❑ Oasis
- ❑ Owosso
- ❑ Palace
- ❑ Pathfinder
- ❑ Phoenix
- ❑ Pierce-Arrow
- ❑ Play-Mor
- ❑ PleasureCraft
- ❑ Prairie Schooner
- ❑ Prowler
- ❑ Rainbow
- ❑ Rancho El Rae
- ❑ Red Dale
- ❑ Ritz-Craft
- ❑ Roadmaster
- ❑ RoadRunner
- ❑ Robin Hood
- ❑ Rod and Reel
- ❑ Rollohome
- ❑ Roycraft
- ❑ Safari

- ❑ Santa Fe
- ❑ Scamp
- ❑ Schult
- ❑ Scotsman
- ❑ Serro Scotty
- ❑ Shasta
- ❑ Siesta
- ❑ Silver Streak
- ❑ Skyline
- ❑ Southland
- ❑ Spartan
- ❑ Sportcraft
- ❑ Starcraft
- ❑ Streamline
- ❑ SunCruiser
- ❑ Superior
- ❑ Swiss Colony
- ❑ Talisman
- ❑ Terry
- ❑ Thunderbird Castles
- ❑ Tour-A-Home
- ❑ Tourette
- ❑ Trailblazer
- ❑ Trailorboat
- ❑ Traveleze
- ❑ Travelo
- ❑ Trillium
- ❑ Trotwood
- ❑ United
- ❑ Utopia
- ❑ Va-ka-shun-ette
- ❑ Vagabond
- ❑ Wally Byam's Holiday
- ❑ Westcraft
- ❑ Westerner
- ❑ Wilderness
- ❑ Williams Craft
- ❑ Winnebago
- ❑ Yellowstone
- ❑ Zenith
- ❑ Zimmer
- ❑ Zipper

Field Notes:

Bob Thompson studied drawing at the Otis Art Institute of the Parsons School of Design and earned a bachelor's degree in design at the University of Oregon. He started drawing vintage trailers on notepads during client meetings at the ad agency where he worked as an art director. When his advertising days came to an end he decided to build custom furniture full-time under the moniker of Bobland, with a focus on midcentury style.

Carl Jameson holds a bachelor's degree in communications from Washington State University. His career began in print production and moved into advertising, where he wrote, directed, and produced hundreds of videos. In addition to this book, Bob and Carl have collaborated on the restoration of a 1958 Cardinal and a 1967 Aladdin, with a 1963 Fireball and a mid-1960s Red Dale waiting in the wings.

To see more of the authors' work with vintage camper trailers, visit www.vintagetrailerfieldguide.com